The Metal Life Car

The Metal Life Car

The Inventor, the Impostor, and the Business of Lifesaving

George E. Buker

THE UNIVERSITY OF ALABAMA PRESS
Tuscaloosa

Hardcover edition published 2008.
Paperback edition published 2012.
eBook edition published 2009.

Typeface: Garamond

Cover photograph: Metal Life Car. Image from James L. Pond's *History of Life-Saving Appliances and Military and Naval Construction* (1885).
Cover design: Erin Bradley Dangar / Dangar Design

∞

The paper on which this book is printed meets the minimum requirements of
American National Standard for Information Science–Permanence of Paper for
Printed Library Materials, ANSI Z39.48—1984.

Paperback ISBN: 978-0-8173-5720-7

A previous edition of this book has been catalogued by the Library of Congress as follows:
Library of Congress Cataloging-in-Publication Data
Buker, George E., 1923–
  The metal life car : the inventor, the impostor, and the business of lifesaving / George E. Buker.
    p. cm.
  Includes bibliographical references and index.
  ISBN 978-0-8173-1608-2 (cloth : alk. paper) — ISBN 978-0-8173-8037-3 (electronic)
  1. Francis, Joseph, 1801–1893. 2. Lifesaving— Equipment and supplies. 3. Lifeboats— History.
4. United States. Life-Saving Service. 5. Marine engineering—United States—History—19th
century. 6. Inventors—United States—Biography. I. Title.
  VK1461.B85 2008
  623.88'87092—dc22
  [B]

2007034628

Contents

Illustrations

Acknowledgments

I thank Susan Buker, my daughter-in-law, for her critique of my early draft. My thanks also go to John Arrison of the Penobscot Marine Museum Library, Jean Vickey of the Erie County Public Library, Cynthia Ploucher of the National Parks Service, Outer Banks Group, and Frances Hayden of the North Carolina Maritime Museum for the information they supplied. I would be remiss if I did not thank the Jacksonville University personnel, especially Anna Large, research librarian; Margaret Dixon, from interlibrary loan department; and Peggy Rickey of duplicating.

Also, I thank the following organizations for their permission to publish a photograph from their archives: the Smithsonian Institution for the photograph of the Francis metallic lifeboat; the Erie County Historical Society, Erie, Pennsylvania, for the print of Douglass Ottinger, Cutter Service; and the Bangor Public Library, Bangor, Maine, for the photograph of the Penobscot Lumberjack's Batteau.

I   THE INVENTOR

I

The Origin of Francis's Metallic Lifeboats

Joseph Francis was an unusual inventor who also had the ability to organize a business to produce his inventions and the salesmanship to sell his products. His metallic watercraft were employed on a variety of missions. Narrating the story of his watercraft casts a light upon many nooks and crannies of nineteenth-century America. His metal lifeboats, first used on survey expeditions in Asia Minor and Central America, were in demand among the world's mercantile marine, the U.S. Navy, and the U.S. Revenue Marine Service. His corrugated iron life car was a key to the development of the U.S. Life-Saving Service. His metallic boats were critical to the outcome of the Third Seminole War in Florida. His metal army pontoon wagon bodies served in the trans-Mississippi Indian frontier. Yet few are aware of these services.

In Europe, Joseph Francis's reputation preceded him. Heads of state, military, and industrial leaders feted him. In return, he sold rights to his patents to shipyards in Liverpool and the Woolwich Arsenal in England, Le Harve in France, the free city of Hamburg in Germany, and Balakna in Russia. While Francis was in Europe, Captain Douglass Ottinger, U.S. Revenue Marine Service, claimed he was the inventor of the metal life car. Ottinger used the United States Congress and the United States Patent Office to support his pretense, and the inventor and the impostor had a decades-long struggle in the patent office and in the congressional chambers. Eventually Congress extolled Francis while it withheld its decision as to who invented the life car.

During the Civil War the task of building bridges to cross rivers and streams fell to the U.S. Army Corps of Engineers. Yet this branch of service had almost no contact with Joseph Francis or his metallic watercraft. Few engineers were aware of his devices. Then, when some Union leaders requested his metal pontoon wagons for their commands, the vindictiveness of Quartermaster General Montgomery Meigs kept the Union army from employing them. Thus the army did not use these superior metal pontoon wagons. Francis was the nineteenth-century embodiment of Horatio Alger's heroes going from rags to riches and from public belittlement to public acknowledgment—but, to begin at the beginning.

1.1 Joseph Francis. Photo from James L. Pond's *History of Life-Saving Appliances and Military and Naval Construction: Invented and Manufactured by Joseph Francis, with Sketches and Incidents of His Business Life in the United States and Europe* (New York: E. D. Slater, 1885).

Into this world, Joseph Francis was born in Boston on 12 March 1801. It is not known if some family member was involved in a shipwreck or if he was a spectator at some traumatic shipping disaster, but from early boyhood he was aware of the perils of the sea and the loss of life during shipwrecks. Gradually, throughout the years, he created the concept of a safe boat. It was a long, slow learning process to convert these concepts of additional buoyancy to float under all conditions, extra strength to withstand the forces of nature and lightweight enough to be employed under normal working conditions. He was about eleven years of age when his father died, and a relative employed him in his boat-building establishment. It was the beginning of a lifelong career dedicated to saving life from the sea. With few exceptions, he directed most of his works and inventions toward that goal. Before his first year of employment was over, he produced a rowboat with cork at both bow and stern that provided the buoyancy to support four men when the boat was full of water. It was his first step along his chosen career. Evidently he had the use of tools and the shop after hours, because in 1819 he entered a fast, unsinkable rowboat in the Mechanics Institute Fair in Boston and received honorable mention.[1]

Encouraged, he moved to New York and established a boat shop at Stryker's Bay on the North River. In 1825 he built many wooden "Life Pleasure Boats," as he called them, using cork in the bow and stern. Because of the extra buoyancy of his craft, he used "life" as part of the title for all his boats. Francis's reputation as a boat builder grew, and in 1830, the newly formed New York Boat Club ordered one of his boats. Soon after, the club presented Francis's boat to the czar of Russia. The club then ordered a second boat from Francis: the *Seadrift*, a thirty-foot, double-decked, sixteen-oared craft that was still in excellent condition fifty years later. Francis's work for the New York Boat Club was a financial interlude; his main objective still was to build a better lifeboat.[2] In 1832, while working for the New York Boat Club, he received his first patent for a portable screw boat. His boat had nothing to do with propulsion, such as a screw propeller, but was a boat made in sections for ease of transportation with the sections literally screwed together when ready to use.

From 1833 to 1838, he constructed many wooden lifeboats modeled after the whaleboat and inserted metal air chambers along the sides and under the thwarts for increased buoyancy. He experimented in the East River at the foot of Wall Street, New York, and in Philadelphia, Pennsylvania, for the benefit of shipping interests in both cities. The result was that he sold many of his boats to passenger ships. Based on this prototype, the U.S. Navy commissioned him to go to the Portsmouth Navy Yard to build lifeboats for the frigate *Santee* and the ship of the line *Alabama*. While working for the navy he met and later married Ellen Creamer, daughter of a Salem, Massachusetts, merchant.[3]

In 1837 Francis built a self-bailing, self-righting wooden lifeboat that he demonstrated to New York merchants and ship owners. The self-bailing devices consisted of a convex, watertight deck just above the load line, the line of immersion when the boat was loaded. Then, above the load line, he placed valves piercing the sides of his boat to complete his self-bailing features. Part of his test took place at the dock at the end of Wall Street where two fire engines poured water into the boat. The incoming streams, confined to the space above the load line, discharged through the open valves.

The self-righting devices were cork bow and stern and air chambers along the sides and under the thwarts. Francis demonstrated its self-righting ability by attaching a line to the stern of his lifeboat and hauling it up to the yardarm of the brig *Madison.* He released the boat after it reached its vertical position with its bow well above the water. The boat plunged into the water, sank a couple of feet, and then bobbed up to an upright position. The cork and the air chambers produced an opposite reaction to the downward pull of the ballast and keel weights. His lifeboat received great approval among maritime interests. Francis repeated his experiments in June 1837, for the owners and shippers of Philadelphia, and received the same enthusiastic response as that given in New York.[4]

News of his superior lifeboats spread abroad to foreign maritime interests. He received orders from the English government to provide boats for the coast of Canada. A British regiment ordered a racing boat from him that, according to Francis, bested the English boats in its first trial. He sold the emperor of Brazil an imperial life barge. As time passed, more and more of the world's commercial ships carried his lifeboats.[5]

In 1838, Francis began to think about an enclosed boat to carry people through a heavy surf during a storm or to transport people from ship to ship at sea under conditions too extreme for the normal open boat. Edward Wardell claimed that his father, Henry Wardell, gave Francis the idea for an enclosed boat when the father and son stood on the Long Branch, New Jersey, shore and watched a broached schooner breaking up in a winter storm. As the crew dropped off into the icy water and died, Henry Wardell said, "If I only had a gun to fire a shot with a line to it over the vessel, we could save them if we had nothing better than a hogshead to haul them ashore in." His father repeated his story to Francis. Shortly after hearing Henry Wardell's account, Francis drew some drawings, but he only had an initial concept for a covered boat, and his business demands limited his time to think of an enclosed boat.[6] It would be three more years before he resumed work on this concept.

In 1839, he patented his life and anchor launch designed to assist ships that had run aground. His launch had two wells fore and aft, each with a windlass on deck, and tackle running down the well, to house a ship's anchor. The launch could then carry the ship's anchor out to deep water and drop it to the bottom. This allowed the grounded vessel to pull against its anchor and warp itself offshore. The packet ship *Duchess d' Orleans* used an anchor launch capable of carrying a seventeen-hundred-pound anchor.[7]

Later that same year the American Institute, after conducting many tests with Francis's lifeboats, recommended their use among all sea-going vessels. Further it stated that his boats were especially desirable for naval ships, reasoning that even if the enemy shot perforated one or two sections of his boat there would be sufficient buoyancy to sustain the crew and allow the sailors to board the enemy ship or to perform other exigencies.[8]

The great interest in his lifeboats exceeded the capacity of his boatyard. In October 1840, he wrote the Secretary of War Joel R. Poinsett requesting the use of the empty Fort Gansewood in New York City to build his lifeboats. He noted the increase in demand for his lifeboats rose after his recent experiments at the Brooklyn Navy Yard. Francis said he would cover the public area and the army guns with canvas awnings to protect them from the elements. Further, he would give bonds as surety for protecting and delivering the government's property back at a moment's notice.

The endorsements appended to his letter give an insight into the workings of the bureaucracy. Poinsett sent the letter to the quartermaster general, asking about the proposed selling of the property. In reply Poinsett learned of the completed plans for the April sale. Still buyers wanted a general warranty from the government before reaching any reasonable price. Later in the year, the price of real estate in the city plummeted. The quartermaster recommended the government withhold the sale until prices improved. Francis's letter then went to Major McKay to report "on the propriety of complying with the request" and on the prospects of selling the property while in Francis's charge. Evidently Francis found the process too drawn out, or the army decided not to enter such an agreement; in any event, no further action took place.[9]

The year 1841 was both encouraging and challenging. On 2 March, the Chamber of Commerce of New York endorsed and recommended his lifeboat to the public. Later in the month, he received his third patent for life and other boats. Then on 11 October, he obtained his fourth patent for building boats, vessels, and other seafaring craft. Finally, he decided to set to work on his ideal lifeboat, one that would be strong enough and secure enough to protect its passengers regardless of the conditions of the sea and surf.[10] Francis transferred his business of providing boats to government agencies and the merchant marine to others to run. He sent his family to the country and moved into a building at 83 Anthony Street in New York City. For a year he experimented on a proper material to resist the pummeling his boat would receive traversing rocks and shoals.[11]

Yet he worried wood might not be strong enough. To decrease weight, he had the deck rest on the carlings, but then it would not support a man's weight. When he put extra frames or knees in the car, it became too heavy and difficult to maneuver, and it reduced the passenger space. After many attempts Francis had to admit defeat; he destroyed his prototype wooden car.[12]

Next, Joseph Francis began experimenting with metal. Most experts were skeptical of a metal boat, believing it would be too heavy and would sink if it shipped water. Yet as Francis worked with metal, his basic concept of a lifeboat changed. Instead of relying on self-bailing and self-righting devices, he thought of a vessel so buoyant that it floated on top of the water. His more pressing problem was shaping the metal and reducing the metal's weight to achieve the desired buoyancy. He began by making a two-foot-long model boat. Then he covered it with paper strips soaked in paste, layered four strips thick, and when the strips dried the paper retained the shape of his model. Encouraged, Francis hammered a sheet of iron to his model, but upon removing the mold, the iron snapped back to its original flat shape. After more thought, Francis made a concave mold to fit his convex piece. The two units now formed matching dies. He placed a sheet of iron between his wooden dies and exerted pressure by hammering the two parts together. When he let up on the pressure, the iron sheet remained between the two dies; however, when he opened the dies, the iron snapped back to its original flat shape.

Francis thought that if the dies were larger the pressure might imprint upon the metal. He made wooden dies 10'6" long, which was his projected length for his life car, just in case it succeeded. It was much more difficult to join the two dies together. He pounded with a hammer and used wedges and even a screw vice to force the two parts to close. Yet upon opening the dies the metal snapped back to its former shape.

Francis now worried that if he had to revert to frames and timbers to force the metal to retain its shape it would share the fate of his wooden car. He wanted a vessel buoyant enough to remain on top of the water regardless of the surf, but he needed to find a practical way to work metal without increasing its weight. After much thought, he recognized that the common tin table waiter (lazy Susan) might be the answer. The table waiter was made of a light tin sheet with its edges rolled up, a process that provided the strengthening element. By plaiting or corrugating sheets of metal for his boat, Francis could strengthen the metal without increasing the weight of the sheet. He then put a half round molding one inch wide on his two dies. Then he placed the metal sheet between the dies and exerted pressure. This time when he opened the dies the metal retained the shape imparted by the dies. This first success led Francis to corrugate the entire side of the metal. This increased the metal's strength so that it resisted the powerful concussions rendered in later tests.

His next problem was to develop some way to shape the iron or copper sheets into a boat. It was an easy process to corrugate a sheet of metal alone; however, a boat's shape was a flowing form running back from the bow to stern, widening at the beam, and contracting at either end. From the keel to the gunwale, amidships contained much more metal than at the bow or stern. How could he shape his sheet to expand and contract its size depending upon its position within the boat? To answer that question, Francis turned to the hydraulic press. Since it is easier to conceive of a metal boat than to find the means to create it, it was a long and slow process, but in the end, Francis thought that a set of dies with corrugations grooved in the dies would produce the desired result.

The realization that more time and money were necessary to improve their product may have damaged the relationship between Francis and his partner George E. McKay, for in 1843, Francis wrote to the Secretary of War John C. Spencer that his and McKay's partnership in the Life Boat Association had been discontinued and he alone would conduct the business. Francis continued telling the secretary of war that his U.S. patent protected his lifeboat from inferior imitations by unscrupulous boat builders.[13]

Continuing with his work, Francis had to produce the machinery to impart great pressure to stamp the sides with one imprint. Francis ordered and received a set of cast-iron dies from Stillwell, Allen & Co., known as the Novelty Iron Works in New York City. Further, Francis had to design a hydraulic press capable of exerting eight hundred tons of pressure to stamp out his metal boat. Horatio Allen, one of the partners of the Novelty Iron Works, became interested in Joseph Francis after he ordered the huge cast-iron dies from his company. The dies cost Francis six thousand dollars, and he still had to construct the hydraulic pump. While Allen was investigating Francis and his business, Francis was preparing to join the Novelty Iron Works because he needed money and the type of equipment the company could provide. Francis submitted to Allen his plan, a list of his patents, and the reasons why the two businesses should merge, resulting in an agreement whereby Francis conveyed half of his patent rights already issued and half of any future patents to the Novelty Iron Works, and in exchange, the company provided the space and machinery for Francis to work. It also stipulated that Francis had complete management and control over his corrugated metal works, including control of orders, contracts, and collection of bills for his enterprise.[14]

Francis's initial metal work was on his open lifeboat. The stamped corrugations

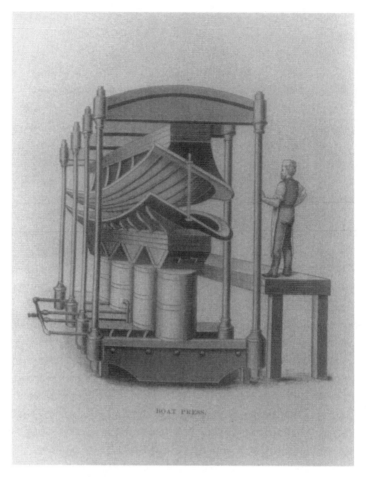

1.2 Boat Press. Photo from Pond's *History*, p. 34.

ran longitudinally at intervals of five or six inches apart that gave the external appearance of being boards straked or lapped as were wooden boats. Two sheets forming a side were lapped about three or four inches and riveted by a double row of rivets forming one half of the vessel. Francis also made metal boats to be shipped in sections and assembled by bolts at its destination. He then formed the two sides of the hull together, enclosing the keel, stem, and stern pieces of oak, and nailed the metal sides to the oak pieces. The upper edging of the metallic gunwale enclosed the oak gunwale frame so that the exterior of the boat presented a complete metal surface. The interior held a wooden keelson with other pieces of planking attached. He placed metal air chambers in the bow and stern sections and under the thwarts. Francis's first metallic boat was the result of four metal sheets pressed between four sets of dies into the four quarters of the vessel. From 1843 on, Francis built his new metallic lifeboats, and the lifeboats could be of any length by using the same procedure. By 1845, Francis used a number of different dies ranging from four to ten tons each that allowed him to manufacture life barges, life cutters, life whaleboats, life surfboats, life car boats, rowboats, and sailboats.[15] Francis's initial labor and manufacturing costs were high, but he persisted. Once he produced metal lifeboats, his business prospered.

Francis already had gained a solid reputation with his earlier wooden lifeboats, but since his metallic boats were costly, he generally asked new buyers to provide him with their assessment of his metal lifeboats. The testimonials he gathered made excellent reading for prospective new buyers. For example, Captain M. Berry built the steamship *Southerner* in 1846, and outfitted it with ordinary wood boats as well as some of Francis's galvanized iron lifeboats. Four years later Captain Berry said his wooden boats "became *leaky, staved,* and *useless,* and have been *replaced with metal.* . . . They cannot either sink, burn, break or remain overset." He found his metal boats, although roughly used, only needed painting to be as good as new. Equally as important, the metal boats gave his crew and passengers a great deal of confidence for their safety.[16]

Almost two months to the day after Berry's letter, the *Southerner* was steaming toward New York City. According to the log, at 2:10 A.M., Friday, 4 October 1850, at latitude 38° 39′ a sail was sighted off the larboard (right) bow. The captain put the helm hard aport (left) and backed his engine strong. Almost immediately there was a collision. The captain backed clear and stopped his engine. The other vessel, the bark *Isaac Mead* went under the *Southerner's* bow. Within five minutes those on the steamship heard cries of distress from the sea. The crew and passengers of the steamer quickly launched three of Francis's boats and were able to save seven crewmembers and two passengers of the thirty-three souls aboard the *Isaac Mead.* The *Southerner's* boats remained in the water searching until the only sound heard was the sea. Not until the search ended was the crew able to check the steamer's damage. The *Southerner* had her cutwater, bobstay, and flying jib boom carried away. The captain said that only Francis's metal lifeboats had the strength to withstand the rigors of lowering and recovering in that sea.[17]

Francis received great publicity from another early metal boat experience that appeared in newspapers and magazine articles. It began when Captain Samuel L. Breese, commanding the U.S. sloop of war *Albany,* wanted to rid himself of his copper gig. The *Albany,* built by the New York Navy Yard in 1846, included

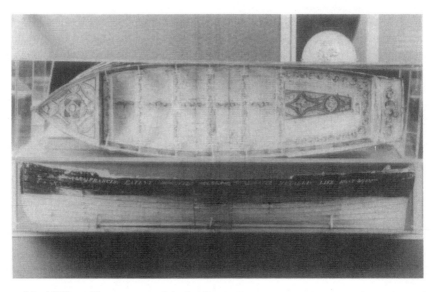

1.3 Metal Lifeboat. Photo courtesy of the Smithsonian Institution.

Francis's copper gig as part of its initial equipment. On 8 January 1847, Captain Breese brought the *Albany* into Antón Lizardo just south of Veracruz, Mexico. The sloop was the first replacement sent to the Home Squadron at the opening of the Mexican War. Eight months later Captain Breese left his copper gig ashore at the Castillo de San Juan de Ulloa off Veracruz. He did this because "of the leanness of the Albany aft, she sends so deep in a heavy sea or lying to, or becalmed, that she often dips up her stern boat full of water, which was the case with the Copper Gig. Not liking her, I left her for the use of another vessel of the squadron." Yet the ending of Breese's extract is quite complimentary of the copper gig. "*This gig had no gripes under the midships, when 'dipped up full of water,' and yet did not break down.*"[18] Gripes were broad bands formed by strands woven together and fitted with thimbles and lanyards used to secure boats when hoisted.

In January 1848, Professor Robert Grant, stationed on the U.S. steam frigate *Mississippi*, had the task of transferring disinfecting material from the Castillo de San Juan de Ulloa to the harbor of Sacrificio Island. Unfortunately for Grant, there were no small boats available for his use. Near the end of the month, Grant learned of a metal boat buried in the sand near the landing for the Castillo. Upon an examination, he found a boat half filled with sand sitting in three feet of water. When he began cleaning out the sand, he found several large pieces of iron, some weighing 150 pounds, and large rocks weighing the boat down. Her seats, rowlocks, and some woodwork lay smashed and buried in the sand nearby. As he cleaned out the boat he noted large concave indentations along the sides. Apparently someone used a heavy sledgehammer or iron bar to crush the sides, yet the indentations had not broken through the metal. Continuing, he raised the boat and found large holes in its bottom where the same instrument or instruments succeeded in punching holes in the bottom of the boat because the metal could not expand beyond the water's bottom. It was evident to Grant that someone had purposely tried to destroy the boat, but the yielding nature of the copper had defeated destruction, except on the bottom.

Grant repaired the holes by placing a sledgehammer on the inside and hammering the burrs on the outside back into place. He removed the concave bulges by hammering them back in place. He then fastened the seat, and everything was as good as new. His new boat was 30' long, had a 4'4" beam, a depth of 23", and a copper thickness of 32 ounces. Grant found his new boat to be excellent at sea as he and two hands managed to go between the Castillo and Sacrificio for several weeks in all sorts of weather. Part of the trip was in the open sea where the boat showed itself to be a sturdy sailor. Grant concluded she "was made in 1846 for the sloop of war 'Albany,' Capt. Breese, and had been thrown one side for what was supposed inefficiency, but she proved to be the strongest, swiftest and safest boat in the Gulf Squadron."[19] One wonders, if Captain Breese left his gig for another vessel, and it was as seaworthy as Grant said, why would anyone try to destroy such a boat?

The 1840s and 1850s provided the bulk of the U.S. Navy's exploration during the nineteenth century. Lieutenant Charles Wilkes gathered information on the Antarctica and explored islands in the Pacific from 1838 to 1842; Lieutenant William L. Herndon led two expeditions to the Amazon River Valley in 1853 and 1854; Commander Thomas J. Page explored the La Plata River in 1856; Lieutenant James M. Gilliss traveled around the southern portion of South America in 1857–1859; Lieutenant William Lynch explored the River Jordan and the Dead Sea in 1848; and Acting Master William G. Temple surveyed the Isthmus of Tehuantepec, Mexico, in 1850–1851. These last two officers used Francis's metal boats.

Lieutenant William F. Lynch, USN, led a scientific-commercial expedition to descend the River Jordan and explore the Dead Sea. His task was an unusual challenge for Francis's metal boats. Lynch's orders from Secretary of the Navy John Mason allowed him to obtain two of Francis's metallic boats. He took a galvanized iron and a copper boat, and Francis delivered both boats in sections for easy shipping.

Lynch reached the eastern Mediterranean shore on 31 March 1848, and offloaded his equipment the same day. The next day he moved near Acre to encamp. While there he heard that Arab tribes on both banks of the Jordan were hostile. An American party told him of an attack two nights earlier under Mount Tabor. The governor of Acre, playing upon these fears, tried to take advantage of the supposed threat by asking an exorbitant price for his men to serve the Americans; Lynch was confident that his men, all armed, would be able to defend themselves, yet he also employed men from two other well-known Arabs to assist the expedition. Thus, while he and some of his men rode their boats, others and the assisting Arabs followed along the shore.

For the next seven days his expedition trekked over high mountain ridges, down deep, seemingly bottomless, gorges to reach Lake Tiberias. Here he assembled his two metal lifeboats, bought a wooden boat, the only one available for sale on the lake, and launched his expedition on the lake's calm waters. Lieutenant Lynch gallantly named his metal boats *Fanny Mason* and *Fanny Skinner* after two young ladies of Washington, D.C. They were the daughters of Secretary of the Navy John Mason and Commander Charles W. Skinner of the Navy Department's Bureau of Construction, Equipment and Repairs. The wooden boat he named *Uncle Sam*. The next day his sailors made their final check of supplies and prepared for their journey.

On Monday, 10 April, the expedition departed in the early afternoon. Leaving the lake they passed the village of Semakh, and just downstream encountered the remains of a ruined bridge. The fragments of the ancient bridge effectively blocked the river, except for a narrow place near the left bank. The pent-up waters shot through the opening with great force. At 5:05 P.M., after reconnoitering the rapid, Lieutenant Lynch decided to take the *Fanny Mason* (the copper boat) down the sluice. He brought the boat head up and let her go stern first over the rapid. "She struck on a rock in mid channel, and broached broadside to, and was for some moments in danger; while in this position, the crew of the 'Uncle Sam' brought their boat unintentionally within the influence of the current, and she was swept down upon us with great velocity, but striking our boat at a favorable angle, she was whirled round, and sliding off the rock, drifts safely down the rapid. Taking everything out of the 'Fanny Skinner,' (the iron boat) she barely touched in passing; but the 'Uncle Sam' was extricated with difficulty."[20]

The next day the river current's speed was two knots, but increased as they continued. Farther on, the river became a foaming rapid with fish weirs and ruins of another fallen ancient bridge. "After five hours' severe labor we got the boats through,—the metallic ones without injury, but the frame one so battered and strained that she sunk shortly after, and we were obliged to abandon her. *Had our other boats been of wood, they would have shared the same fate.* A blow that only indents a metallic boat would fracture a wooden one."[21]

Wednesday, 12 April, they traversed two cascades and six rapids where the current was never less than four knots and at times reached twelve knots. The next day they swept down rapids safely with only a few indentations to the metal boats. As they approached the region of the hostile Arabs, Lieutenant Lynch mounted his heavy blunderbuss on the bow of the lead boat. "At 10.40, *descending an ugly, brawling, shelving rapid, she struck on a rock just beneath the surface of the water, and broaching, broadside on, was thrown upon her bilge*—taking in a great quantity of water—but all hands jumping overboard, her combined strength and buoyancy carried her safely over, though for some minutes we feared she would go to pieces."

Tuesday, 18 April, at three in the morning Lieutenant Lynch learned that some pilgrims would be passing by. He moved his tents higher up and, in respect for the pilgrims, moved his boats downstream and moored them on the other side. Yet he kept a crew in readiness to rescue any pilgrim who might fall into the river. It was early afternoon before Lynch left for the final journey to the northwest shore of the Dead Sea, a couple of hours away. As he rounded a point of land and rowed into the Dead Sea, a fresh northwest wind blew that soon freshened into a gale. The sea became heavy and his boats more difficult to handle. Added to that, the salt spray pained their eyes and any open wounds on the skin. The water from the spray evaporated rapidly, leaving incrustations of salt all over them.

On Wednesday, 19 April, Lieutenant Lynch made arrangements for camels to transport his metal boats, in sections, back to Jaffa. The lieutenant concluded, "It gratifies me to state that the boats are in almost as good a condition as when we received them."[22]

Shortly after Lieutenant Lynch's expedition, Commander Charles W. Skinner, of the Navy Department's Bureau of Construction, Equipment and Repairs, sent a model of a copper lifeboat under construction to the minister of marine of France. Skinner said that if the copper boat successfully completed a severe trial, the U.S. Navy would adopt that type for other navy vessels. He mentioned the recent Dead Sea expedition, saying the only damage inflicted on the boats were indentations because of striking rocks during descent through twenty-seven rapids. A hammer removed all of these dents. Further, he noted that the boats did not leak, their air chambers remained secure, keeping the boats very buoyant. Then he pointed out that the boats might come in sections for easy portage or shipping.[23]

Two years later, 19 July 1850, Commander Skinner wrote to Senator Daniel S. Dickinson to express his views on safety measures to reduce steamboat disasters. From naval experiences he determined that the best item was a metallic boat with air chambers installed. "A cutter so fitted, 26 feet in length, furnished to the United States frigate 'Savanna,' was reported to this Bureau by the commanding officer, New York, to be capable of sustaining inside 25 to 30 men, when filled with water." Again he cited Lieutenant Lynch's expedition. Metal boats will not leak from exposure to the sun, are fireproof, and when mashed can be easily repaired. He concluded: "Many vessels of the navy have been furnished with one for the purpose of crossing dangerous bars, landing in a heavy surf, or lowering at sea in the event of a man falling overboard; for such purposes I consider them superior to any others heretofore used in the navy or mercantile marine."[24]

About 1850, although the exact date is unclear, the success of Francis's corrugated lifeboat and life car (discussed in the next chapter) caused his business to exceed the limited space allotted within the Novelty Iron Works factory. Joseph Francis moved his operations to Greenpoint, Brooklyn, New York, and set up a larger manufactory named Francis' Metallic Life-Boat Company. His company began with a capital of $250,000, with Horatio Allen as president and Francis as manager with full control of the business, as he had back at the Novelty Iron Works.[25]

Acting Master William G. Temple, chief hydrographic assistant, Tehuantepec Survey, sent his comments on metal boats to Joseph Francis. His expedition used only the galvanized iron boats. Unlike Lieutenant Lynch's expedition that used camels for transportation, Temple's group used local Indians, who carried the boats over mountainous mule paths, and "no other boats could stand the rough usage and the heavy thumps which they unavoidably got, from the snags" and rocks while traversing the rivers of southern Mexico.[26]

Captain E. Crabtree of the U.S. mail steamship *Hermann* wrote a series of letters in praise of Joseph Francis's metal lifeboats. In June 1848, during a gale his two larboard side metal quarter boats blew over their davits several times before his crew could secure them on deck. He knew that wooden boats could not have withstood the bashing endured by his metal boats. He also was present when the U.S. mail steamship *Washington* backed into a post at the Novelty Iron Works dock. The metal boat on the stern "was twisted by the pressure at least two feet, and very much crushed." Such damage to a metal boat cost little to repair, whereas a wooden boat, with the same damage, was beyond repair.

Two years later, Captain Crabtree wrote that he added two larger size metal boats to his compliment. He considered that all four of his boats were equally effective. Being hurriedly used and roughly handled did not affect them. The boats were impervious to fire and secure from leaks at all times. He recommended Francis's metal boats for all vessels.

Six months later the captain wrote again to tell of another event testing his metal boats. On 21 January 1851, the steamer *Prometheus,* while maneuvering to tie up to a slip, ran into the stern of his vessel. The *Hermann's* gig, on the stern davits, bore the brunt of the collision. The broadside blow to the gig resulted in breaking the gunwale and thwarts and forcing the gig's sides to crush together. The gig bore all the shock and saved the *Hermann* from damage.[27]

Captain Charles L. Moses of the bark *Henry* wrote to the owners about the loss of the bark. He left Valparaiso, Chile, on 28 November 1851. On 31 December in the French Polynesia, at latitude 22° 47′ south, longitude 151° 07′ west, he struck a coral reef and his vessel swung to it broadside. In two hours the *Henry* leaned far enough to put the starboard side of its deck eight feet under water. Captain Moses and crew worked desperately to free the bark without success. By 5:30 P.M. the captain and crew abandoned the *Henry,* leaving the stricken vessel in their metallic lifeboat. Captain Moses, being windward of a south-southeast gale, worked his lifeboat three hundred miles in a heavy sea before reaching land. Moses praised the seaworthiness of his metal lifeboat, and he thanked Francis profusely for his invention.[28]

The Treasury Department readily accepted the metal boats, and on 28 May 1851, contracted for seventy-five boats. The copper boats were to be made of 34 or 36 gauge, 24′ to 26′ long, 5′6″ beam, and 2′ depth. They would have bow and stern air chambers that together had a buoyancy of at least 12 cubic feet, all for $15 per foot, or at $8 per foot for galvanized iron boats. Near the end of the year the department ordered a galvanized iron sailboat for the collector of customs at Providence, Rhode Island, with dimensions of 26′ long, 8′ beam, and 3′ depth. The following year the collector of customs, New York, received an iron barge. In 1853, the department ordered eight metal boats, six for revenue cutters and two for collectors of customs.[29]

The U.S. Navy generally ordered metal boats for specific ships. The U.S. Navy Yard in Boston ordered a copper quarter boat for the USS *Princeton.* It was to be 27′ long, 6′6″ beam, 2′4″ deep—to top of gunwale, wash-strake 4.5″ wide (boards or thin planks fastened to the gunwale of boats to keep out spray), and a 3′8″ stern. The yard also inquired about when its dingy for the *Portsmouth* would be ready.[30]

Captain Napoleon L. Coste, U.S. revenue brig *Washington,* wrote to Francis on 8 August 1852 to present his testimonial. His last cruise had been off the Florida coast for several months. Coste said he had used copper and iron quarter boats and a dingy. He felt the metal boats made good sea boats, as they were buoyant, inexpensive to maintain, and not injured when firing the heavy guns. He was particularly impressed with his last boat from the Metallic Boat Company because her speed surpassed any sea boat encountered. Coste noted that his small metal boats were light enough for two men "to pick up and throw them overboard," yet they could carry eight to ten people in the water. He told Francis that these small boats would be ideal for passenger steamers. He thought their small size and large carrying capacity would be beneficial for that class of steamers.[31]

Later that month Francis received a letter from Messrs. Everet & Brown stating that they had used his metal boats of various sizes for their three steamers in the South American trade and found them excellent for use in the Tropics. Then they continued saying that their Liverpool Packets also used his metal boats. As far as they were concerned his boats were superior to wood or other forms of construction. They were delighted with the boats' safety aspects as well as the small cost for repairs. They felt safe recommending his boats to friends, knowing from experience the intrinsic value of all his boats regardless of size or design.[32]

Undoubtedly the most spectacular episode relating to the safety provided by Francis's metal boats came from the explosions at Hurlgate in the East River. Long Island Sound connects to the Upper New York Bay by the sixteen-mile-long East River. Hurlgate, a section of the East River, had immense rocks that impeded safe navigation. Professor Benjamin Maillefert undertook to rid Hurlgate of these rocks and open navigation along the East River. His modus operandi was to place numerous powder charges of about 125 pounds in canisters, lower the charge to the river's bottom, and detonate the canister. Detonation took place by attaching wires from the canister to the boat above where the wires attached to a galvanic battery. Each explosion would split some of the rock it rested upon, and repeated assaults broke the rock until eventually a channel was cleared for boat passage. In August 1851, Joseph Francis lent Professor Maillefert two of his metal boats to work on the excavation.

In February 1852, Francis requested the return of his boats for overhaul and repair after the long and severe trial of seven months. Maillefert strenuously objected to losing the boats, even for a single day! He said that wooden boats could only stand the strain of the underwater explosions for a few days before their planks loosened and leaked so much that they required constant bailing. Yet his two metal boats "have been subjected to constant and extreme rough usage, having been knocked about amongst sand, ice and rocks, and more or less severely shaken by every one of my great charges of 125 pounds of powder each which has been fired at Hurlgate as well as on Diamond Reef, and the effects of which they fully endured, being placed at a distance of some thirty or forty feet only from the explosion. They are still in perfect order, and as sound and safe as ever; not a rivet is out of its place, and if they were only painted afresh, it would be, in fact, impossible to distinguish them from new ones." The professor continued, saying that on 12 November 1851, when a metal boat was inadvertently placed directly over an explosive charge, neither the crew nor the boat suffered injury. After that his men had such confidence for their safety in a metal boat that they would work directly over a charge again if necessary.[33]

Professor Maillefert considered it providential that he insisted on keeping the metal boats, for a month later, 26 March 1852, a far more serious accident occurred. This time the wire to the submerged canister was confused with another attached to a canister in one of the professor's wooden boats. When Maillefert touched the wire to his galvanic battery the canister in the wooden boat exploded shattering it into atoms and killing the two men instantly. Maillefert and his brother-in-law, in the nearby metal boat, rose upward about 150 feet. At the time, his boat was stern to the exploding boat. The air chamber in the stern of the metal boat flew out, but the metal end of the boat bent up, protecting the two men from the flying shrapnel that had been the wooden boat. Both men landed in the water. After what seemed an eternity, the professor struggled to the surface. Nearby he saw his metal boat with his brother-in-law hanging on to the side. Rescuers picked up both men, but Maillefert temporarily lost his sight and had a badly injured arm. On 19 April 1852, the professor's sight returned and he was able to write about his near brush with death. He was ecstatic over the buoyancy of his metal lifeboat, and he emphasized that his boat carried no cork, India-rubber buoys, or other devices to increase its buoyancy. Even after the loss of the rear air chamber, his boat was buoyant enough to support the two men waiting for rescue.[34]

While the previous examples concerned the metallic lifeboat, other forms of metal boats were in use. Colonel H. Amrey Brown wrote to Joseph Francis how pleased he was with his metal barge. Francis used the term "life" for all his metal boats, including metal life barges. Colonel Brown said his barge "rows easy, and is buoyant and dry, riding the waves like a duck."[35]

The Honorable John A. Dix testified that he had two of Francis's metallic lifeboats. His largest was a schooner-rigged boat that he kept afloat throughout the summer and fall for five years beginning in 1847. Twice gales drove him ashore. He lost some rigging, but never sustained injury to the hull.[36]

The available data clearly show that Joseph Francis had invented a metal boat with sufficient buoyancy and strength to answer most of his demands, and naval and merchant ships increasingly added his metal lifeboat to their vessels. Yet by this time, he realized that open boats could not provide the protection necessary to save people trapped aboard ships broached on shoals offshore during storm conditions that kept open boats from making the journey from shore to shoal. He turned his attention to his enclosed lifeboat, a watercraft that could make that journey.

2

The Metallic Life Car and the U.S. Life-Saving Service

Of the thousands of miles of sea and lake shores of the United States, the most deadly reach for shipwrecks was the sandy coast from Cape Cod to Cape Hatteras. Here local fishermen skilled in launching their light fishing boats crossed the surf to reach shoaled shipwrecks. The Great Lakes coasts allowed the use of heavy self-righting and self-bailing lifeboats launched down rails into deep water from the artificial harbors common to most of its ports. The least dangerous was the Pacific shore for its current flowed parallel to the coast and its offshore dangers were widely spaced.[1]

The first half of the nineteenth century, Francis's most active inventive period, was fraught with storm-tossed shipwrecks. It was that last voyage from shoaled vessels to shore that spelled the difference between life and death for passengers and crew. Often when open surfboats could not force a passage to those shipwrecked, their plight became disastrous. To make that final trip was the ultimate goal Francis set for his enclosed lifeboat.

Why were shipwrecks so prevalent? Sailing vessels and steamboats crossed the oceans employing a simple form of navigation. These vessels sailed from point to point on the earth's surface generally striving for the shortest time of travel, the least wear and tear on the vessel, and, in the case of steamers, using the least amount of fuel. Throughout its voyage, each vessel tried to maintain its present position at sea as accurately as possible. In practice, four methods provided the vessel with its location: by sighting one or more known landmarks while using an accurate map or chart; by sighting and determining the latitude and longitude from one or more heavenly bodies; by dead reckoning, that is, calculating the direction and distance from the vessel's last known position; and by sounding the depth and character of the bottom when in less than one hundred feet of water.[2]

The first method provided a precise position, if the vessel had an accurate map or chart. Determining latitude and longitude provided an accurate position, if the vessel carried a qualified navigator to make the observations. Dead reckoning could be satisfactory in the hands of a knowledgeable navigator, although there were a number of variables to lessen his accuracy, such as wind force, current, and the helmsman's ability to hold the course. Finally, depth soundings and the character of the bottom were dubious position indicators, but at least a decreasing depth gave some warning of impending danger. At sea away from land, the last three methods could produce an accurate enough position, for pinpoint positioning was not necessary for the vessel's safety on the open waters of the sea. Yet the closer to shore, the more accurate the position must be to avoid danger. Sailing close to shore amidst a winter storm when the sky was overcast or obscured by fog, when the wind howled, the sea lashed heavy, and the cold rain or snow enveloped the vessel increased the danger exponentially. This last scenario was the shipwreck season.

While ships could flounder and wreck along any shore for countless reasons from human or design error, to nature's fury, the two locales most prone to winter shipwrecks were the ports of Boston and New York. These two ports carried a large maritime trade during this period. Heading for Boston, a ship braved New England's rockbound coast. As early as 1789, the Massachusetts Humane Society built huts along the more desolate sections of its coast to shelter shipwrecked survivors fortunate enough to reach shore. If one looked at the sea approach to New York, the south shore of Long Island and the east shore of New Jersey resembled a funnel directing ships toward New York's harbor. The sandy shores of this funnel had sandbars and barrier islands between the shore and the Atlantic Ocean. Unfortunately for navigators of approaching ships, winter storms sculptured and moved the bars and barrier islands, making their position dubious and dangerous. Shippers from these two ports suffered high deaths rates and property losses during the shipwreck season, although official statistics did not begin before the fall of 1871.[3]

These conditions would subject a normal boat to impending risk of destruction. The wave or swell motion of the ocean formed when wind blew over the water's surface creating friction that caused the up and down motion of the water. This rising and falling energy moved in the direction of the wind, but generally the water remained stationary with a limited circular motion. If one observed a free-floating cork in water, one would note that the cork bobbed up and down but did not move forward with the passage of the wave. As the swell approached shore, the gradually shallowing water caused the wave to lose its support beneath its crest causing the crest to fall vertically on the beach. These incoming waves, known as rollers, presented little danger to ships at sea. Breakers were waves suddenly breaking over reefs, rocks, bars, or other obstacles offshore. Breakers had a different appearance and sound. Breakers covered the sea with foam and produced a loud roaring sound. This turbulent, destructive region among offshore breakers was where the metal lifeboats and surfboats reigned, for Francis believed his metal lifeboats were comparable to surfboats that were specially built to traverse heavy seas and breaking water during storms.

To handle a lifeboat in this region took considerable skill. In rowing to seaward, a heavy sea might up-end the boat, or turn it broadside on. If the surfmen had sufficient command over the boat, they avoided the sea. Thus their craft did not meet the sea at the moment of its breaking. If impossible to avoid the sea, the surfmen gave the boat sufficient speed to prevent the wave from carrying it back.

In rowing before heavy surf, the effect of the sea was to raise up the stern and to depress the bow. If the boat had sufficient stability, it would assume in succession the descending, the horizontal, and the ascending positions, as the wave passed under its stern, amidships, and bow. If the boat had little stability and a heavy roller overtook her, the stern rose, and the wave carried her along bodily on the front of the wave. Meanwhile, the bow immersed in the hollow of the sea met water comparatively stationary that offered a resistance. The boat then might turn end-over-end, or broach to.

There were certain safety procedures to follow rowing in before surf. To avoid the sea one should try and place the boat ahead or behind a breaking sea. If the boat was small and square-sterned, head the bow to seaward and back to shoreward, but row ahead against each surf to allow it to pass the boat quickly. If going to shore bow first, back the oars against each surf on its approach. If using sails and oars, the crew should take down the sails before reaching the broken water and rely only on oars.[4]

Prior to 1838, the national effort was limited to providing lighthouses and lightships to designated dangerous places along the nation's shores. In 1837, the government's shipwreck support consisted of 208 lighthouses and 26 lightships. A congressional act of December 1837 authorized the president "to cause any suitable number of public vessels adapted to the purpose to cruise upon the coast in the severe portion of the season to afford such aid to distressed navigators as their circumstances and necessities may require." At first, some naval vessels had that task, but they were too large and deep draft to serve effectively just offshore. Then revenue cutters substituted for naval ships.[5]

Before the federal government was involved in rescue operations, the sparse population along the coast did the best it could to save victims with its limited means. In New Jersey, after a storm, the flotsam from the wrecked ships drifting ashore drew people from inland settlements to the beach; salvers would visit the smashed hulks and gather whatever could be found.[6] In due time, more than one owner of a worn-out coastal schooner sent his vessel out with little or no cargo under a captain and crew skilled in crashing on the bar, getting ashore, and waiting for the sea to destroy the vessel. Then the captain reported to the owners, who filed their claim for insurance on both ship and cargo.

The New York underwriters soon understood what was happening and initiated the wrecking system, the first organized rescue and salvage scheme along the New Jersey shore. The board of underwriters appointed and paid wrecking masters to control specific sections of the beach. Thereafter, when a vessel went aground, the first report went to the wrecking master, who then would call upon a number of wrecking boat crews to respond. He took command of the men on shore and of the cargo as he represented the insurance companies. Wrecking boat crews utilized boats built to work in the turbulent surf. Naturally they would take off crew and passengers before off-loading cargo. Rebecca Harding Davis recorded a conversation with a crewman from one of the earlier wrecking boats:

> Well, I've seen vessels pretty well smashed up, sir. There was the Alabama, coast-schooner: all the crew went down on her in full sight; and the Annandale: she was a coal-brig, and she run aground on a December night. It was a terrible storm: but one surfboat got out to her. They took off what they could—the woman and part of the crew. I was a boy then, and I mind seein' them come ashore, their beards and clothes frozen stiff. After the boat left, some of the crew jumped into the sea, but they couldn't live in it two minutes. It was nigh dawn when the boat got out to the brig agen, and there wasn't a livin' soul aboard of her: only the body of the mate lashed tight to the mainmast, a solid mass of ice. He couldn't be got down, and I've heerd my father say it was awful to see him, with one hand held out as if p'inting' to shore, rockin' to and fro there overhead till the brig went under. Months after, some of the bodies of the crew was thrown up by the tide; they was as fresh as if they'd just gone to sleep.
>
> How could that be? Where had they been?
>
> Sucked into the sand. Them heavy nothe-easters always throws up a bar, an' they was sucked under it. When the bar gave way the tide threw them up. But as soon as the air tetched them they began to moulder.[7]

In the winter of 1839, William A. Newell, a recent graduate from medical school, was ashore when the Austrian brig *Count Perasto* ran aground below Barnegat Inlet, New Jersey.[8] The villagers dragged thirteen drowned bodies from the water, but the surf and wind were too violent for those on shore to launch their boats. Newell watched as the hapless brig thumped helplessly on the bar just a short distance from shore. The doctor thought how different the outcome would be if those on shore could have gotten a line out to the brig. Later he began experimenting and ultimately he melted several bullets into a ball heavy enough to haul a stout cord out beyond the surf when shot from the mouth of a cut-down blunderbuss.

Meanwhile, Francis envisioned his covered boat would be 10'6" long, 4'6" beam, 19" depth, with a flat bottom, full bilge, and full ends. He thought his life car, as he called his covered boat, could go from shore to a distressed ship during times when the elements were too rough for open boats. His life car, suspended from a hawser, stretched from shore to ship could make the trip. The surfmen on shore and the crew on the vessel would pull the life car back and forth rescuing people.

Initially, there was no indication that William Newell and Joseph Francis knew each other; each man's work complemented the other's. Newell worked to put a line from shore to ship; Francis worked to build a boat to go from shore to ship. His metallic life car was the answer when the elements were too severe to launch a surfboat.

In 1841, while Francis continued his experiments to design his metal life car, the "International Shipwreck Society for all Nations," headed by King Louis Philippe of France, asked him to describe his latest work. Francis responded immediately, telling of his work with metallic boats and his concept for an enclosed metal lifeboat. In return, the society enrolled him as a member of that organization on 1 February 1842, and recorded him "among the benefactors of the society."[9] The following year the "Royal English Section of the International Shipwreck Society of France unanimously awarded him a Medal of Honor" on 4 July 1843. Both societies urged him to aid them in establishing an American Shipwreck Society. Francis presented the subject to his fellow members of the American Institute. The result was the creation of the American Shipwreck and Humane Society.[10] Although the American Society had some success over the years, it became evident that the task was too great to be in private hands.

Gradually during the mid-1840s, the national government began a policy toward a federal lifesaving program. In June 1846, two navy lieutenants wrote to the secretary of the treasury recommending he apply for appropriations to provide government assistance from shore to shipwrecked victims based upon the British system. The next year, Congress removed from the president control over marine relief and gave that responsibility to the secretary of the treasury. In addition, Congress enacted its first federal appropriation for shore support over ship-

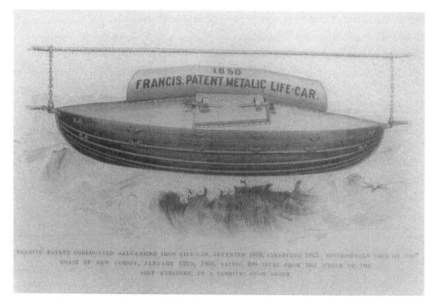

2.1 Metal Life Car. Photo from Pond's *History,* p. 44.

wrecks. At the time the allocated funds had no impact on the coast of New Jersey. In fact, Congress did not use the money immediately, but carried it forward and ultimately gave it to the Massachusetts Humane Society that already had boat-houses and refuge shelters along its coast.[11]

Newell's election to Congress in 1846 gave him the opportunity to put his ideas for lifesaving into being.[12] Congressman Newell of New Jersey provided the impetus necessary to bring the federal government into the task of providing assistance to shipwrecks. From the time he observed the disaster of the *Count Perasto* through his first term in Congress, William Newell devoted his energies to developing a plan to save lives and property offshore. Early in January 1848, Representative Newell submitted a resolution that the Committee on Commerce inquire into a plan to protect the New Jersey coast, from Sandy Hook to Little Egg Harbor, with safeguards to preserve life and property. Fearful that the committee might not understand his resolution, he appeared before the members to clarify his position. When he found that the committee did not receive his plan seriously, that it refused to even consider any of its aspects for further consideration, he doggedly refused to surrender. In August, while the House considered the Senate's lighthouse bill, he asked for an amendment: "For providing surf boats, rockets, carronades, and other necessary apparatus for the better preservation of life and property from shipwreck on the coast of New Jersey between Sandy Hook and Little Egg Harbor, $10,000, the same to be expended under the supervision of such officers of the Revenue Marine Corps as may be detached for this duty by the Secretary of the Treasury." Congress accepted his amendment unanimously. This was the first legislation leading to the later formation of the U.S. Life-Saving Service.[13]

Meanwhile, Francis found it was not an easy task to build a life car. He made, experimented with, and rejected nine prototype life cars between 1845 and 1849, before he made what he considered the perfect life car in February 1849. While the nine rejected corrugated iron life cars failed to withstand the pounding over rocks or sandbars offshore during conditions of heavy surf and high wind, they could transfer people between ships at sea when these conditions kept open boats off the seas. Therefore, Francis sold them to the U.S. Navy and to the Collins line of steamers for use between ships at sea.[14]

His life car, completely enclosed by its convex deck, resembled a cocoon suspended beneath a hawser as it carried four or five passengers lying horizontally. Amidships was a hatch through which the passengers embarked and disembarked. Joseph W. Casey, who worked on the first perfect life car from start to finish, and John Downey got into this car to test it. They rose up sixty feet in the air to the yardarm of a Collins steamer then at the Novelty Iron Works dock. Once up to the yardarm, the sailors cut it loose and it plunged into the water and bobbed up to the surface. After the test, Francis wrote to the secretary of the treasury and offered to sell his life car to the government as a means of saving people from stranded vessels. The secretary replied that he had no money for experiments, but suggested that Francis should test his life car, at his own expense and, if it proved effective in an actual disaster, the government would consider buying his craft. Francis shipped his life car to a dock in the North River near the Battery for shipment to the New Jersey coast. He selected a boathouse at Squan Beach as the site to await the final test of rescuing people from a broached ship.[15]

At this time the secretary of the treasury, in carrying out Newell's plan, detached Captain Douglass Ottinger, Revenue Marine Service, to establish life-saving stations in New Jersey. Ottinger's previous record included duty on the Great Lakes revenue cutter *Erie* for eleven years. Shortly thereafter, he superintended construction of the *Dallas* for two years, served aboard her during her shakedown at Buffalo, New York, and then stationed aboard her in Erie, Pennsylvania. Ottinger had no prior experience with shore to shoal rescues. His new orders directed him to report to a committee from the New York Board of Underwriters that would assist him. The officer plunged into his assignment determined to become familiar with all facets of his task. He soon learned that two subjects were vital to cross the surf from shore to shoal. He must establish physical contact with the stranded victims and provide the rescuers with a suitable vessel. Captain Ottinger had excellent advisers for both problems.[16]

Mr. Walter R. Jones, of the committee, contacted Mr. R. B. Forbes, of the Massachusetts Humane Society. He asked about his society's procedures. Forbes sent detailed instructions on its methods and equipment. The Massachusetts Society began its lifeboat stations in 1807. Over time, it developed close ties with the British Royal National Life Boat Institution. Thus the society knew of the English captain G. W. Manby, a merchant master, who shot line by a mortar to stranded vessels in 1806. Manby wrote a treatise in 1826 detailing his work with mortar and line. Therefore, Captain Ottinger learned of Manby's early work and later improvements. In the winter of 1848–1849, Ottinger tested rockets at Sandy Hook. In the summer of 1849 he tried his mortar and line at Long Branch.

The underwriters selected a committee of surfmen and wreckmasters to assist Captain Ottinger. Henry Wardell, a recognized authority on shipwrecks, led the committee. Ottinger and the committee set about designing a suitable surfboat. The end product resembled the standard New Jersey surfboat, a boat that had Viking lines brought by early Swedish colonists of south Jersey. Thus a light, wide-beamed, lapstraked craft, narrow flat bottom flaring out to an abundant sheer, pointed bow, and raked square stern was the answer.[17]

When the time came for Ottinger to build his surfboat, the Board of Trade spoke highly of Joseph Francis. The captain brought his model surfboat proposal to Francis. He asked for a larger craft than Francis's standard metal lifeboat. He wanted his surfboat to carry at least ten air chambers. He wanted India-rubber fenders outboard of the gunwales to protect the surfboat while alongside the wreck. Most surprisingly, he wanted the flat bottom to be of wood. It seemed that the surfmen believed wood would withstand the abrasive beach sand better than the thin galvanized iron. Thus Captain Ottinger's surfboat had metal sides down to and surrounding the wooden bottom.[18] Francis, in turn, showed the captain his latest metallic life car that he considered perfect. Captain Ottinger was impressed.

On the first of the year, Congressman Newell asked Captain Ottinger for a progress report. The Revenue Marine officer was ready. He said that "although it may appear that we have not progressed rapidly," much had been done. Ottinger acquired eight sites where he planned to construct wooden frame houses. He and the surfmen selected a surfboat for use along the coast. In addition to the galvanized iron surfboat, he proposed "to have a 'life car' at each station, which is designed to be sent to the stranded vessel when the wind and sea is [*sic*] too heavy for the best constructed boats to live."

Ottinger told of experimenting aboard the revenue schooner *Pleasonton* off Sandy Hook, firing rockets with line attached. He managed to project his line 250 yards to shore. He planned to try a mortar and shot at a future time, and, if successful, to include a mortar, shot, and line at each station, as these items would not be standard equipment on most merchantmen.

He continued, "I can scarcely answer your inquiry respecting the persons to whom the boats are to be intrusted; but from what I learn on that point, my opinion is, that the *surfman* who arrives at the boat house should have the privilege of taking charge of her for that occasion, *provided* he has the ability to take the 'steering oar;' and if he has not, none of the others will place themselves under his command." He said he intended to recommend to the secretary of the treasury that the commanders of nearby revenue cutters visit the person entrusted with the upkeep of the station every three months to ensure all was well. In a postscript, Ottinger concluded his report by recommending that Long Island, New York, also needed surfboats and houses for shipwrecked victims. Yet, in Newell's report to Congress, he felt there was no need for government to intervene. Newell believed that beyond supplying the station and its accessories, private associations should shoulder the burden of day-to-day affairs.[19]

On 17 February 1849, Congressman Newell sought to extend the limits of his first act to include the remainder of the New Jersey shore as far south as Cape May and all of Long Island, New York. Congress agreed and appropriated $20,000 to build six lifeboat stations for New Jersey south to Cape May and another eight for Long Island.[20]

On 21 May 1849, Captain Ottinger submitted his last report to the new secretary of treasury William M. Meredith before going on a leave of absence to captain a private ship to California for a group of investors. He stated that "the galvanized iron surf-boats were adopted on account of their durability, and not being likely to need repairs for a long time. . . . The life-cars are also made of metal, with air chambers of the same material, and, in addition, are fitted with the India-rubber floats and fenders. . . . These cars are constructed on the principle of a buoy and intended to pass through the surf when the surfmen dare not venture off. They are to be hauled to and from the stranded vessel by means of hauling lines attached to each end, and are protected from injury by contact with the ship's side by the inflated floats." After listing the other items included in the surf-boat stations, he continued: "As it was of much importance that the apparatus should be reliable, all the articles, except the life-cars, have been practically tested, and these are approved by most of the intelligent surfmen, and also by Mr. Francis, boat-builder, at the Novelty Works, who has spent much time in obtaining information on the subject of life-boats and life-saving apparatus; and we availed ourselves of his experience in constructing them."[21] The nascent Life-Saving Service was taking shape and employing both of Francis's boats, the metal life surfboats and life cars.

One day in the summer of 1849, bathers at New Jersey's Long Branch, near New York, were spectators to an unusual demonstration. Captain Ottinger, whose leave of absence did not begin until late June 1849, conducted a practicality test of the life car. Henry Wardell, an agent for the New York underwriters, had general supervision of the boathouses along the Long Branch shore. At that time the boathouses were under the control of the Shipwreck Benevolent Association of New York. Henry Wardell's son, Edward, remembered the distribution of Francis's life cars to several houses in 1849. He said he was present when Francis, Captain Ottinger, and Mr. Newell visited the boathouse (later known as No. 4) to experiment with the life car.

After the initial inspection, Edward Wardell went aboard the experiment's mock wreck, a boat stationed a half mile from shore in calm water, while a group of men on shore assembled a mortar. When ready, the men aimed and fired the mortar. As the shot arched out over the bobbing boat, the bathers could see a long line trailing from the projectile back to shore. The round shot flew over the boat to splash into the water to seaward. Crewmen on the target grabbed the line and began pulling it in. Soon two other lines, a hawser and a smaller line, began traveling from shore to the boat. The sailors made the hawser fast to a raised stanchion and continued pulling in the smaller line. This second line pulled a metal life car, suspended from the hawser, from shore to the boat. When it reached the boat, the crew opened its hatch and Edward Wardell got in. The hatch's latch was on the outside with no way for the passengers inside to open it. With the hatch secured, those on shore pulled the life car back. Thus Edward Wardell became the first man to cross the surf in a life car.

What the bathers observed was a trial of one of Joseph Francis's metallic life cars, but not his first perfect life car—that was on Squan Beach under Francis's control. This was a life car purchased by Captain Ottinger and stored at station 4. In a calm sea the life car carried Edward Wardell, the mock shipwreck survivor, to shore. Earlier his first perfect life car had withstood the pounding of rolling over paving stones and the smash as it dropped from the yardarm of a Collins's ship. All of these tests were in imitation of a coastal ledge or bar under extreme weather conditions. The final test awaited a winter's storm. If it passed that test, then the life car was the link in the chain between shore and ship in a storm's fury.[22]

Captain Ottinger left on leave of absence just as Congress expanded the life-saving stations to south New Jersey and Long Island, New York. Three people assumed the unfinished business. Captain John McGowan, USRMS, superintended building six life cars from August through October 1849. The cars were for stations from Brigantine Beach to Cape May. McGowan said, "The cars that I built were precisely the same as those built by Captain Ottinger, with the exception of a handle inside the scuttle-hatch put on by me."[23]

Edward Watts, a civil engineer, supervised Long Island's stations. He had ten stations in all, eight from Coney Island to Montauk Point along the outer shore of Long Island, and two along Long Island Sound, Fisher's Island and Eaton's Neck. Watts worked with the New York Life-Saving Benevolent Association.[24]

In early November 1849, First Lieutenant John N. Toner, USRMS, who had relieved Captain Ottinger, submitted his final report. He stated that the surfboats and life cars made by Mr. Francis were those recommended by Captain Ottinger. Yet he received a number of reports that the wooden bottoms cracked and leaked. Two probable causes were the wood drying out while sitting in the lifesaving station and while crossing from shore to ship and back the violent thumps of the surf sent tremors through the ridged iron sides to the more flexible wooden bottom. To correct that deficiency the whole inside bottom was galvanized iron with an additional wooden bottom attached outside the iron one. Apparently the Jersey surfmen still worried about the abrasiveness of the beach sand.

Richard C. Holmes, collector of customs for the Great Egg Harbor District on Cape May, assisted Toner in selecting the government sites, getting deeds from the owners of the land, and securing numerous other acts in the local area so helpful to the government. When Toner completed the final lifesaving stations on the New Jersey shore, he asked Holmes to take control of the general superintendence of the whole southern line of shelters. Further, Toner gave him keys to the two stations nearest his home. The government's task was complete and only awaited the winter storms to test the metal life surfboats and life cars.[25]

It was not a long wait before the life surfboat received its call. Near the end of November or the first of December 1849, the steamer *Eudora* went ashore on Ludiam's Beach, Cape May, in the vicinity of Richard Holmes's place. Holmes supervised the rescue operations. A few days later he wrote to the president of the New York Board of Underwriters to tell of the performance of the metal life surfboat he used. He thought that a surfboat properly manned and managed had "little danger of loss of life by shipwreck." He continued: "They will live in almost any surf, and it must indeed be a terrific storm when a stranded vessel can not be boarded by them." Holmes said that "if they are not entirely proof to the waves, nothing has ever been made to outlive them. . . . When kept head or stern to the sea, they cannot be filled or swamped."[26]

The true test for the life car took place on 12 January 1850, when a winter tempest of wind, snow, and freezing spray drove the *Ayrshire*, with two hundred and one souls aboard, upon the bar off Squan Beach, New Jersey. The ship breached abreast of the station house. Mahlon B. Chapman was among the first to arrive and assisted in carrying the hawser, life car, mortar, lines, and so forth to the shore. He noticed one ring from the chain at the end had broken. He put rope grommet in its place. John Maxson, the wrecking master, fired his mortar sending the line across the wreck. While the crew hauled in the hawser, Maxson prepared to send off the life car; however, the government official ordered him to attach an India-rubber float to each side of the car. That accomplished, the metallic life car journeyed back and forth carrying four or five at a time. Chapman kept renewing the worn grommets after several trips. Finally he wrote on the car asking the sailors to send a leading block from the ship to shore.

Just after that Samuel Chadwick launched a metal life surfboat while the tide was low. He succeeded in getting alongside the ship and a sailor attempted to throw the leading block and to jump into the boat. Both the sailor and the block fell into the icy water. Fortunately for the sailor, the surfmen rescued him and brought him ashore. Chadwick made two other attempts to get alongside the *Ayrshire*, but it was so rough that it was impossible.

All during this time the life car continued its journey back and forth bringing passengers and crew ashore. John Maxson said the life car passed "through *a terrific foaming surf. Every soul—men, women, children, and infants—came through the surf during that cold snow-storm, dry and comfortable.*" During the time of its travel, one rubber float filled with water while the other maintained its air. Maxson concluded by saying that this event showed "the ability of the Metallic Boat to do her work, even under such disadvantages." He believed that had the *Ayrshire* landed even four miles from the station many of the rescued people would have perished from the cold. As it was, the people landed, left the car, and went immediately into the station house where a fire warmed them.[27]

The passengers of the life car had a frightening trip, for once inside, with the hatch shut and secured from the outside, the journey was in total darkness. There were no ventilation openings in the car. The time of travel was considerably less than the amount of oxygen in the craft, so there was no need for openings for any purpose. In later versions of his life car, the convex cover was raised enough to allow the passengers to sit up at both ends. Regardless of the model employed, the trip to shore subjected its passengers, sitting or lying in pitch-blackness with no reference to the outside world, to powerful shocks and concussions as the car traversed the breakers.[28] Rebecca Davis's captain told what happened to the passengers after a rescue in the life car. "Some men stagger out of the car sick, some crying or praying, some as cool as if they'd just stepped off the train."[29]

Of the two hundred and one souls aboard the *Ayrshire,* two hundred survived. The one fatality was a man caring for his two young nieces. When it came their turn to leave the wreck, he placed the girls in the car, but he refused to go aboard. After the crew secured the hatch and pushed the car to begin its return journey back to shore, he jumped on the outside of the life car. When the first blow of the surf struck him, he lost his grip, plunged into the icy water, and perished.[30]

John Maxson, the *Ayrshire* wreckmaster, years earlier watched when the *John Minturn* came ashore on 15 February 1846 on the same beach. He believed that if the mortar and life car were on the beach then, many, if not all, the people could have survived the shipwreck. He evaluated the importance of the *Ayrshire* rescue, saying: "We can also now communicate with the ship, by means of the mortar and car, as soon as she strikes, without waiting, as heretofore, for the storm to cease, by which time she may go to pieces, and all be lost."[31]

There was an interesting footnote to the *Ayrshire* wreck. At the time of the rescue, no one expected the ship to survive the beating of the sea. Yet the hull did ride out the battering. After the storm, the beaten hulk slowly settled to the bottom and sand covered the remains. About twenty-three years later another storm's erosive actions exposed the remains of the *Ayrshire* and revealed John Maxson's shot that initiated the life car's rescue. The Treasury Department kept the shot as a distinguished relic of the first rescue by a metallic life car.

It was obvious to all that the life car was a success. Not only could it go from shore to shoal and return during extreme weather, it allowed untrained persons to rescue victims from stranded ships. Surf rescues required specially designed boats and skilled crews to make rescues on stormy seas. The life car needed few testimonials. Yet the metal life surfboats, following the modifications of Ottinger and the wrecking masters, needed testimonials. One night during a violent storm, the booming of a gun at stated intervals awakened Richard Holmes. He got dressed and went to the shore, but could see nothing. Yet the measured boom, boom,

boom continued. He aroused neighbors until he had a full crew for the metal life surfboat. Using a compass, he tried to establish a heading before launching his boat. They would listen, then row, then stop to listen again, but the storm's noise almost drowned out the gun's boom. It was so dark that Holmes was not sure if his boat was making any headway. Some of the crew thought that the send of the sea was keeping them motionless. Yet the men pulled on their oars a half hour, an hour, one and a half hours, and two hours. By that time the gun's boom definitely was louder; then Holmes saw a faint flash before hearing the sound. Now he knew they were approaching a distressed vessel.

Gradually the black hull of the ship took shape apart from the dark violent storm. A little closer and they saw the ship beaten by the sea was on her side and overwhelmed by the crashing waves that slammed her back and forth. Holmes brought his boat to the leeside to communicate with the people huddled on deck hanging on for dear life. It was not possible to bring his boat too close. He could hear the cries of the crew and passengers borne down upon him by the wind, but those on the ship could not hear their rescuers. Daylight began and Holmes more clearly saw the problem. The ship lay on a shoal held there by the storm and the ship's anchor that the crew had dropped just before hitting the bar.

Holmes rowed around to the windward side. Now the ship's crew could hear him. He called for them to let a line down the leeward yardarm. The crew complied. Holmes then rowed to the leeward side where he brought his boat up to the rocking, swaying line, but distanced from the ship's side. Holmes turned his steering oar over to another and ran to the bow of his boat. The next time the line swung by he grabbed it, and the new steersman veered the surfboat farther to leeward leaving Holmes hanging on the line. In no time Holmes was up the line, over the yard to the ratline, and down on deck.

The crew surrounded him looking for advice. Holmes told them they were on a sandbar parallel to shore with deeper water between them and the shore. He thought they should release the anchor and allow the wind and surf to push them off the bar toward shore. The crew followed his suggestion and after some terrible concussions the ship thumped over the bar, gathered speed, and drifted toward shore. Once again the ship struck shallow water off the beach. During this time the surfboat followed the derelict.

Holmes knew his men were on the point of exhaustion from the hours of rowing in the storm. He signaled his surfboat alongside the ship. When close, he jumped into the boat carrying a line with him, the other end fastened to the derelict. On reaching shore, Holmes borrowed from the life car procedure and tied a line on shore and to the stern of the surfboat. Now the ship's crew pulled the surfboat out to the ship. Once loaded, the surfmen pulled it back ashore.

When all the passengers landed, Holmes suggested that the crew take down some of the sails and spars to build a tent on shore. Later the crew sent provisions ashore. Soon the rescued, safely ensconced in a huge makeshift tent, sat by fires eating provisions sent from the shipwrecked vessel. The metal life surfboat proved its ability. In all 121 souls were saved from death.[32]

Selah Strong, keeper of Fire Island Light, New York, wrote that he used Francis's surfboat to board the *Minerva* when she grounded off Oak Island in 1850. At the time most people believed it impossible for any boat to live during the storm. Strong concluded his letter, saying, "the principle of surfboats and station houses along our coast, is an excellent one; their present management, in detail, I deem bad; government should appoint a qualified man to take charge of each boat, with power, in extreme cases, to employ men and fairly remunerate them for services rendered."[33]

On Thursday, 2 December 1852, Long Branch, New Jersey, was in the throes of a violent southeast gale. The wind blew toward shore, fog covered the area in a dense white blanket, and the offshore breakers lay hidden between the howling wind and the thick white blanket. Captain Marshall Brodie of the ship *Georgia* was not aware of his danger until his vessel slammed hard aground at midnight. The *Georgia,* only a half mile from shore, lay invisible in the white blanket, unseen until noon on 3 December.

When Captain Thomas Bond discovered the broached ship, he gathered his men and headed to the station house to haul its life surfboat to the beach. Yet the waves were too high for his boat to board the *Georgia* by normal means. Captain Bond sent some men back to the station house for the mortar and lines. His first shot dropped a line between the fore and mizzenmasts. Bond attached a large line to the one draped over the *Georgia* and signaled the crew to pull it in. When the sailors received the heavy line, Bond attached the line to the bow of his surfboat. Then he fastened a second line to the stern and signaled the crew to pull the boat to the ship.

On the outbound trip Bond's men guided the surfboat to keep her bow headed toward the *Georgia.* The surfboat reached the ship half full of water. The sailors quickly bailed out the boat and loaded twenty-two women and children in the boat for the return trip. The metal boat reached shore half full of water, yet its cargo was safe. On the second trip outbound the current set strong to the north and it took three men on shore to hold the bow to the *Georgia.* The sailors watching the second inbound trip noticed that as the boat passed the bow of the ship going from the lee shelter to the fury of the storm a tremendous sea swept over the surfboat filling it with water; yet it remained afloat and continued on to shore. From that time on they did not waste time bailing. In trip after trip until nine at night the metal life surfboat carried passengers and crew ashore. In all, Captain Bond estimated 296 souls saved.[34]

Meanwhile, Captain Ottinger was on the Pacific Ocean far from the Atlantic's storms and shipwrecks. His leave of absence ended in December 1850. He then served on the *Lawrence* and the *Frolic*, both Revenue Marine vessels in San Francisco. From April through September 1853 he was in transit back to the Atlantic. He commanded the *McCelland* out of New York from September 1853 to November 1855. While he established the first eight stations in New Jersey, he was not present during the early trials of the life surfboats or the life cars nor was he officially concerned with them on his return.[35]

During this early period there developed a division of labor on the coast. The underwriters initiated the wrecking master and wrecking crews to reduce their loss due to storm wrecks, whereas Congress established lifesaving stations to save lives. The two systems developed differently. Rebecca Davis's narrators, Jacob and the captain, succinctly described the two systems:

> We understand the noble work which these wrecking-crews have done— By the way, how do they choose their captain, Jacob—the man in the stern, as you call him? The most brave, heroic fellow, I suppose?
>
> "I dunno about that," with a perplexed air. "We don't calcoolate much on heroism and sech: we choose the man that's got the best judgment of the sea—a keerful, firm man. These six men hes got to obey him—hes got to put their lives altogether in his hand, you see. They don't want a headlong fellow: they want a man that knows the water—thorough."
>
> "Besides," added the captain, "it is as with any other business—the best crew is surest of employment and pay. Each owner of a wracking-boat chooses his men for their muscle and skill: and the wracking-master chooses the best boat and crew. There's competition, competition. On the contrary, the life-saving service, like all other government work, for a good many years fell into the hands of politicians: the superintendent was chosen because he had given some help to his party, and he appointed his own friends as lifeboat-men, often tavern loafers like himself. A harness-maker from Bricksburg held the place of master of the station below here for years—a

man who probably never was in a boat, and certainly would not go in one in a heavy sea."[36]

Between September 1850 and August 1854, congressional appropriations provided for lifesaving stations from Rhode Island south to Florida, on the Great Lakes, and Texas. Yet the lack of responsibility and supervision for these stations continued. The illegitimate private use of the lifeboats and the deterioration of the station buildings took its toll on the lifesaving apparatus along the nation's coasts.

In 1854 immigrant shipping flourished in the Atlantic. Yet it was a deadly year with the loss of the *City of Glasgow* carrying 460 souls disappearing without a trace. Then in a mid-April gale two sailing vessels with about 500 immigrants floundered at sea. Luckily, rescuing vessels took all off the sailing craft before they went under. This same storm broached the *Powhattan* off Squan Beach. The *Powhattan* an old ship bound from Le Havre to New York with 200 German immigrants aboard. The northeaster slammed her ashore about six miles from the nearest lifesaving station. The wrecking master found the ship Sunday morning "thumping on the bar one hundred yards from shore." Passengers filled the decks waiting for rescue. The wrecking master sent helpers to fetch the lifesaving equipment a mere six miles away. All day Sunday the captain of the *Powhattan* bellowed through his speaking trumpet appeals for help. His voice carried over the huge waves to the helpless wrecking master. Some passengers, swept overboard, drowned in the cold water and drifted ashore. At dusk "a tremendous wave struck the *Powhattan* 'and in one moment the hull was scattered into fragments.' The wreckmaster could hear shrieks but could do nothing, no one survived." Aid from the lifesaving station arrived Monday morning too late to assist the doomed passengers and crew.[37]

Senator Hannibal Hamlin, chairman of the Senate Committee on Commerce, asked the secretary of the treasury for an accounting and recommendations to improve the service. Secretary James Guthrie replied that once the government established and equipped the station the government's responsibility ended. He recommended that the Treasury Department appoint a superintendent for each coast and station keepers for each shelter. During Congress's investigation of the wreck of the *Powhattan,* another wreck took the lives of over two hundred people.

The *New Era of Bremen* grounded on 13 November 1854 off Deal Beach, now part of Asbury Park, New Jersey. It carried over 500 German immigrants. Contrary to the tales of the captain being the last to leave his ship, this captain and three crewmen fought the passengers to launch a lifeboat. They made for shore while terrified passengers screamed for help. At least the captain reported his ship's grounding, and equipment from the nearest lifesaving station set out. Unfortunately for the shipwrecked, the rescuers found the *New Era* beyond shot range of the mortar. Further, night set and the surfmen were unable to operate in those conditions. In the morning circumstances were better. The surf pushed the hulk closer to shore, within mortar range. Yet the first shot failed when the metal spiral wire connecting the shot to the line broke. More shots had the same result. The rescuers fired until they expended all their powder and shot. In a last effort the surfmen waded waist deep in the cold water to bring in those people fortunate to make it ashore alive. About 163 survivors made it. Investigation later determined that during storage corrosion set in on the metal spirals. This disaster energized Congress. The following month it enacted the secretary of the treasury's recommendations. Superintendents for each coast and keepers for each station received $200 per year. Yet, the money to carry out this change was not available until 1857.[38]

That same year Congress continued work to bolster its system for saving lives from shipwrecks. It recommended extending the telegraph line from Squan village to Barnegat village with a connector to the Squan, Long Branch, and Sandy Hook telegraph. This would allow communications between Barnegat Inlet, the intermediate stations, and the steam revenue cutter at Sandy Hook.[39] Such rapid communications allowed other stations to send aid if the disaster was great enough to require additional help.

In 1881, Congressman Samuel S. Cox, while reviewing the government's feeble and spasmodic efforts to create a lifesaving organization from 1849 to 1878, found that the one positive theme that promoted success was the employment of local fishermen and surfmen. These men knew "the coast and its local navigation, its currents, eddies, and bars." The deepwater sailor was ill equipped to wield surfboats against the raging breaking sea. Fortunately for the service, these fishermen and surfmen, from the beginning, served as the corps saving life from the sea.[40]

While the government struggled to formulate an effective on-shore organization to aid shipwreck survivors, Joseph Francis was securing his rights to his life cars. He believed his two patents of 1839, for life and anchor boats, and of 1845, for boats and other vessels of sheet-iron, protected his life car. Yet on the advice of his attorney, he filed a caveat on 9 February 1850 with the patent office to cover the peculiar hatch and trip-cylinder to the life car. Actually he had invented the deck hatch and trip-cylinder in 1843, when he first began work on his covered wooden boat, but he failed to patent it. On 11 April 1851, referring to his caveat, he applied for his patent. The patent office rejected his claim, stating it contained nothing new or patentable. The rejection also referred to a patent of J. D. Greene granted in 1849 for a ducking boat, and because "air chambers are at the present day such ordinary devices that their application to any form of boat is not patentable, [and] the last claim likewise can not be allowed."[41] Francis was not too concerned because he knew that his two previous patents covered his life car.

The evolution of Francis's life car and Representative William Newell's legislative efforts to involve the federal government into lifesaving stations ashore progressed coincidently. Through the labors of Francis and Newell, Captain Ottinger had the means to launch lifesaving stations along the New Jersey shore equipped with both of Francis's metallic boats, the life surfboat and the life car. Having succeeded with his life car, Francis now became more concerned with expanding his customer base to include the U.S. Army.

3

Metallic Boats for the U.S. Army

Having established his metal lifeboats and life cars with the U.S. Navy, U.S. Revenue Marine Service, and maritime shipping interests, Joseph Francis turned his attention to the U.S. Army. When contacted by Francis, the commanding general of the army, General Winfield Scott, issued General Orders Number 55, appointing a board of officers to examine and report on Francis's metallic lifeboat, directing it to meet in New York City on 15 November 1851.[1]

Meanwhile, Francis, never one to wait patiently, forwarded a letter to Quartermaster General Thomas S. Jesup on 14 November 1851. With his letter he enclosed a model of his metallic man-of-war life cutter and seven testimonials. Five printed references, probably prepared for his book published that year, and two longhand letters. In the body of his letter he outlined the advantages of his metal boats over wooden ones. Two months later Francis took a more direct route and had his friend John A. Dix give him a letter of introduction to General Jesup.[2]

General Scott received the army board's report on 3 December 1851. The report was detailed and encyclopedic in coverage. The members first met with Francis and visited all aspects of his manufactory at the Novelty Iron Works. As time passed and Francis informed more people of the superiority of his metal boats, his reasons became a litany: great strength, lightness, durability, impervious to worms in tropical waters, tightness, fireproof, may be shipped in sections, and, because of its long life, it was economic. Then they viewed many of his testimonials, interviewed merchant captains using his metal boats, and delved deeply into the subject. The board's list of advantages was similar to Francis's litany. The members spent much time analyzing the cost and expected repairs of wooden barges and metal barges, noting that the longevity of the metal boats were estimates derived from the maritime service since no data existed from army uses. Thus they cautioned that army land operations might be more severe on metal boats than naval usage, especially as army crews would have less nautical skills. The notes at the end included pages 165 and 167 of Abbott's "Some Account of Francis's Life-Boats and Life-Cars" in *Harper's New Monthly Magazine,* July 1851, and a handwritten marginal note on page 167 of the article giving a naval officer's account of how to satisfactorily repair a hole or crack in the metal boat sufficient to keep it in operation until a permanent repair could be made.

The board agreed in all aspects to the superiority of the metallic boats. Yet it considered it prudent to recommend a year's trial of both copper and iron craft at some principal posts, particularly New York and Boston harbors, the coast of Florida, and on the Great Lakes before ultimately deciding whether or not to introduce these boats for general service. The Board forwarded its findings to General Jesup, who concurred. Jesup ordered a boat for the New York and Boston harbors, Key West, and Fort Capron in Florida. He said that if he received additional appropriations perhaps other locales could test the metal boats.[3]

Francis reasoned if letters to the commanding general of the army and the quartermaster general were inadequate, he would write to the secretary of war. On 15 June 1853, he sent a model of his metallic life barge and his book *Francis' Metallic Life-Boat Company* with its illustrated testimonials to Secretary Jefferson Davis, who acknowledged receipt on 20 June 1853.[4]

It was a year after Francis met Jesup, about the time he wrote to Secretary Davis, that he received a letter from the general requesting more information on his copper whaleboat. Francis replied that his boats were made in sections, so that any inexperienced persons could assemble a boat from sections of old or new boats, or a combination of the two, to create a new watertight craft. He said that a twenty-seven-foot whaleboat used six hundred pounds of copper. The current cost of copper was forty cents a pound. Thus the material cost of the whaleboat would be $240. Yet if the army obtained its copper from the government copper rolling mill at the Washington Navy Yard, as the navy did, it would cost twenty-two cents a pound, or $132 per boat. Of course, there were his fabrication costs. Still he pointed out that at the end of the boat's useful life of ten or twenty years the intrinsic value of the copper remained. The copper could go through another cycle as a new boat.[5]

Unknown to Francis, the army was making preparations for its third war with the Seminole Indians in Florida. Quartermaster General Jesup followed the events in Florida closely. In the Second Seminole War, 1835–1842, he had been the military commander in the territory for almost eighteen months from 9 December 1836 to 15 May 1838. He knew the locale and the Seminoles. He kept current on operations in the Everglades long after he left Florida. He was aware of the vital role played by the navy's Florida Expedition, a riverine task force, that eventually included four schooners, three revenue cutters, six gunbarges, and over a hundred canoes and flat-bottomed boats, manned by 622 officers, sailors, and marines. The Florida Expedition, serving under the army, employed its schooners and cutters to blockade the glades from Cuban fishermen who might bring powder to the enemy. The gunbarges patrolled the reef and shore of south Florida to keep the Indians from fishing or resting away from the severe environs of south Florida's swamps. The canoes and flat-bottomed boats scouted the Everglades seeking the enemy. General Jesup began to plan for the coming war with the Seminoles without the benefit of the navy's Florida Expedition, for naval units were no longer assigned to the army; he turned to Joseph Francis to provide the necessary metallic boats.[6]

The Third Seminole War or the Billy Bowlegs War, December 1855 to March 1858, was the final conflict in the American attempt to move Florida's Seminole Indians westward. It was a unique struggle. The theater of operations was terra incognita in a semi- to tropical waterland of bays, lakes, rivers, and almost impenetrable swamps. From the outset the senior military commanders knew the proper tactics to succeed, and they employed a variety of Joseph Francis's metallic boats to match Florida's aquatic settings. Unfortunately for these commanders, it took over two years to develop an amphibious force capable of carrying out their tactics.

The theater of operations may best be described as the watershed of the southern portion of the peninsula beginning at Lake Apopka, flowing south through a chain of lakes, including Lake Kissimmee, to Lake Okeechobee where the water then oozed into the Everglades, Marjory Stoneman Douglas's river of grass. During the summer wet season almost daily thunderstorms, occasional tropical storms, and infrequent hurricanes dumped copious amounts of water on the peninsula inundating an extended area of the theater of operations. Water from the overflowed lakes and streams meandered south as it followed the land's slight southward gradient. Thus Lake Okeechobee and the Everglades's wet season stretched beyond local rains to include the tardy arrival of northern lake waters weeks and months after the rainy season's skies cleared. The summer season was the sickly season with high temperatures, insects, and floods. The military pulled back from its forts in the center of the peninsula to the more healthful regions of the coast. During late fall and winter months the high water of Lake Okeechobee continued to ooze off into its indistinct southern shore. To the east the Hillsborough, the New, and the Miami rivers moved water through breaks in the limestone ridge to the Atlantic coast. To the west Lake Okeechobee waters filled Lake Flirt, which fed the Caloosahatchee River. Yet most of the water continued imperceptibly southwestward down the river of grass's 120-mile-long, 70-mile-wide swath with a gradient of a few inches loss to the mile before mixing with Atlantic,

Florida Bay, and Gulf of Mexico waters. During late fall and winter months the temperatures moderated, insects decreased, water levels dropped, and military operations resumed.

Events leading to a third war with the Seminole Indians began when Colonel William J. Worth terminated the Second Seminole War in August 1842. He temporarily set aside two and a half million acres in south Florida for the remaining three hundred Seminole Indians. The boundaries were from the mouth of the Peace River up the left bank to the fork of the south branch; follow that branch to the northern edge of Lake Istokpoga to a stream emptying into the Kissimmee River; thence the left bank of the river until it empted into Lake Okeechobee; thence due south through the lake and the Everglades to the Shark River then follow the right bank of the Gulf shore to the starting point. Many Floridians were not content to allow even that small number to remain in the state. That same month the Armed Occupation Act allotted 200,000 acres south of Gainesville for settlement of family and single men over eighteen years of age able to bear arms. They would receive 160 acres. While this act was in effect only nine months, it produced a thin settlement line from the Indian River west to Tampa Bay across central Florida. In 1845, President James K. Polk, embroiled in land disputes with England and Mexico, wanted to defuse an internal land dispute between Floridians and Seminoles. He issued a twenty-mile neutral zone around the Indian reservation to further isolate the red man from white settlements. Then the federal Swamp and Overflowed Land Act of 1850 gave the state about twenty million acres, most of which were located around Lake Okeechobee and in the Everglades. Yet south Florida's survey had not begun. Therefore, Congress could not select nor set aside those lands until surveyors distinguished what land fell under the provision of the 1850 act. Thus, eliminating the Seminoles from south Florida and surveying the swamplands became intertwined problems.

On 20 June 1853, the surveyor general of Florida, John Westcott, asked the commissioner of the General Land Office in Washington for permission to extend "the lines of the public survey across the present lines assigned to the Seminoles" between Peace Creek and the Kissimmee River. The commissioner deferred to the secretary of the interior for instructions. Meanwhile, Westcott sent surveyors into the land and then kept the army informed of his work with a plat showing the status of surveys through September 1853.[7]

Almost a year later Indian agent Captain John C. Casey submitted to Secretary of War Jefferson Davis a plan for removing the Seminoles. First, all trade with the Indians should cease so that their gunpowder supply could not be replenished. At the same time, there should be a systematic encroachment upon their land by survey teams operating between the Kissimmee and the Caloosahatchee rivers. The U.S. troops moving into the region to build roads and forts would back up the civilian survey teams. In the second and final phase, military survey teams would move into Big Cypress Swamp, the heart of the Indian land. Casey acknowledged that this might provoke the Seminoles to retaliate, but with their diminished supply of powder, he believed that the war would be brief.[8]

Meanwhile, John Westcott prepared to send as many survey teams into south Florida as he could hire. Apparently he needed more men than he could find in the state, so he sent an agent to New York City to gather crews for his assault upon Indian country. Tom Agar, a newly arrived Englishman, answered an ad in the *New York Sun* offering work on a survey expedition in south Florida for five months at forty dollars a month plus board. Agar said his group left New York on 9 December 1854 aboard the *Ravenswood*. They landed at Key Biscayne where they were "armed with a rifle, a six barrel [*sic*] revolver and a large knife." They immediately went to the Miami River to run their survey to Lake Okeechobee. Agar reached Spanish Town, not far from Tampa Bay, where he received his wages on 25 May 1855.[9] Civilian surveyors worked in the center and eastern portion of the peninsula north of Lake Okeechobee.

Colonel John Munroe, army commander in Florida, sent military units into the western and southern section of Indian country. Between March 1854 and June 1855, he dispatched at least twenty-four surveying expeditions into Seminole lands. The soldiers laid out trails, established a few blockhouses, and searched for forts from the Second Seminole War that had been lost due to poor map-making.[10]

Still army orders were slow in coming, for Francis had little communication with the army other than requests for a few metal boats for evaluation. Obviously General Jesup was not going to expend money until the need developed, and Joseph Francis was not aware of the happenings in Florida. Yet, on 4 November 1853, Francis tried to prod the army. He informed the quartermaster general that he had all the necessary machinery prepared to manufacture metal life whaleboats of either copper or galvanized iron in any size the army desired. Francis again related the advantages of metallic boats. He then made an offer to produce an iron boat deliverable in New York City for $8.50 per foot. Thus a twenty-eight-foot iron boat would cost $238, or a copper boat at $15 per foot would cost $420. Again he said if the army provided the copper from the Washington rolling mill the twenty-eight-foot copper boat would cost $216. Francis further demonstrated the value of his boats over wooden boats by noting that the U.S. quartermaster of Philadelphia bought wooden boats for California at $124 per boat. The boats lasted only two years and during that time repairs amounted to the original price of the boat. To use a wooden boat for ten years would cost $2,240; whereas, his iron boat would last at least ten years with an initial cost of $238, freight to California at $200, and repairs at $50. The total cost for ten years of service would be $488. Further, if his metal boats were made in sections to be packed for shipping, the transportation became heavy freight stored compactly in a ship's hold and the cost of shipping would be $10, saving the government $190.[11]

Meanwhile, on 10 October 1854, Colonel John Munroe sent headquarters his military plans in the event that the Seminoles took hostile actions rather than leave Florida. It was a simple plan to draw a line across the peninsula along the Caloosahatchee River, Lake Okeechobee, and then southeast from the lake to Fort Dallas on the Miami River. He believed that transportation south of this line must be by water. To accomplish this he had six companies on the western side and one on the eastern side. Three companies stationed at Fort Meade, forty-five miles east of his headquarters at Fort Brooke in Tampa. Three companies placed at Fort Myers fifteen miles up from the mouth of the Caloosahatchee River on the south bank. His eastern company was at Fort Capron on the Indian River. He planned for the Fort Meade soldiers to man the boats on Lake Okeechobee during the winter months. During the rainy season they would be withdrawn from the lake. Fort Myers troops would construct a road along the south bank of the Caloosahatchee eastward to the ford at Fort Thompson. They also would blaze trails southward to Billy Bowlegs Town and Waxy Hadjo's camp. Fort Capron's men would conduct expeditions into the Everglades in hopes of linking up with the Fort Myers soldiers. Colonel Munroe asked the Topographical Bureau for all the information and maps it had on south Florida. He hoped his actions would annoy the Seminoles enough to prod them into accepting terms to move.[12]

When General Jesup received a copy of Colonel Munroe's letter to the adjutant general saying that six wooden boats and ten canoes were to be built in Tampa for service on Lake Okeechobee with another ten canoes for Fort Dallas on the Miami River, he wrote to Colonel Munroe to tell of his plans to aid his Florida command. Jesup had ordered two barges and four whaleboats. One barge was of galvanized iron and the other of copper, and all of the whaleboats were galvanized iron. He planned to send half to the west coast and half to the east coast. Jesup also said that several Durham boats would follow just as soon as they were completed. He continued saying that when he had commanded the army in Florida during the Second Seminole War, he had planned to put a steamboat on Lake Okeechobee. If Munroe wanted a steamer for the lake, he would order an iron steamer built in sections. The steamer, shipped in sections, allowed for assembly at the lakeshore. Yet he failed to mention another small boat he had in mind because his arrangements with Francis were still ongoing.[13]

Jesup's choice of boats displayed an extraordinary knowledge of that form of transportation. Traditionally barges were transports, and the other three (batteaux, whaleboats, and Durham boats) performed stellar service in previous wars. General Jeffery Amherst, during the French and Indian War, used 800 batteaux and whaleboats to ship 10,000 men down the St. Lawrence in 1760. General George Washington employed the Marblehead Massachusetts Regiment to ferry his 2,400-man main force across the Delaware River in Durham boats in 1776, contrary to Leutze's famous painting.[14] The six-oared barges, designed to carry heavy freight on Lake Okeechobee and the larger rivers of south Florida, were thirty and forty feet long, with six-and-a-half- to ten-foot beams, and they were propelled by oars or poles. Some officers jury-rigged square sails to use wind power, and later the army provided a mast and sloop-rigged sails.[15] Francis's whaleboats had a narrow square stern, although most whaleboats were sharp at both ends. Those used in Florida were four-oared, twenty-seven foot long, five-foot beamed, and used as a troop carrier on Lake Okeechobee, on large rivers, and for scouting along the Atlantic and Gulf coasts, and were well fitted for any task at sea.

Because of Munroe's plans, on 2 November 1854 Lieutenant Colonel Charles Thomas, deputy quartermaster, wrote to Joseph Francis ordering three or four of his largest metallic whaleboats, and two barges or square-sterned rowboats for service in Florida. Thomas said troops and supplies would leave New York on 20 November 1854, and if possible he would like to include these boats at that time. Thomas then asked Francis if he could make "a light draft metal Batteau, about twenty feet long pointed at both ends, flat bottomed, with air chambers at each end, same as the whaleboats and barges." He said he could provide a model or description of a Maine Penobscot River lumberjacks' batteau for his edification. He wanted to know the cost and time to build the batteau, and said that he needed ten to twelve.[16]

That same day Colonel Thomas wrote to Thomas Mason of Bangor, Maine, asking him to describe the construction of a Penobscot River batteau. Then later in the day he telegraphed Mason and asked him to ship a batteau to Joseph Francis. Mason received the telegram first and set about obtaining a batteau, which cost him $17 locally. When the letter arrived a day later, he gathered information on the batteau's construction and forwarded a detailed diagram of the Penobscot River lumberjacks' batteau.

Later, Mason told Colonel Thomas that he would forward the batteau by steamer on the Fall River route to New York City. He also procured a model of the batteau, but now that an actual batteau was en route he would forward his model to Colonel Thomas to add to his collection of watercraft. In addition, Mason said the batteau could carry two men and four thousand pounds and draw 12 to 15 inches. When light she would draw 1 1/2 to 2 inches. Its propulsion was by paddle, pole, or oars. If carrying men, she carried as many as the seats could hold, about twenty-five men.[17]

Joseph Francis told Thomas that his order for four whaleboats and two barges, with oars and awnings, would be available for shipping by the November 1854 date. Four days later Francis received the batteau from Maine. He said it was "the queerest craft extent," but he thought it had excellent qualities. Francis said the batteau lacked seats and wanted to know if Jesup desired seats. He suggested that the batteau would nest beautifully and suggested building a nest of three or four; he also said it would take a little time to prepare dies for such a boat. Jesup's endorsement on Francis's letter said to order a nest of boats, and the equipage to include oars, poles, and seats.[18]

Colonel Munroe, a member of General Jesup's staff during the Second Seminole War, knew the conditions in south Florida. It was a forbidden region of swamps, tangled vegetation, and water impenetrable to wagons, pack mules, and horsemen. It had been the realm of the Seminoles since midway through the last Florida war. For a decade and a half the Indians carved a homeland for themselves in a strange region seldom visited by white men. The colonel knew it would take foot soldiers in boats to penetrate the Seminole lands.

Yet Colonel Munroe received bad news concerning his water transportation. On 12 December 1854 Lieutenant Ambrose P. Hill reported Fort Capron had two Mackinaw boats, two whaleboats, one barge, and one sloop-rigged sailboat. The Mackinaw boats lacked sails and had to be rowed, therefore reducing their capacity to carry freight. Both were old, had lots of rotten wood, and were not suitable for rough usage. One had been condemned years ago and recently patched up. Neither could meet the service's demands. The sloop was in good repair, of about a ton burden, able to carry twelve barrels of flour. Neither the whaleboats nor the barge were suitable for carrying freight. A little over a month later, Lieutenant Hill revised his report, saying that Forts Capron and Jupiter had four Mackinaw boats. Three of them were condemned as unserviceable three years

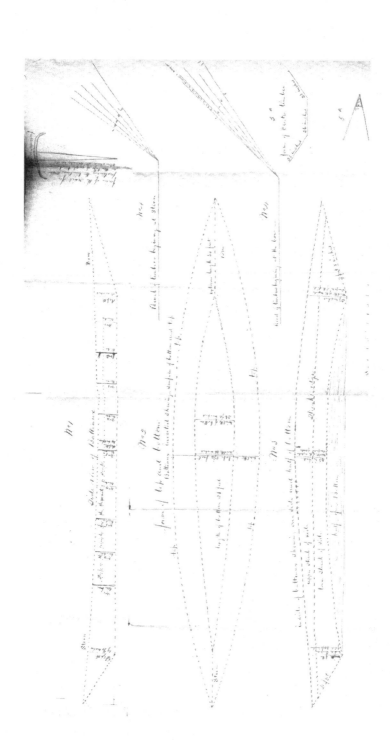

3.1 Plan for Maine Penobscot River Lumberjack's Batteau. Photo courtesy of the National Archives.

3.2 Batteau with Lumberjacks Breaking Log Jam. Photo courtesy of the Bangor, Maine, Public Library.

earlier, and the fourth was a fit subject for a Board of Survey. He said to carry supplies from Fort Capron to Jupiter, a fifty-mile journey, required strong, tight boats. In a headwind the Mackinaws would need to lay by in the open river, and for six months of the year the prevailing wind was southeast, dead ahead. Depending on the weather, Hill estimated the journey would take from four to twenty days. Further, he opined that it would take fifteen Mackinaws to transport a three months' supply to Fort Jupiter. He recommended getting some of the old surfboats used in the Mexican War at Vera Cruz, for they drew only three feet loaded. Yet Lieutenant Hill's commanding officer told headquarters that "the four Mackinaws will be put in order as far as practicable and as soon as possible."[19]

When Colonel Munroe began the task of carrying out his operation plan, he needed to do many things. He needed a better understanding of the terrain. Many of the Second Seminole War forts were not located precisely and needed relocating. He had to examine transportation routes and in many cases improve them. He had to know where the Seminoles lived, and for that he needed boats to reach them.

On 14 January 1855, Captain Alexander Montgomery reported difficulty finding civilians in Tampa willing to make canoes. He suggested that soldiers could make their own canoes on the shore of Lake Okeechobee at much less cost, but the colonel did not approve that scheme. Montgomery had completed fourteen of the twenty canoes, and they varied in size from twenty-one to thirty feet in length. The work was so slow that he suggested the larger canoes might replace the need for boats. In any case Montgomery concluded not to make any boats until he received further orders from the colonel.[20]

Captain Harvey A. Allen received orders to examine Lake Okeechobee and to find old Fort McRae and determine if it was suitable for use again. On 19 February 1855, he departed Fort Myers with one of Joseph Francis's metal lifeboats loaded on a wagon. He took the road to Fort Thompson, crossed the ford, and continued on to Fort Center on Fisheating Creek, arriving in the evening of the twentieth. The next day he launched his lifeboat in the creek and discovered that one of its air chambers where it joined the bottom of the boat was broken. It was not serious enough to delay his expedition, and he set out for Lake Okeechobee. The mouth of the creek was full of grass and plants that had to be pushed aside to allow passage of his boat. Once on the lake Allen found that the shore seemed one continuous green growth, but about a half a mile north of his exit was a dead tree that made a good mark to find the creek on his return. He also noted that there were no islands southeast of the creek's mouth as his map indicated. Everywhere they landed the shore was white sand, there were no rocks, and the water was shallow; therefore, they were forced to off-load their boat in waist-deep water before hauling the boat on shore to protect it from the wind.[21]

The day after Allen reached Lake Okeechobee a copper barge and a large skiff from Tampa departed Fort Myers for Fort Deynaud, destined for service on the lake. Colonel Harvey Brown kept the other Tampa-built boats at Fort Myers because he did not believe they were strong enough to make the distant and hazardous journey to Okeechobee. He instructed the commanding officer at Fort Deynaud to place the two boats on wheels in preparation for the overland trip to Fort Center. Meanwhile, he assembled a detachment under Lieutenant John T. Greble to take the boats to Lake Okeechobee to add to Captain Allen's group. Brown hoped that Major William Hays had some men who knew something about rowing to add to Greble's detachment, saying, "I suppose good oarsmen cannot be found—but something of the use of the oar should be known as the row will be a long one."[22]

Lake Okeechobee was a unique body of water. Its peculiarities would have challenged most professional seamen, and Captain Allen's crew, a corporal and five privates, were far from professional seamen. Storms whipping across the lake sometimes created storm surges wherein the waves rose to heights where the troughs between waves were shallow enough to slam the boat upon the lake bottom. Such conditions played havoc with barges and whaleboats. Captain Allen reported that during a thirty-six-hour period his boat was subject to strong wind and impressive swells. After that encounter he sought shelter, if possible, at the approach of a storm. He also discovered that between shore and wooded area farther inland there was a marsh of varying widths separating the lakeshore from land.[23]

Shortly after he arrived on the lake, he received a small iron boat from Fort Deynaud. His vague description "a small iron boat" raised a question as to whether it was one of Francis's batteaux or another type of small iron rowboat. In the official records there were several similar references to iron rowboats that lend belief that Francis may have produced other craft beyond his already mentioned boats. At any rate, after Lieutenant Greble arrived, Allen decided to send Greble back with the three large boats and to keep the small iron boat for his work constructing Fort McRae's blockhouse. He needed the small boat to tow logs down the lake to his site, but he did not need the larger boats. He felt that at the exposed construction site the large boats might receive more damage from storm and wind than they would at Fort Center.[24]

Companies L and M of the First Artillery had recently reactivated Fort Dallas and had received ten large cypress canoes built at Fort Myers under Lieutenant

Greble's direction. On 1 March, Captain Samuel K. Dawson led the first expedition out of the fort to the cheers and handkerchief waving of the artillerymen, wives, and children left behind. Dawson headed for Prophet's Landing and then skirted the shore of the Everglades in the direction of Waxy Hadjo's Landing to communicate with the troops at the recently established blockhouse of Fort Shackelford. He led seventy-one men guided by the Seminole Chia, whose services had been invaluable during the Second Seminole War. They paddled up the Miami River to its fork and took the left bank. The water was shallow, and at times the men had to haul the canoes. Because of the boggy land, they covered only six miles before darkness overtook them. Chia brought them to a small key or island to spend the night, but the ground was so damp that part of the troops slept in the canoes and the rest cut and piled brush to raise them above the water. That night a norther blew in and many of the men spent the night huddled around the fires just waiting for daylight so they could move about and warm up.

The second day Chia found the water low and shifted his course. He followed a winding slough that Captain Dawson said seldom allowed them to be on a course for more than five minutes. While dragging their canoes the men often sunk almost to their waists in the oozy mud. The sawgrass cut their arms and legs repeatedly as they pushed and pulled their canoes onward. They covered twelve miles that day. The next day the expedition made ten miles, for the men were losing strength in the sharp, soupy, morass. That third day Dawson made an interesting observation. They had finally entered a sinuous slough where the water was deep enough for the troops to remain in their canoes and paddle. As the expedition passed around a nearly mile long turn, Dawson looked "across a grassy mud bank, not fifty yards distant" and saw his rear canoe going in the opposite direction. Dawson was convinced that this had happened repeatedly in the serpentine slough without having a clearing to confirm this phenomenon. The next day was a repeat of the earlier days, and by midafternoon Dawson had had enough. He told Chia to turn back, and on the seventh day the expedition reached Fort Dallas with little accomplished except lacerated arms and legs, torn shirtsleeves, ripped trousers, and exhausted soldiers.[25]

On 5 May, the government contract steamer *Texas Ranger* hauled Captain Henry C. Pratt's nine-boat expedition from Fort Myers to Malco Inlet on the southwest coast. After off-loading and establishing a base camp, Pratt directed Lieutenant James Robertson to examine and check all creeks north and eastward of the camp. Robertson found a creek flowing from the northeast listed on his map as the Malco River. Only skiffs drawing less than two feet could navigate up the Malco; the deeper draft ones needed hauling. The skiffs were Francis's batteaux, also known as gondola skiffs. Three miles up from its mouth, Robertson found an Indian field under cultivation, but no Seminoles were in sight. Meanwhile, Captain Pratt explored east and southward. He visited White Horse Key by passing from Malco Inlet to Gullivans Bay. As with Robertson, only his skiffs drawing less than two feet could proceed afloat. He had to haul his boats through parts of the channel. White Horse turned out to be a small mangrove island with no drinking water on it. Captain Pratt's guides had led him to believe it had potable water. The group returned to base camp where drinking water from the steamer was stored. Pratt then sent Lieutenant Matthew Blunt to Chokoliska to check if Indians were there. Although he found no signs of Seminoles, Blunt left a package of tobacco at a field planted in watermelons and continued on his scout. Upon his return he found the package gone, but still no signs of Indians.

When the *Texas Ranger* returned, it had orders for Pratt to proceed to the Shark River, but the steamer captain reported he only had fourteen cords of wood and he would need at least twenty-four to go to the Shark River and return to Fort Myers. Pratt sent men to gather dry mangrove wood, and they brought in eight cords. On the trip to Chokoliska Inlet to pick up Lieutenant Blunt, the steamer captain tried to use the mangrove wood, but his engineer reported it did not produce enough heat to create the necessary steam. On 3 May, Captain Pratt returned to Fort Myers with little to report other than that expeditions must carry adequate water for future treks into the southwest coast.[26]

On 11 June 1855, Colonel Brown, commanding at Fort Myers, submitted his views on boats required for Florida. He thought one small sailboat of ten- or fifteen-ton burden should be used on Lake Okeechobee, the barges should be thirty-one feet long with six-foot beams, and the whaleboats should be twenty and a half feet long with five-foot beams, and there was a need for some smaller boats of light draft. Then in a postscript he reported a weakness in the air chambers of some of Francis's metal boats. He stressed that this problem should be attended to immediately, for "remedied they are by far the best boat for the service." By the time Brown's comment reached New York Joseph Francis was in Europe, but Marshal Lefferts must have made a proper correction because there were no more comments about this weakness.[27]

One of Colonel Munroe's most active officers was Second Lieutenant George Lucas Hartsuff, Second Artillery, who, working for the Topographical Engineers, made four survey treks into Indian Territory, three of them into the Big Cypress Swamp, the very heartland of the tribe. In June 1855, he reported his arrival at Fort Deynaud after more than three months in the swamps. Along with his map, Hartsuff submitted a report that the land was worthless for anyone but Seminoles.[28] Yet Lieutenant Hartsuff did more than survey during the first six months of 1855. He built Fort Simon Drum. He cut a trail north from Fort Drum to Fort Deynaud. He traveled east to examine Waxy Hadjo's campsite; then he built Fort Shackelford nearby. He rediscovered Fort Keais, one of the abandoned and lost Second Seminole War forts. Lieutenant Hartsuff, and others like him, made the army visible to the Seminoles in their swampland fastness.

About this same time, Joseph Francis went to Europe and became immersed in selling his metallic watercraft throughout the continent. When he departed from the United States he was not aware of the Indian problem in Florida, nor later that his metal boats participated in combat operation in that state, for he never gathered testimonials from the military who used his boats nor did he write about the Third Seminole War. Yet throughout his life Francis's modus operandi was to use testimonials to publicize his inventions. Thus, the conclusion that he did not know about the small Indian conflict in south Florida is sound. As far as Francis was concerned, he had just introduced the U.S. Army to his metal boats.

On 24 December 1855, Colonel Munroe sent three wooden boats from Tampa to Fort Myers by schooner for Fort Thompson. Second Lieutenant Stephen H. Weed received orders to go to Fort Myers to pick up the boats. When he arrived at Fort Myers, he found the schooner had left the boats at Punta Rassa at the mouth of the Caloosahatchee River. Borrowing a boat from Captain Henry C. Pratt, Weed set out to retrieve his watercraft. Arriving at Punta Rassa, he found all three boats had their ribs separated from their stem. One also had its bottom boards broken. He had to leave that boat at Punta Rassa. The other two he towed up river to Fort Myers for repairs. On closer examination he discovered that one of the two needed extensive repairs necessitating leaving it at Fort Myers. Lieutenant Weed returned to his post with only one of his three boats after a fourteen-hour row covering about thirty-three miles.[29] Francis's metal boats would have been stronger vessels.

Chief Billy Bowlegs anxiously watched the incursions of surveyors and troops into his land. He was one of the last of the Seminole chiefs left in Florida. He knew the power and might of the white man. In 1852 he went to Washington to talk with the Great White Father about migrating west. Billy Bowlegs traveled by horseback, coach, steamboat, and train on his way north, visiting Tampa, Palatka, Savannah, and New York. He had no illusions concerning the Americans. Yet he resisted going west. Instead, he moved deeper into the Big Cypress Swamp to avoid white men. By 1855 Billy Bowlegs could ignore the crisscrossing survey parties no longer. On 20 December he struck at Lieutenant Hartsuff's command deep in his land. Captain Casey's plan worked; the Third Seminole War began, and Francis's metal boats of all descriptions were dribbling into south Florida. Although Joseph Francis was out of the country and not in contact with the Department of Florida's commanders, his metal boats were in combat operations and valued by these officers.

4

The Third Seminole War

Strategy and Tactics

During the Third Seminole War, the three overall commanders in Florida carried out the strategic goal of removing the Seminole Indians from the state. Their basic tactic to achieve that goal was to scour the Everglades and swamps south of a line from the Caloosahatchee River east to Lake Okeechobee then southeast to Fort Dallas to locate the Indian settlements. Their methods of operation varied for many reasons, including local conditions over which they had little control. Yet Colonel John Munroe, 9 October 1853–22 November 1856, General William S. Harney, 22 November 1856–27 April 1857, and Colonel Gustavus Loomis, 27 April 1857 to the war's end, 7 May 1858, hewed closely to the basic tactic of sending foot soldiers in boats into the interior.[1]

The Seminole strategy was to remain isolated from whites in their homeland in south Florida. Their tactics were the result of a great council in April 1841, a little over a year before the end of the Second Seminole War (1835–1842). At that time the chiefs decreed that they should travel in small groups, use ambush, fire, and flight to counter the Americans' superior force. It was sound advice in 1855 also.[2]

It is strange that although the Americans provoked the Seminoles to conflict, when the war arrived the army was not ready. During the first six months most action took place under the Indian initiative, such as against three white men tending a cootie flourmill near Fort Dallas, a military wood party from Fort Deynaud, upon Colonel Hamlin Snell's house on Sarasota Bay; and killing two oystermen at Charlotte Harbor.

On 31 March 1856 a party of Seminoles approached the Braden Castle, a one-thousand-acre sugar plantation along the Manatee River. The Indians fired upon the house and the inhabitants went to the second floor to return fire. Later the Seminoles tried to burn the house, but the thick stucco walls were fireproof. The warriors left with seven blacks, some mules, and food. Militia units set out after the hostiles, following the mule tracks, and found their prey camped on the south bank of the Big Charley Apopka Creek. Surprising the Indians, the militiamen fired and killed two. The remaining fled into the creek, hiding in the extensive vegetation along the banks. After firing into the banks the militia left convinced they killed two more warriors. They also retrieved the slaves and mules. Later Lieutenant Henry A. Crane complained that Lieutenant John Addison and his men stopped to gather war trophies and refused to cross the river and continue after the Seminoles.[3]

An important and bloody encounter took place on 14 June. The Seminoles attacked the Willoughly Tillis farm on the Peace River just south of Fort Meade. Again the besieged whites held off their attackers. Seven militiamen from the fort responded to the attack, and the Indians fled to the safety of a hummock, a very dense heavily wooded area well suited for the hostiles to hide. In the encounter at close quarters the fatalities were three whites and one Seminole. The next day a larger detachment of militiamen set out after the Indians and a day later surprised their foe. This time several Indians and two whites died. Oscen Tustenuggee, an important war chief, died in this engagement and hereafter most of the Seminole hostilities took place in south Florida.[4]

Historians of the war summed up the role of the Florida militia efforts in the first six months as unimpressive. Contemporary Floridians considered the engagements at Big Charley Apopka Creek and Peace River as victories. Yet they were defensive actions responding to Seminole attacks.

Meanwhile, Captain John C. Casey, Indian agent in Florida, gave Colonel Munroe his views on the conduct for boating parties in the Everglades. A compass was necessary for any expedition, and, if possible, all noncommissioned officers should carry one. It would be a sound policy for all men to be told where the closest road lay so that if lost, they had a basic direction in which to head. The troops must be prepared to cook and sleep in their canoes. They must learn how to use their guns to build fires without making much noise. Each canoe should carry grains and fish lines to catch soft shell turtles and fish. The men must learn how to catch gophers, for a roasted gopher could provide nourishment for several days. A roasted snake was as good as eel. The cabbage tree also provided additional nourishment for the troops. Sometimes water could be found by digging with a knife into the ground for surface water, if not, a man could relieve his thirst by gathering the dew from air plants. According to Casey this last water was "sweet and wholesome." The captain concluded by saying, "Nothing tends to bewilder a lost man so much as the fear of dying from want of food and water."[5]

Even before Governor James Broome could react to the Seminole attack, the people on the frontier, too impatient to wait, took matters in their own hands. In Tampa, the people held a meeting as soon as news arrived of Billy Bowlegs's attack on Lieutenant Hartsuff's command. On 24 December 1855 the people selected

William B. Hooker to command the local militia charged with taking action. He sent detachments to a string of forts along the frontier and sent a group down the Peace River to halt the expected Seminole advance toward Tampa.[6]

On 7 January, five days before the governor's action, Secretary of War Jefferson Davis authorized Colonel Munroe to call upon Florida for three mounted militia companies and two infantry companies.[7] On 12 January 1856 Governor Broome, acting with comparable speed, raised six mounted militia companies immediately, but knowing the state lacked the money to pay for such a large organization, he offered all of them to the secretary of war for federal service.[8]

When Munroe received his authorization from the War Department he forwarded his request to Governor Broome. The colonel was quite specific in his desire that the infantry "be composed exclusively of good woodsmen" versed in the habits of the Seminoles. The Florida foot volunteers would be "employed as hunters and trailers in the swamps and morasses where horsemen can not go and where alone the Indians are to be found and overcome." Munroe entrusted his letter to militia general Jesse Carter of Tampa to take it to Tallahassee. The colonel apologized to the governor for being unable to take it to the capital himself.[9]

In recent months Colonel Munroe had learned a great deal about his troops during their expeditions and surveys prior to the opening of hostilities. Many of his soldiers were German and Irish immigrants from the urban poor: men unskilled in boating, hunting, and woods craft; these three attributes were critical for the coming struggle. The colonel decided early that he must rely upon the Florida foot volunteer militiamen to assume the lead role in finding the Seminoles.

While he waited for his Florida foot volunteers, Colonel Munroe set about getting his boats. He wrote to Colonel Daniel D. Tompkins, quartermaster of the Department of the East in New Orleans, that back on 16 September 1855, General Jesup told him that among the quartermaster's property destined for the troops in Florida were six of Francis's metallic barges. As of this letter his command had not received them. Munroe requested either the mentioned barges "or others of the same general description either of Iron or wood be furnished with the least possible delay—These boats being immediately and absolutely required for service." He continued by saying that "if wooden boats were sent then the six metal ones were still necessary for proposed operations."[10]

This request brought a flurry of replies from the Quartermaster Corps. Colonel Tompkins said that he had no metal boats on hand, and there was no way to make them in New Orleans; however, he telegraphed the quartermaster general regarding the "Six Francis Barges or Life Boats" desired. Meanwhile, he found three wooden boats near Munroe's description that he bought and would ship on the steamer *Fashion*. He hoped to have three more boats built that may be ready when the *Fashion* returned.

The next day Tompkins received a telegraph from General Jesup that he had ordered the six lifeboats together with twenty metal batteaux from New York.[11] General Jesup said that as soon as he had received Munroe's earlier letter that the Tampa canoes were too heavy for the Everglades, he had ordered eight metallic barges and twenty metallic batteaux. When the crafts were ready, Jesup would send them to Fort Dallas and the Caloosahatchee as follows: Ten iron batteaux to Fort Dallas, eight metal barges of thirty-foot length, and ten iron batteaux to the Caloosahatchee River. All of the boats and batteaux would include oars and paddles.[12]

Colonel Munroe even called upon Captain Israel Vogdes of Key West to ship his metal barge to him. This was one of the early barges first procured when the army issued them to New York, Boston, and Key West harbors for experimental purposes. Vogdes asked for its return as soon as possible.[13]

In the first week in February, Colonel Harvey Brown, commanding the forces along the Caloosahatchee, sent a list of boats in his command. On Lake Okeechobee there were 2 six-oared metallic barges "long in use and nearly worn out," a large wooden batteau "not at all fit for service," and one four-oared metallic whaleboat "in good order." At Fort Deynaud there were the following: "all from . . . one scow . . . unserviceable: one scow—good, one small [unintelligible], two oars skiff—not fit for service 1 canoe. *Fort Myers* 1 six-oars metallic barge, good,—1 four oars metallic whale boat—good—6 small metallic gondola skiffs—serviceable but not adapted for this water—of little use, 2 wooden four oars skiff—good for nothing—3 small skiffs—good for nothing—2 canoes—not adapted to the service—1 scow *Fort McKenzie* 2 small gondola skiffs—Kissimmee River 1 canoe not serviceable."[14]

Sometime during February Colonel Brown received a letter from Daniel Stemson in New York City telling him that several batteaux and iron barges were being built for his neighborhood, and if he wanted to make any alterations he had better send them direct to General Jesup, for he made all the purchases of metal boats without consulting with other quartermaster personnel.[15]

Colonel Munroe's metal boats proved less sturdy than intended. The army board that examined Francis's metallic boats had been correct when it suggested that army usage might be more damaging to metal boats than that employed by the maritime forces. In January 1856, First Lieutenant Albert J. S. Molinard, with eighty-three men, set out from Fort Deynaud to transport two metallic boats to

Fort Center. The boats' crudely built boat cradles, the rough road, and the heavy metal boats caused the cradles to frequently break down. All travel halted while repairs made on the cradle were undertaken. It was a difficult and frustrating journey that took five days instead of the expected two days' trek.

When Molinard arrived at Fort Center, he found the wooden boat scheduled for his use needed recaulking, and that would take at least three days. The boat cradles wore holes in his two copper boats at the four pressure points, and the green copper boat had a lengthy rip in its side when at one time it fell completely out of its cradle. Molinard reported that all of the air chambers received damage; although, he thought he could make repairs if he had the proper tools. Instead Colonel Munroe dispatched a coppersmith from Fort Myers under military escort to Fort Center.

Once repairs were completed Molinard left his sick troops at Fort Center and moved into Lake Okeechobee, spending his first night on Observation Island. On 18 January he reached Cypress Point and the following day Fort McRae. During his journey he ran into a heavy blow and, because of the poor handling qualities of his flatboat, he had to hug the shore, doubling his distance traveled. With metal boats he could have gone directly across the lake. Leaving Fort McRae he again ran into strong wind and torrential rain violent enough to force him back to beach his boats. Evidently the repair work on his green boat was unsatisfactory for he had to repair two leaks in it before he could launch again.[16]

Colonel Munroe's metal boat problems were minor compared to his difficulty recruiting Floridians with boating, hunting, and woodcraft skills to use the boats, although the early reaction of citizens indicated they were ready to serve. It seemed that the militiamen refused to walk; most frontier Floridians were cattlemen and preferred to ride to war. The quick response to raise six mounted militia companies demonstrated that. Yet the colonel knew only skilled boatmen could penetrate the Everglades to reach the Seminoles.

Governor Broome wrote to Colonel Munroe authorizing him to select three of six Florida Mounted Volunteers for federal service. The colonel graciously declined, saying that such decision should come from the highest authority in the state. Then he shifted to Florida's two companies of infantry that he had requested and not yet received. He reiterated that the composition must be woodsmen and trailers. These volunteers will aid the regulars in finding, pursuing, and securing the Seminoles. These select Floridians operating from boats were of the first importance. Munroe regretted that he could not offer a greater monetary inducement to these special troops.

The colonel continued, saying that Richard Turner of Tampa, who had been a captain in the militia during the last Seminole War, offered to raise a company of boatmen and hunters. Munroe recommended that Florida accept Turner's offer. Even if he raised only a fraction of a company, the governor should accept the detachment with the table of organization of a platoon's assignment of officers and noncommissioned officers.[17]

Two days later Munroe wrote to the adjutant general of the army telling of his request to the governor to accept Turner's offer. Anticipating acceptance, he now requested permission to accept Turner's company or detachment regardless of the raising of the other two infantry companies. He assured the adjutant general that Turner's men would be woodsmen and boatmen, efficient in arms and hunting and that they would be immediately available for service on the southwest coast among the islands where boats can approach the interior. The colonel believed that Turner's men would "render valuable services."[18]

Later Governor Broome told Munroe that General Jesse Carter was now the state's special agent responsible for filling the army's request for militia. This system would eliminate the governor as a middleman and speed up the flow of Floridians to federal service, although Broome wanted to be kept informed at a later more convenient time.[19]

Colonel Munroe did not intend to wait upon the Florida militiamen. He wrote Colonel Harvey Brown that he planned to bring Company L at Fort Dallas to Punta Rassa for temporary service with one of Brown's companies to operate around Malco Inlet. Munroe felt that Company L had gained experience in their treks into the Everglades and it would be advisable for troops from the east and west coast to jointly explore Florida's southwest coast.

Then he told Brown of his requisition to Governor Broome for two infantry companies of volunteers. These two companies of Florida foot volunteers would be hunters and trailers operating with regular troops in expeditions south of the Caloosahatchee. He stressed that Brown must not accept any Floridian for these companies unless he was a good woodsman. Unfortunately for planning purposes, he did not know when the Florida foot companies would be ready for service. Finally, he told Brown that the secretary of war directed three hundred rifles "prepared for long ranges" and supplied with sword bayonets be sent to south Florida as soon as possible.[20]

On 15 February the schooner *Libby Shepard* loaded Company L, a metal barge, and three large canoes and headed for Punta Rassa. Yet, Munroe's plan to merge east and west coast companies in joint operations around Malco Inlet were set aside when Company L had to open the abandoned Camp Daniels just west of Fort Myers.[21]

Colonel Munroe wrote to Governor Broome that Captain Richard B. Turner's foot detachment, received at Fort Brooke on 3 March, mustered only twenty-five privates. Thus Turner had to accept a first lieutenancy. Munroe again voiced his opinion that the present pay for foot soldiers on duty in the Everglades, hammocks, and swamps of south Florida needed doubling. He believed "the severity of the duties, and the dangers they will incur when compared either with the mounted troops, and the price of ordinary labor which is always expected to form the basis of compensation" was not reflected the foot soldier's pay.[22]

The colonel moved rapidly once he had his first Florida foot unit. First Lieutenant Turner and his men, armed with the long-range rifles, went to Punta Rassa to await the shipment of metal boats from New York City and then go to the Malco River to assist Captain Pratt exploring the southwest coast. Pratt had had that same assignment a year earlier. While Turner waited at Punta Rassa, Colonel Munroe requested permission from the secretary of war Davis to place a certain force at Manatee, Florida, into any of his volunteer militia companies. With Davis's approval, Munroe then accepted a second lieutenant, a sergeant, a corporal, and nineteen privates into Turner's foot company. Thus Richard Turner's detachment had enough men to increase his rank to captain.[23]

Shortly after the federalization of the first Florida foot, Captain Casey modified the war's operational rules when he announced a cash premium for capturing or enticing Seminoles to move west. The premium was $250 to $500 for a warrior, $150 to $300 for a woman, and $100 to $200 for a boy over the age of ten. "The maximum or highest rate will be paid for all except the infirm, bedridden and helpless, in which cases the rate will be decided by a Board."[24] Now the goal to capture rather then kill prevailed.

Captain Turner received his batteaux from the steamer from New York City and departed Punta Rassa on 1 April. He arrived at Malco Inlet but found Captain Pratt was not there. He headed south looking for him. Just south of Malco Inlet, Turner encountered a severe storm and three of his batteaux swamped. Evidently the unfortunate batteaux had defective air chambers, for otherwise they should have remained afloat. Not wanting to jeopardize all of his party, Turner placed the rescued men and some supplies ashore at a temporary camp before proceeding south.[25]

Meanwhile, Captain Pratt had moved and established his camp on Chokoliska Key. On 31 March he was low on fresh water. There was no fresh water on the island. Pratt sent two boats to proceed up the river for three or four miles to get water. Three hours later, hearing shots from the interior, he sent two officers and twenty-five men in the two remaining barges to investigate. His water party ran into an ambush, were fired on, and lost two men. Captain Pratt sent a letter relating the incident and requested ammunition to replace that lost on his expeditions and more skiffs to carry out his task. Immediately, Colonel Brown sent two skiffs to Pratt by schooner.[26]

On 6 April, just after Pratt received the new skiffs, Captain Turner arrived with his forty-three men. Captain Pratt turned his new skiffs over to Turner and sent the Florida foot to check an Indian field at the mouth of the Wekima Creek and then continue into the interior. When Turner reached the head of navigation, he left a guard with his batteaux and continued on across the prairie. Turner said that when the prairie was dry it was possible to use pack mules, but it was filling with water causing the ground to be boggy and difficult to travel through the tall brown grass. With great effort, Turner crossed the prairie and reached the cypress swamp before returning to camp.

When Captain Pratt reported Turner's accomplishment, he again asked for more small boats or skiffs. He noted that his two sailboats, while good for towing the small boats along the coast, were unable to move close to the mainland except at high tide. He also added that Turner needed one thousand rifle percussion cartridges with caps and that he did not have enough to supply both his company and Turner's.[27]

Captain Turner was active while attached to Captain Pratt's command. Beginning at Chokoliska Key, he guided his detachment inland and discovered a mound on the prairie, about five or six acres in size, with an acre and a half planted in corn and pumpkins. The corn was almost two feet high. Turner destroyed the plants. He also found several trails about three weeks old indicating that the Indians had moved north. Pratt later assumed that the military actions on the coast caused the Seminoles to move.

While Turner examined the Fakahatchee and Wekima creeks, Pratt examined the coastline from Chokoliska Key to Paviony Key and the Paviony River then on to White Horse Key before returning to his Chokoliska camp to meet Turner. Pratt decided to send Turner back into the interior, and he would follow going up the Fakahatchee River. Two days after Turner left, Pratt saw smoke in the direction that Turner had gone. He took three boats and eight men to investigate. When he had gone up the river a couple of miles, he saw three canoes heading toward him from a small tributary. As near as he could tell, there were fifteen men in the canoes. Then it struck Pratt that this was a decoy to draw him off so that other Indians could attack his base camp. He immediately returned and prepared for a fight, but nothing more happened.[28]

Then Pratt moved to Camp Malco where he launched three different expeditions. The first led by Captain Pratt examined the Fakahatchee River trying to reach Depot 1. The scout did not reach Major Arnold's command, but they believed that they were within five or six miles of their destination when they were halted by thick hammocks and cypress. The second trek, under Captain Arnold Elzey marched between the Fakahatchee and Wekima rivers. The intervening land was pine barrens. The country was difficult to march over and contained groundwater that was too salty to drink. The third trip led by Lieutenant Henry Benson examined the east and southeast reaches of the cypress swamp and eventually the Everglades. Turner continued his examination of the Fakahatchee and its tributaries by batteaux and on foot, trying to find a better water route to the Big Cypress Swamp. At the end of these treks Pratt concluded that the only entrance to the Big Cypress Swamp was through the Fakahatchee or Wekima rivers. Turner spent so much time on the Fakahatchee that its name became Turner's River.[29]

Meanwhile, First Lieutenant Richard C. Duryea led a detachment of forty-five men out from Fort Dallas with orders "to act offensively against the Indians." He ascended the Miami River to the Everglades and then took a course to the southwest staying as near to the mainland as possible. During the first two days he examined five of the largest islands without finding any signs. On the third day he found a trail and followed it for four miles before losing it. Later in the afternoon he picked up the trail again that led to an Indian encampment that showed occupancy a few weeks earlier. Lieutenant Duryea camped there for the night. The next day he saw a large island between his group and the mainland and headed for it. He got within two or three miles before the water became so low it was useless to attempt to haul his canoes any farther. He took a patrol on foot to the island, but found no signs of Seminoles. On the fifth day, he found a trail of a canoe and followed it until he lost it in deep water. One of the islands examined had the remains of an old plantation of about four acres now fallow. On the sixth day he found numerous abandoned Indian campsites not used for months. Duryea turned back on the sixth day and reached Fort Dallas on the tenth day. At the end of his expedition Duryea noted that on the way into the glades they had to drag their canoes about a third of the time and on the way back the water level had risen so that they only had to drag their craft one-fifth of the time. Lieutenant Duryea found it difficult to act offensively against an enemy that he could not find.[30]

The accumulation of negative reports and the absence of finding Seminole family communities on the treks from Fort Dallas into the Everglades and from the probes along the southwest coast led Colonel Munroe to assume that the

Seminoles must be in the Big Cypress Swamp. The colonel determined to mass as large a force as possible to assault the Indian homeland. He called upon the state to send its three mounted volunteer companies to Fort Deynaud to serve with the federal troops. During that time the U.S. government would provide provisions and forage.[31]

Munroe then wrote to Colonel Brown that he had received news of the attack upon Major Arnold's command and that arrangements were in progress to gather both the state and federal Florida mounted volunteers to work with the regular army units in an attack upon the Seminoles in the Big Cypress Swamp. The Florida volunteers received orders to go to Fort Deynaud as soon as possible.[32]

From Fort Deynaud they moved to Fort Simon Drum where Captain Lewis Arnold led the combined forces of volunteers and regulars down to Billy Bowlegs's village on their way to the Big Cypress Swamp. Only twenty of the Floridians were mounted; the rest were on foot. The volunteers were in an unaccustomed milieu, tramping in the hot weather subjected to sand fleas, and later, as the water rose, to mud and water. When the water became too deep for the horses, the mounted men stabled their mounts at Depot 1 and sloshed along with the infantry. Unfortunately for the force it was the same old routine of trading a few shots with the hidden enemy and failing to be able to trail them in the morass that was their homeland. Yet according to Captain Arnold and Lieutenant Hartsuff the Florida mounted volunteers performed their duties on foot with energy and zeal.[33] By the end of May the attack into the Big Cypress Swamp had ended with few Indian contacts due to excessive flooding and lack of boats for the soldiers.

Colonel Munroe began his post-operations critique to the adjutant general, Colonel Samuel Cooper, saying that during the early days of his combined operation he had received a letter from Colonel William J. Hardee, whose *Rifle and Light Infantry Tactics* had been officially adopted by the army the year before, recommending employing Indians as trailers to find the Seminoles. Munroe already had reached the conclusion that the lack of good trailers had been confirmed through the experience of his troops during the past season. He concluded that good Indian trailers conforming to Colonel Hardee's description would have been desirable.[34] Yet Munroe felt that the lack of an adequate number of competent Florida foot volunteers operating in boats also contributed to the poor performance of his forces in penetrating the Indian homeland. Again he voiced his belief that if the foot troops were paid on the same scale as the mounted men, or "if the rates of wages in civil life were made the standard," more men would be induced to serve in foot companies.[35]

When Colonel Munroe wrote to Governor Broome, he told him he had re-

ceived permission from the secretary of war to call for three to five companies of
Florida foot. He pointed out that his first request, back in January, for two companies of foot still were lacking. Only Captain Richard Turner's detachment had
served, and his service was exemplary. Almost all of Turner's operations took
place while using metal batteaux. The colonel was aware of the difficulty the state
faced in finding foot troops, but they were the only force able to operate in the Big
Cypress, the Everglades, and the swamps. The only way to stop Seminole depre-
dations on the frontier was to find and attack the Indians in their swampland fastness, and that required infantrymen traveling in boats.[36]

Back on 10 October 1854 Colonel Munroe asked the Topographical Corps of
Engineers for all the information and maps it had on south Florida. Almost two
years later, while waiting for a good map, he sent Major Hays and Lieutenant
Hartsuff's explorations in the Big Cypress Swamp to Washington to assist the car-
tographers. On 14 June 1856, the adjutant general told Munroe that Lieutenant
Joseph C. Ives had completed a detailed map compiled from U.S. Land Office
maps and various army reports from his operations area that should be ready in
a few weeks.[37]

In July, Colonel Munroe and Governor Broome still were corresponding over
federalizing Florida militia. In answer to the governor, Munroe stated rather
bluntly that until he received his first request of two foot companies he would
not ask for more infantry units. That same day, 6 July 1856, the colonel wrote to
Colonel Samuel Cooper giving his views of the Florida militia. The mounted
troops, drawn mainly from the frontier, had families living in danger of Indian
raiders. This situation "seriously affected the efficiency and usefulness" of those
companies. "Their domestic obligations and personal interests have in great measure led them to attend to their own affairs at the expense of the public." In his
conclusion, Munroe again referred to Turner's small detachment as being an effective Florida unit, and noted that he was still waiting for his two full companies of foot militia.[38]

Perhaps to make amends for his earlier remarks Colonel Munroe wrote to
Governor Broome in August to say that Captain Turner's detachment completed
its service on 1 September, and in all of its assigned duties that small batteaux
force received the highest commendations at headquarters from all of the officers
who worked with that unit. He suggested that if Turner could raise a company
or less, the state should immediately accept it for active duty. He ended by saying
that for the coming campaign those militia foot companies were vital.[39]

Colonel Munroe had his staff develop a plan for operations during the 1856–
57 winter campaign. The northernmost defensive line consisted of one mounted

company to patrol from Fort Brooke to the upper St. Johns River. A boat command stationed on Lake Okeechobee, one-fourth mounted, was to patrol from Fort Meade south on the Kissimmee River and the eastern shore of Lake Okeechobee. One column in boats was based at Fort Dallas, scouting in the Everglades and patrolling using pack mules to examine the east coast north of the fort. Four boat columns operating from the mouth of the Caloosahatchee would probe all points of the southwest coast into the interior. Three columns on foot would operate in the Big Cypress Swamp with its supplies based at Fort Deynaud. This was an ambitious program calling for mounted, foot, and boat troops.[40]

Quartermaster Major Justus McKinstry estimated this plan would need thirty-three boats. The 30 September inventory of Fort Myers listed forty-seven boats and Fort Dallas twenty-five, and of these seventy-two boats forty were Francis's metallic boats. Fort Myers had five iron whaleboats, nine barges (six iron and three copper), and twelve iron batteaux. Fort Dallas had one iron whaleboat, three iron barges, and ten metallic batteaux, and, in November, it received ten small iron rowboats from the Metallic Boat Company.[41]

It was during this planning period that Colonel Munroe finally received the Ives's map. It seemed that the Government Printing Office delayed its work so long that the topographical engineers made a copy from the original map to forward to Munroe immediately.[42] While the map showed many army trails, Florida's southwest coast, within the Ten Thousand Islands area, still was terra incognita.

Colonel Munroe was not the only one making plans for the 1856–57 winter campaign. That summer Secretary of War Davis sought the advice of General William S. Harney, who had inflicted a resounding defeat upon Little Thunder's Brulé band of Sioux in the 3 September 1855 battle of Ash Hollow on the Blue Water Creek, Nebraska. During the winter General Harney sent word to all the Sioux bands to meet in council with him in the spring. The council met during the first five days of March 1856. The minutes of the meeting were forwarded to the secretary of war, submitted to President Pierce, and referred to Congress by 24 July 1856. In addition to his current activities, Harney had extensive action in Florida during the Second Seminole War. Chakaika's band had attacked Harney's camp in July 1839, killing half his men. A year and a half later Harney found Chakaika's camp, killed him, and broke up his band. Harney and Lieutenant John T. McLaughlin of the U.S. Navy's Florida Expedition conducted joint scouts in the Everglades. In seeking advice from General Harney, Secretary Davis selected a knowledgeable Indian fighter.[43]

General Harney carefully read the documents furnished him by the adjutant general Colonel Cooper relating to the Florida war. His letter to Secretary Davis was in effect his campaign plan. He said there should be at least two full regiments of regular troops in Florida, and the state should provide an equal number of foot regiments. This combined force should operate "*almost entirely* in canoes and small boats." No boat or canoe should carry more than seven men, and it should be equipped with thirty days' provisions. The boatmen needed Colt's repeating rifles because of the difficulty of loading ordinary weapons while chasing the Seminoles in watercraft. In addition, the effect of Colt's repeating rifles would be a great demoralizer upon the Indians. He did not know how many mounted troops might be needed, but set a minimum of eight or ten companies. He stressed that the mounted troops must be most active while the boatmen are on expeditions into the interior because the Seminoles might try to flee their swampland and it would be up to the mounted men to stop their flight. After submitting his views, Harney left Washington, D.C., and returned to St. Louis, Missouri.[44]

Secretary Davis concurred with Harney and issued instructions necessary to carry out the campaign, including ordering Harney to become the commander of the Department of Florida. On 4 November 1856, he wrote to Harney telling him that on his arrival in Florida both Colonel Munroe and Captain Casey had been instructed to bring the general up to date on the Florida situation, including the Department of the Interior's plan to set aside a western tract of land for the Seminoles separate from the Creeks, and to pay $100 to $200 for all Seminole children captured regardless of their age. Davis hoped the general would "be able to find among the citizens of Florida, hunters and woodsmen who will serve a valuable purpose as guides, especially in following the trails of retreating parties." The secretary continued, saying that he would furnish Harney with whatever means or force necessary for his purposes.[45]

General Harney's itinerary to his new command in Florida called for a stop at Key West where a steamer would be waiting to take him to Fort Brooke. Upon his arrival the general found there was no steamer. After waiting from 7 to 13 November, the collector at the post placed a revenue schooner at his service and Harney arrived at Fort Brooke on 21 November 1856. Because he had pondered over the documents in Washington and the vitality with which he carried out his military duties, General Harney relieved Colonel Munroe of command of the Department of Florida the next day.[46]

General Harney brought several innovations to the Florida war. Most significantly he wanted to continue operations throughout the year. No more closing the interior forts and moving troops back to the coast for the summer sickly season. Second, he wanted his boat crews to have not just rifles, but also Colt's repeating rifles. Third, he wanted more Florida mounted volunteers to keep the Indians from fleeing south Florida when pressured by his boat crews. Fourth, he asked the secretary of war for authority to employ civilian trackers, boatmen, guides, interpreters, and spies. By this time there were about fifty iron boats in south Florida.

Once the general reached Florida, he submitted his detailed memorandum of operations for the summer of 1857. That document left no doubt of his view that boat operations were essential. Yet his opening sentences revealed his erroneous impression that the Seminoles, with their families, could not live in the Big Cypress Swamp and Everglades during the rainy season. His plan called for boat operations to contain them to the swamps. Harney's scenario was that the Seminoles would break up into small family units and strive to go to the coastal islands or to higher ground north and east of Lake Okeechobee where mounted soldiers could easily capture them in their new positions, provided military operations continued throughout the summer months. "The experience of the writer has proved this."[47]

Following his introduction, Harney laid out his disposition of the troops. He wanted six boat companies to patrol the southwest coast from Punta Rassa to Cape Sable. These companies would examine the islands and, as the water rose, probe the interior. Fort Cross and the depot near the Malco River were to be their supply bases. Two boat companies at Fort Dallas served the same function on the east coast operating between Dallas and Cape Sable. They would have a depot at Key Largo and were to penetrate the Everglades when the water rose. The company at Fort Jupiter patrolled between Fort Capron and Dallas in boats, examining islands and rivers along their route. The company, in boats, on the Indian River scouted as far north as Smyrna. Two boat companies at Fort Kissimmee were to cover the river and Lake Okeechobee and also enter the Everglades. Fort McRae would house a company of Florida mounted volunteers. Depot 1 would continue to house two foot companies. The mounted volunteers on line from Fort Brooke to Capron would scout under its existing orders. Finally, Harney established a weekly express from all points to report to headquarters.[48]

There followed a flurry of orders emanating from his headquarters. On 28 December 1856, the general ordered the chief quartermaster at Fort Brooke to hire Turner as a guide for boat services along Florida's southwest coast.[49] He ordered Captain Joseph Roberts to take two schooners, the *General Harney* and the *Major Page,* from Fort Deynaud to Fort Center for duty on Lake Okeechobee. The schooners arrived at Fisheating Creek on 4 January in good order; however, later

Roberts reported that the schooners had problems navigating on the lake and he submitted a requisition for "two Francis' life boats of large size."[50] By 5 January 1857, the general began his activities along the southern east and west coasts. On 30 January, he wanted the troops moving into the interior to be equipped with the smallest skiffs available.[51]

General Harney ordered Colonel Justin Dimick to scout the Everglades and attempt to reach the Big Cypress Swamp. Colonel Dimick was an odd commanding officer who seemed oblivious to the tactics necessary to engage the Seminoles in south Florida. When he first brought his detachment to Fort Dallas in October 1856, he was in the habit of riding off into the countryside on daylong excursions with only a junior officer to accompany him. Captain Abner Doubleday, invited after breakfast for such a ride, said the two did not return until nightfall. Doubleday thought, "The Indians might easily have cut us off for we took no precautions. We soon found that Dimick was addicted to these long excursions." The colonel continued such scouts on foot and even had a detachment of disabled soldiers on mules looking for the enemy, but seldom into the interior where the Seminoles were. One officer said, "This is all nonsense. It is merely to look well on the recap of our exploration which is sent to Genl Harney."

Even when Dimick did employ boats, they were the wrong kind. He did not like the metal batteaux and obtained two Whitehall boats, which were faster. Evidently he did not realize that once in the glades the paddled or poled batteaux were more efficient than the double-oared Whitehalls in the narrow sloughs boarded by hanging tropical vines. Thus on 6 February, in response to Harney's order, Dimick sent two Whitehall boats and one copper alligator or batteau up the Miami River. The water was falling in the glades and at times the men had to haul their boats as they pushed into the interior. Yet when the group reached a stretch of rocky rapids the scout stopped because the rocks might seriously damage the wooden Whitehalls.[52] Had Francis's metal boats been used exclusively, the scout could have continued.

Unfortunately, General Harney was not in Florida long enough to carry out his extensive plans. On 10 March, he received one hundred Colt's repeating rifles. On 22 April 1857, Harney received orders to "repair without delay" to Fort Leavenworth in preparation for an expected conflict with the Mormons of Utah. He departed Florida 27 April 1857. Yet later on the day he received his orders, he issued a contract to Lewis Daugherty and Edward Beezly to bring his circular of 19 April to the Seminoles. His circular told the Indians that the Department of the Interior had made arrangements to set aside a tract of land for them separate from the Creeks. Daugherty and Beezly had told him that they had good relations with the Seminoles and that the Indians were ready to leave Florida. Harney wrote, "I consider this so important that I must respectfully suggest that these arrangements may not be disturbed."[53]

Thus when Colonel Gustavus Loomis assumed command of the Department of Florida, he was shackled with the general's plan. Harney had issued instructions to continue existing orders until Daugherty and Beezly returned. On 6 May, Loomis received the adjutant general's letter telling him to carry out General Harney's memorandum of operations, with an enclosed copy of the memorandum. On 14 May, Loomis received notice of the secretary of war's permission to Harney to hire up to 150 civilians for boatmen, guides, and so forth. Loomis had only to obtain the guides and foot volunteers.[54]

When Colonel Loomis needed a guide for a forthcoming scout, he selected Jacob E. Mickler, who had been a private in Captain Turner's detachment. At the time, Mickler was a paymaster clerk for the U.S. troops in Tampa; however, he craved more action than a paymaster clerk offered. Based on his duty with Turner, he accepted a position to guide the regular army troops under Captain Thomas Williams, Fourth Artillery, at Fort Center. The expedition examined Lake Okeechobee and then went up river to Fort Kissimmee. Captain Williams was well pleased with his services.[55]

Colonel Loomis was busy carrying out General Harney's plan for continued operations in the interior during the summer sickly season. Earlier, on 10 April, Colonel Munroe, now the commander of the First District, Department of Florida, submitted a drawing to the commanding officer of Fort Kissimmee illustrating how to build a platform over several boats to house troops above the water during the rainy season. Evidently the platform over boats for living quarters was specific to Fort Kissimmee because on 5 June 1857, Dr. Richard D. Lynde suggested to his commanding officer at Fort Center that "with the rain falling in torrents daily covering the ground with several inches of water" it was necessary to construct platforms not only for a hospital tent, but also for all officers and men. By early September, floodwaters isolated Fort Center, washed out two bridges on the road to Fort Deynaud, and immobilized two wagons on the road in both directions.[56] Some historians claimed that before the Second Seminole War the Florida Indians lived in cabins and only developed the "chickee," an open-sided shelter with a raised floor and roof, when driven south into the swamps. It seemed ironic that in the Third Seminole War the American military developed a similar shelter when forced to live in similar circumstances.

Colonel Loomis had no better luck than his two predecessors at getting the state to raise foot volunteers. On June the Fifth Infantry moved from Florida to Bleeding Kansas because of the slavery/anti-slavery clashes, and on 13 June Daugherty and Beezly returned with a negative report that they made no contacts with the Seminoles. Thus he reported to the adjutant general that with no real pressure on the Seminoles south of the Caloosahatchee River the Indians "felt no need to move or fight."[57]

Loomis took steps to pressure the enemy. Richard Turner again raised a detachment of boatmen and hunters. This time the colonel had the detachment registered as employees of the Quartermaster Department. At the time Turner had thirty-eight men and expected at least two more from Fort Myers. In addition, Loomis authorized Turner to recruit Daugherty and Beezly, if possible. A week later Loomis entered a similar agreement with Jacob Mickler to command forty-five men for special service. All men, employed at $3 per day and a ration, were under the Quartermaster Department of the Department of Florida as civilian contractors. The leaders carried the title of captain. Financially, this was a great improvement for as militiamen their pay scale would have been as follows: privates, $11 per month; sergeants, $17 per month; second lieutenants, $64.50 per month; captains $79.50 per month; and captains acting as commanding officers, $89.50.[58]

It did not take Captain Jacob E. Mickler long to demonstrate his ability. On 17 July 1857 while scouting along the Kissimmee River, he noted a small stream in the sawgrass flowing into the east bank of the river. He investigated and found an island in the midst of the sawgrass. He landed his boats, left a boat guard, split his men into two units, approached, and charged the unsuspecting Seminoles. He captured six women and nine children, and lost one warrior who made good his escape.[59]

Colonel Loomis created his third boat party when he gave a contract to Mr. A. N. Pacetty, who at the time was a civilian foreman of a group repairing bridges from Fort Brooke to Fort Meade. Evidently Pacetty needed more volunteers to attain the rank of captain and desired some sailors. On 27 July 1857 he visited Fernandina and offered four sailors forty or forty-five dollars a month to serve in his company. They accepted, and, on the way back to Tampa, he recruited two more men. Captain Pacetty mustered his men into service in Tampa, arrived at Fort Kissimmee on 26 August, and received eight metal lifeboats. From that time forward he operated on Lake Okeechobee. His task was to penetrate the swamps and sawgrass surrounding the lake searching for Indians.[60]

Yet as the colonel's boat parties increased in number, his federal troops decreased. In September 1857, the War Department withdrew the Fourth Artillery from Florida. Loomis wrote that that happened "just at the time that a foot force could be rendered most available in the Everglades." He continued, saying that the unit's departure was most inopportune and had "checkered a most important movement from which the troops were recalled for embarkation."[61] The pace of military operations slowed. Colonel Loomis and Governor Browne pleaded for an increase in the number of volunteers activated. Washington finally agreed and activated ten Florida mounted companies under militia colonel S. St. George Rogers.

Yet during this period of transition, Loomis's three boat parties were actively prodding for Indian communities. It was a serious game of hide-and-seek. The fact that they seldom found the enemy was not important; it was important to force the enemy to continually move to avoid discovery. The continual flight began to demoralize the Seminoles. After Captain Pacetty's boatmen were organized and operating on Lake Okeechobee, Captains Turner and Mickler turned their attention to the southern coastline. Generally Turner operated from Punta Rassa to Cape Sable and Mickler from Cape Sable to Fort Dallas. Of course, regular army units also scouted the coast. Occasionally, Captain Abner Doubleday and Jacob Mickler met and joined forces while scouting the Everglades.

The federalization of Colonel Rogers and his ten companies of Florida Mounted Volunteers was the force that unlocked the Seminoles' homeland for the Americans. Prior to this time the regular army colonels were locked in place at their home forts. They dispatched their troops concerned only with their own territory; that is, Colonel Brown from Fort Myers prodded the southwest coast and Colonel Dimick from Fort Dallas the Everglades. Fortunately Colonel Rogers was not bound to a particular fort, his command was large enough to cover south Florida, and he was an astute, energetic, and capable military leader.

Under orders from Colonel Loomis to keep pressure upon the Seminoles, Colonel Rogers began to place his troops in accordance with his instructions. He placed five companies on the Caloosahatchee River with plans to move south as the ground between the river and the Big Cypress Swamp dried out. He ordered seventy-five to one hundred supply wagons to follow and support these companies. He sent three detachments to Lake Okeechobee to support Captain Pacetty's boat party. He intended to penetrate the interior from the southwest coast. By mid-November, he shifted his commands so that he had "as many Efficient boatmen as possible, for the forth coming Coasting Expedition."[62]

Captain William Cone made the first move heading south from the Caloosahatchee River with 115 militiamen on 21 November. His destination was south of Fort Doane and west of the Okaloacoochee Swamp. He surprised a portion of Billy Bowlegs's band and captured an aged warrior, five women, and thirteen children. He found several towns of about forty houses, stores of food, and a daguerreotype photo of Bowlegs taken on his visit to Washington in 1852.[63]

Meanwhile, Rogers arrived at Chokoliska Key on 18 November. The colonel was ill and was not able to go on the first scout. Captain John Parkhill led his men with Captain Turner as his guide. Parkhill landed nine miles up the river in a mangrove area and from then on his men walked in water "from half leg to half thigh." He found a trail and followed it into areas not previously scouted. Parkhill found a large Indian settlement of thirty buildings and forty acres of cultivated land of pumpkin, peas, potatoes, corn, and rice in Palm Hammock. He destroyed everything of value. On his second scout he found two more villages of fifteen buildings and more cultivated fields. Again he destroyed everything. Then he found a large trail. Taking only the six soldiers with him he walked into an ambush. Captain Parkhill died in the initial enemy salvo. His men carried his body some fifteen miles before burying him on the shore of a small lake.[64]

Colonel Rogers was dissatisfied with his maps. According to him the maps were so poor that it was doubtful what was the name of any river crossed. Captain Turner said he took Captain Parkhill up the Fakahatchee and that the Seminole villages were on Palm Hammock. Rogers thought differently. Therefore, he led the next scout of eight days and had Turner go from the Malco River to Palm Hammock again. They traveled from Malco to the headwaters of the Wekima without finding Palm Hammock. Rogers brought his men back to Fort Myers exhausted. He wrote triumphantly that he had located the Seminole Nation in the glades. Yet of his 110 men, only 57 were physically able to continue, and they refused to go against the enemy again because their federal service was nearly over.

In his critique he said that the scouts of Captains Cone, Parkhill, Stevens, and his own trek had definitely found the Seminole homeland. Cone penetrated the Okaloacoochee Swamp from Fort Keais going southward and found a goodly portion of Seminoles. Parkhill penetrated the Okaloacoochee from the south and found even more villages and cultivated fields. He believed that Cone and Parkhill were between eight and ten miles apart. Stevens search proved the Seminoles were fleeing east of Camp Rogers. His scout proved Turner wrong and the Seminole Nation centralized in the Okaloacoochee Swamp. Rogers believed that Turner had an uncanny ability to enter south Florida from any point and return to his entrance, but he did not have a mental geographic image of south Florida. Yet these scouts destroyed almost two hundred acres of cultivated land and two hundred houses. He felt the Seminoles had two choices. They could gather for a last stand or escape into the Everglades. There the Indians could hide living off wild food, but they could not put in another crop until the next growing season.[65]

Rogers recommended mustering out his regiment and trying again with another group of volunteers. With fresh troops he felt the conflict would end in three months, but he doubted that the army could raise the needed foot troops because the service was too grueling and the pay too small, but foot soldiers "might Easily be raised in the same manner as the Boat Companies heretofore in the service." He felt that that decision was best made by the Department of Florida and Washington.[66]

Interestingly, Francis J. Sweeny, one of Pacetty's four sailors recruited in Fernandina, recorded that upon returning to Tampa they "mustered out of the company and were paid at a settler's store in Tampa by a man of the name of Mr. McKay, who kept the store. The captain was present at the same time." The variance in the amount of pay and its disbursement from a settler's store rather than from the quartermaster department raises some questions of propriety.[67]

By this time however, the Department of the Interior and the western Seminoles had reached an agreement that called for the military in Florida to cease operations while talks were conducted between the Florida and western Seminoles. Billy Bowlegs and a majority of his people realized that the last six weeks of Rogers's campaign foretold their future if they remained in south Florida. Billy Bowlegs agreed to terms. On 4 May 1858, the Seminoles boarded the steamer *Gray Cloud* at Fort Myers to begin the journey to the west.

The importance of small boats, especially Joseph Francis's metallic boats, to the successful conclusion of the war was evident in the numerous batteau treks into the Big Cypress Swamp by Captain Turner, into the Everglades by Captain Mickler, and the metallic lifeboats patrolling Lake Okeechobee by Captain Pacetty. The fact that most of the Tampa manufactured canoes were withheld from operations into the interior because they were not sturdy enough, the three damaged wooden rowboats sent from Tampa to Punta Rassa, and the wooden Whitehalls that could not cross a rocky rapid all demonstrated the superiority of Francis's metal boats. Further, it must be remembered that during the Second Seminole War most expeditions into the Everglades employed sailors and marines from the navy's Florida Expedition either singularly or jointly with army units; whereas, in the Third Seminole War most of the American units were non-sailors composed of Irish and German urban immigrants of the army and Florida militia cowmen who were equally unfamiliar with boat handling. The Department of Florida's three commanders were aware of that importance.

5

Metal Army Pontoon Wagon Bodies

In 1852 while the salesman Francis initially was trying to promote his metal boats, his inventive side was looking for a new project. In the previous decade the nation had gone through a tremendous increase in size. The annexation of Texas in 1845, title to the southern portion of the Oregon country by the Buchanan-Pakenham Treaty in 1846, and the present-day southwest by the Guadalupe-Hidalgo Treaty in 1848 added about 1,200,000 square miles to the United States. Army expeditions into this vast domain were necessary to explore and discover its resources. For that task, the army had to haul supplies into a primitive land by boats, pack trains, and wagons. Mr. Francis decided to develop a floating metal army wagon body to assist the army. When he had completed the concept for his plan, he asked Major Crossman to evaluate his premise. Crossman thought it was sound.

Then it was time for Francis to contact General Jesup. He launched a lengthy letter reminiscent of his earlier letters extolling the virtues of both his metal boats to explain his new metal army wagon body, which still was only a concept.[1] He began by saying that his metal wagon would be of the same capacity as the current wooden ones, except the corners would be rounded and, like his boats, corrugated for strength. The corrugation would provide the strength to carry heavy freight over the roughest road with impunity. With the body one continuous metal enclosure, it was a boat with buoyancy great enough to float its cargo and running gear; therefore, there was no need to carry the India-rubber pontoons. Two standard rubber pontoons, with stiffening of planks, bars, bolts, and bellows, weighed about 328 pounds. Thus by using metal army wagon bodies, the army wagon trains eliminated the weight and space of rubber pontoons. Francis listed other advantages including the necessity of unloading and reloading the rubber pontoon every time a river was crossed. Further, securing two metal wagons together side by side with several boards would make a water vehicle large enough to carry the heaviest ordnances and horses. Joseph Francis also planned to make a magazine wagon with a metal cover to secure the powder and fixed ammunition. Finally, he would produce portable metal chambers for attachment to the sides of the wagon for more buoyancy under special circumstances. All of his metal wagons would attach the rolling gear in the same manner as the wooden wagons did. Of course, one must realize that Francis's letter was just his concept for a metal wagon; he had not progressed to the state of creating the metal dies to make his wagon.[2]

On 4 March 1854, Francis informed Jesup that he was prepared to manufacture corrugated galvanized iron army wagon bodies, and he asked permission to furnish two wagons to the army for testing. Because he had not made any wagons at the time, he did not know his cost per wagon. Yet he would provide the standard metal wagon for one hundred dollars. His second metal wagon would be a magazine wagon specifically designed to carry powder and fixed ammunition for one hundred and twenty-five dollars. Francis also stated that by modifying the feed trough it could become a small one-man boat to allow messengers to cross back and forth, keeping communications open between the groups on both sides of the crossing.[3]

A month later Francis wrote to Mr. William A. Gordon of the War Department in Philadelphia that he had completed his first water trial of the metal wagon, and it performed admirably. When floating light it drew one and a half inches. With seven men aboard, average weight 150 pounds per man, the wagon's draft was six inches while carrying 1,050 pounds. With four men on board they dropped the tailboard and the draft was four inches, two inches below the fixed tailboard. Next Francis broke out oars and the wagon went out into the East River with considerable speed for a rectangular box. Then he told Gordon, in accordance with General Jesup's orders, he would ship the wagon to Philadelphia for his examination.[4]

Francis received a letter from Colonel Charles Thomas asking him to price his metal wagons for orders of 100, 150, and 200 units for wagons similar to the one exhibited at the United States Arsenal, including the feed trough. Also Colonel Thomas asked for the price if made of a lighter gauge of metal. Francis replied that he would deliver the metal wagon bodies in New York up to 100 in number, 18-gauge, for $145, 200 at $135, 300 at $125, and 500 at $115. The 20-gauge would be $5 cheaper.

When he received Francis's letter, General Jesup endorsed it with a recommendation to the Secretary of War that the army buy one hundred to provide a fair trial for these metal wagons. He noted that the wagons were true boats and also could serve as pontoons. Secretary Jefferson Davis approved the purchase on 26 July 1854.[5]

Acceptance of metal pontoon wagons proceeded at a rapid pace. On 27 September 1854, the board assigned to examine the wagon reported that it had completed the examination and found no defects in either construction or workmanship, nor did it have any alterations or improvements to present. Less than a month later Joseph Francis received a contract for one hundred corrugated, galvanized, sheet iron gauge no. 18, wagons of the size and dimensions as the wooden army wagon provided to him as a model for his dies. The contract called for five corrugations per side and a corrugated iron box permanently attached to the front of the wagon for stowing spare articles. The body and feed trough must have two good coats of zinc paint, the first of white and the second of brown oxide zinc. The first day of June 1855 was the delivery date for all items under contract.[6]

In addition to the basic order for metal wagons, the quartermaster general added eight wagon bodies to the order of four whaleboats and two barges for the Department of Florida. Francis confirmed that the order for the boats would be ready for the 20 November 1854 shipping from New York, but he had not received the galvanized iron for his wagons. Francis noted that he had three bodies ready and if the two then at the arsenal at Washington could be used for this order then five could meet the November date and others made later could be sent to Florida and to the arsenal. Yet before the critical date of 20 November arrived, the Quartermaster Corps told Francis that the shipping date was now the first part of December because of the transport vessel's delay in scheduling. Everything must have proceeded well because by 16 February 1855, the U.S. Quartermaster Department paid Francis $7,105 for forty-nine wagon bodies.[7]

With things doing well at the factory, Joseph Francis decided to take his doctor's advice to ease up from work and take a restful trip to Europe. Of course Francis's idea of a restful trip was different from his doctor's concept. Before he left he had confided to Colonel Thomas that his trip would combine rest and work. The result was that the colonel sent a letter to his friend stating that there was nothing that he could add to the reputation of Francis's lifeboats and barges. Yet he could testify about "the wagon body which has been made under the direction of the Secretary of War for army purposes." Having a wagon that was capable of being a boat or pontoon in crossing rivers and streams was desirable "in our widely extended Country west of the Mississippi river."

He was happy to state that Joseph Francis had been "entirely successful, and that after repeated experiments and tests in the presence of the Secretary of War and members of the Senate & House of Representatives of the United States— the Quarter Master General and other officers of the Army it has been adopted into our service & is now being used on our frontiers in the Indian country." Colonel Thomas continued, explaining that the metal wagon was lighter than the wooden one. Its buoyancy was such that it could sustain its running gear while carrying a moderate load. Further, when the body was detached from the gear it was a boat, and by planking over several wagons the resultant vessel could carry the heaviest artillery pieces.[8]

After Colonel Thomas's letter to Francis, headquarters received other reports telling of the metal wagon's employment on the frontier. On 28 May 1855, four companies of the Sixth Infantry augmented by a detachment of a hundred recruits left Fort Leavenworth on a seventeen-day trek to Fort Kearney to meet General Harney. This was part of Harney's force to deal with the Sioux previous to his assignment to the Department of Florida. On leaving Leavenworth the acting quartermaster Captain Stewart Van Vliet received six metallic wagons for testing to ascertain if they had the qualities claimed for them. They carried the same load as the regular army wagons, 2,000 to 2,500 pounds per wagon. The only difference Captain Van Vliet noticed was that the metal wagons took slightly longer to load and offload because the bottom portion of the tailboard was a permanent part of the wagon body. The captain considered that was a slight objection.

Van Vliet's first water crossing did not take place until they reached the Big Sioux River, the boundary of Minnesota and Iowa. The river was eighty yards wide and deep. He took the metal body off its running gear and crossed and recrossed four or five times loaded with several men on each crossing. He found that the body indeed made an excellent boat. As he became accustomed to his new boat he kept increasing its load until he carried a full cargo. He was amazed that the metal bodies, after being subjected to a rough treatment during their march of twelve hundred miles, were watertight; however, he noted that the last row of rivets along the tailboard had worked loose and allowed some leakage—but not much. He recommended reducing the rivets on the bottom of the tailboard for he did not believe it affected the strength of the boat. Then he thought it might be possible to eliminate the rivets altogether for it was only the working loose of the rivets that allowed water to enter the wagon.

The captain had two other comments. First, that the upper edges of the body have a projection attached to allow the use of oars, which would truly make the wagon a boat. Second, if the boards supplied to form the floor of the wagon, upon which the cargo was placed, could be cut lengthwise instead of crosswise the flooring could be used to attach two or more wagons together to carry large objects, or to create a pontoon bridge. In his summary Captain Van Vliet considered the metal army wagon to be of great importance for the army in the field.[9]

General Harney was so impressed with the metal wagon that he ordered one for his own use. Upon receiving his wagon, Harney thought it was too large and heavy. He wanted Captain Van Vliet to ask the quartermaster department to buy it for the army. Shortly after that, Harney went to Florida, leaving his unpaid wagon with Van Vliet! The captain wrote to General Jesup that if Mr. Francis would "let us have it for what one of ours costs, running gear & all, it will be fair transaction as it is a much better wagon than those made for Govt." Jesup's cryptic endorsement on the Van Vliet's letter stated, "We pay less than H the lower price it can be taken—J." Unfortunately for posterity, there was no correspondence in that file with Joseph Francis to know if he accepted the lower price.[10]

In early December 1855, Colonel Brown ordered Major Lewis Arnold to assemble a survey team of one officer, two noncommissioned officers, and six privates to survey a route from Fort Adams on the Caloosahatchee River to Fort Bassinger on the Kissimmee River, then travel northeasterly to find the road from Fort Kissimmee to Fort Capron on the Indian River. The group had a six-mule team, one of Francis's metal army wagon bodies, a riding horse, and two canoes. The metal army wagon, carrying equipment and forage, could cross any streams encountered. This was an early mention of Francis's metal army wagons in Florida.[11]

Major Arnold replied that he did not have enough wagons. He sent one of his wagons to Fort Myers to bring back a missing rudder for his copper boat. He would have to provide the survey party with an additional wagon because the metal wagon could not carry the equipment, forage, and two canoes. Further, he had the colonel's previous orders to transport the two metal boats and the wooden boat to Fort Center. He awaited instructions.[12]

By November 1856, Fort Dallas had three of Francis's iron wagon bodies. Colonel Justin Dimick, commanding at that post, had no use for the metal wagons and reported that they "were only fit for crossing streams."[13] It was obvious that the colonel did not use his metal wagons during an exchange of companies in October 1857, when Captain Abner Doubleday's company at Fort Dallas received orders to exchange places with Captain Truman Seymour's company at Fort Capron. Doubleday's men thought this their just reward for enduring the rigors of scouting the Everglades while Seymour's men lolled in ease at Fort Capron remote from such arduous tasks. The distance between the two posts was 120 miles. Doubleday left Fort Dallas in mid-month with a train of twelve wooden wagons.

His first river crossing took place at the New River, thirty miles north of Fort Dallas. Doubleday's problem was how to cross a wide stream with twelve wagons and eighty animals with no boats. One of his men was not afraid to swim across the stream even though alligators were quite thick in the waters. The soldier had a small cord tied to his waist, and on reaching the other side he pulled a larger rope across. After the soldiers secured the two ends to trees on both banks, Doubleday then took a wagon body and covered it with a canvass tent making it nearly water-proof. With his improvised boat pulled along the rope, he sent his wife and her maid in the first crossing. Then repeated crossings took place until all the bag-gage and part of his men were on the other side. The soldiers drove the animals across and then only the empty wagons remained to cross. Doubleday tied rope to the tongue and rear of each wagon. The men on the opposite shore pulled on the tongue and the men on the near side steadied each wagon crossing. The wag-ons gradually sunk to the bottom of the river, and, with no obstructions on the sandy bottom, each wagon rolled over to the far side.

A few days later Doubleday reached Jupiter Inlet where the Indian River de-bauched into the Atlantic Ocean. The river was a long lagoon that flowed paral-lel to the coast for considerable miles. If Doubleday could cross the Indian River, the remainder of his journey would be easy traveling along the hard-packed sea beach. Scattered about were the ruins of Fort Jupiter, a Second Seminole War fort, and his troops found boards and sections of the post defenses strung about or buried in the sand. Doubleday had his men, directed by a few carpenters, spend the night making a boat. Meanwhile, other soldiers gathered pine pitch to caulk his watercraft. By daylight the boat building was over and the crossing began. During one of his trips, Doubleday found a sunken flatboat just offshore. He raised, caulked, and provided a blanket sail for it. Then as the teams plod-ded up the beach, the captain sailed upriver overseeing the operation. Captain Doubleday reached Fort Capron at ten o'clock that night, much to the surprise of Captain Seymour and his company who had imagined that they would not be re-lieved so soon. It would have been much easier for Doubleday if Colonel Dimick had given him the three metal wagons.[14]

At the end of 1856, Colonel Charles F. Smith, commanding the Tenth Infantry at Fort Snelling, Minnesota, reported that the four metallic wagons attached to his command "were invaluable as boats or floats in ferrying or bridging streams." In his expedition to explore the country of the northern Red River he could not have accomplished his task without their aid. First Lieutenant J. Y. Forney, his assistant acting quartermaster, suggested that if the army desired to establish a military post on the northern frontier of Minnesota it would be imperative to use metal wagons to carry supplies from Fort Snelling.[15]

General Harney, who was familiar with metallic wagons, in January 1857 or-dered his quartermaster to supply Fort Kissimmee with eight wagons, four of them pontoon wagons. He wanted a platform built over the pontoon wagons to serve as a causeway to carry land transportation across the swamp to reach the road beyond.[16]

Sometime after 30 April 1855 when Colonel Thomas sent his letter praising the metal army wagon and before 28 June 1855 when Marshall Lefferts told Jesup that thirty-five metal wagons were ready for delivery, Joseph Francis had removed himself from business in New York and moved to Paris, France.

6

Francis's European Associates

Francis probably selected Paris because three years earlier he sent William H. Navarro to Le Havre to assemble the sections of his metallic lifeboat and a life car for the Royal Imperial International Shipwreck Society. Now he carried Deputy Quartermaster General Charles Thomas's glowing testimony of his metal army pontoon wagon with two local endorsements verifying his basic letter.[1] Evidently the bureaucratic chain of command moved slowly in France. Francis moved to England, establishing himself at the Atheneum Club, Pall Mall, close to the English War Department. Joseph Francis had a fertile field for his metallic inventions. Although the English Section of the International Shipwreck Society acknowledged his work on metal boats on 4 July 1843, it had not followed up on his work. Later, because of the upsetting of lifeboats along the coasts, the Duke of Northumberland offered one hundred guineas for the best model of a lifeboat sent to the Admiralty by 1 January 1850. The Northumberland Prize Committee said all of the submissions were of wood, although there were some testimonials in favor of galvanized corrugated iron or copper boats. It noted that Lieutenant Lynch, USN, had used a copper boat to successfully descend the rapids of the River Jordan in 1848. The committee concluded a full and fair trial of metal boats should be made, but there the subject matter lay for five years with no apparent interest until Major Vincent Eyre, Bengal Artillery, returned from service in India.

Major Eyre also resided at the Atheneum Club where he met Joseph Francis and learned about his metal boats and wagons. The major concluded "that the fame of these inventions had failed to reach the ears, or to arouse the sleepy faculties of John Bull." He decided to bring these superior watercraft to the Admiralty and the War Department. He felt that his "communications met with very prompt and courteous attention in both quarters . . . nor am I without good hopes that the results may, ere very long, prove important." Thus through Major Eyre, Francis became acquainted with several influential people such as Lord Panmure, Captain J. R. Wood, RN, secretary of the Royal National Life-Boat Institute, and Colonel Alexander T. Tulloh, RA, superintendent of the Royal Carriage Department.[2]

6.1 Pontoon Army Wagon Uses. Courtesy of the National Archives.

On 13 August 1855, Lord Panmure ordered Colonel Alexander Tulloh to purchase a metal army wagon from Mr. Francis and, when received, forward his evaluation on it. The colonel immediately ordered a wagon from New York that arrived the end of November. On Friday, 30 November 1855, Tulloh accompanied by Francis began his experiment. The wagon alone weighed 5 cwt, 7 lbs, with its gear about 17 cwt, 4 lbs. He first placed the wagon in the water with its full gear, including the pole. Then sixteen men got on board, their weight was 25 cwt, and the wagon settled so that the water was about a foot from the top. The men rushed from side to side trying to upset the wagon, but to no avail. "The upper edge of the wagon *could not be brought to the water!*"

After dropping the running gear and letting it sink, the colonel loaded the body with planks and two men, in all weighing 34 cwt, but still could not bring the upper edge to the water. Francis told the colonel that by making the wagon in sections it would ship as compact cargo aboard ships at a much lower rate. He also mentioned that the feed troughs could be one-man boats for communications between the two parties crossing a river. Colonel Tulloh opined that four of these bodies lashed together would make a raft capable of supporting heavy ordnance.

Finally, the colonel asked Francis what terms would he accept to transfer the right of patent to the government? Francis furnished a statement of his terms and a price, that Tulloh marked enclosure A. The colonel told his superiors that he thought the price too high and listed what he considered acceptable. In conclusion, Tulloh enclosed Francis's testimonials listed B to G.[3] On 1 January 1856, in answer to Francis's request, J. Wood sent a copy of Colonel Tulloh's report to Francis in care of Major Vincent Eyre, Atheneum Club, Pall Mall; however, the copy did not contain either Francis's price or the one the colonel recommended.[4]

Major Eyre stated he was not alone among the Indian officers who learned of or viewed the metal wagon. Upon learning of the wagon, General Brooke, commander of the Horse Artillery throughout the Sikh War, wrote that these wagons would replace the clumsy carts that retarded progress, and afforded "no aid in any other way than as a cart." Sir George Pollock, after he had personally tested a metal wagon, wrote, "If I could have had the benefit of Mr. Francis' carts when I crossed the five rivers of the Punjab, the soldiers would have been saved some days' hard labour. I was detained a day or two at each river; whereas, with this carriage I could have crossed each river in three or four hours without difficulty, and without fatiguing the troops."[5]

Francis did not limit his selling to the metal wagon, for in January the Admiralty had Commander Bevis, RN, test his lifeboat at Liverpool and then again in July in the Woolwich Dockyard. During the test sailors rowed full speed at the stone dock, knocking the rowers about, but not injuring the boat. The sailors tossed the boat over stone pavement violently with little effect. Then they filled the boat with large stones, hoisted it high in the air from lines on the bow and stern, and dropped it into the water again with little effect. Almost in desperation "they were battered on the sides with large hammers on one spot, with all the force a strong man could master," and were still in good condition, and watertight![6]

More proof of the closeness of Francis and Eyre may be found when the major said, "It is a further gratification to state that, my operations in this country have been indirectly instrumental in bringing this subject to the notice of the Emperor Napoleon, whose eagle eye allows nothing that bids fair to benefit his country to escape him." On 3 February 1856, Francis demonstrated his metal wagon to Napoleon III in Paris. He put the wagon through its paces on the Seine, while he circulated his drawings of all the functions it could perform during river crossings, such as a boat carrying supplies and soldiers, or two carrying cannon, or several wagons used as a pontoon bridge. The next day the emperor presented a jeweled snuffbox to Francis to show his appreciation of the inventor's ability. The imperial letter also hoped that his inventions "may establish in France the foundation of a new branch of industry applicable to the public services for war and for the navy, as well as for the mercantile marine."[7]

Emperor Napoleon III urged Francis to work with his ministers of war and navy to continue testing his inventions. Of course, ordering material from the United States for Europe took time. Thus for a while Joseph Francis crossed and recrossed the English Channel.

Back in England, Captain J. R. Wood, RN, Royal National Life-Boat Institution, tested the life car on 22 July 1856. It had recently arrived from New York and Captain Wood was among the participants at the North Yarmouth Regatta putting the life car through its paces. It was reminiscent of the first test by the American Revenue Marine Service on the New Jersey coast. A rocket fired a line over a boat 120 yards offshore. Then the hawser with its life car floated out to the anchored vessel. Five men, including Captain Wood, made the return journey to shore. Many of the spectators were familiar with other lifesaving devices such as slings, seats, and breeches buoys, but all agreed that this life car was superior to the earlier devices.[8]

About this time the French minister of the navy wanted to test some of Francis's metal boats. The tests took place at the port of Le Havre. The Board of Examiners watched as Francis placed a metal rowboat seventeen feet long with tackles at each end between two upright posts ten feet high. Then he filled the boat with paving stones even with the thwarts. The rowboat, hoisted to the top of the posts, cut loose, and dropped to the rocky surface below with no injury to the craft. Next sailors rolled the rowboat over the pavement then launched it into the water and rowed stern on into a stone pier. The craft was uninjured and watertight. The minister said that before entering combat, sailors removed the ships' boats from davits to keep the wooden boats from injury during the concussion of cannon firing. Francis placed his boat in davits and the navy brought up its largest cannon beneath the metal boat and fired it, expecting the concussion to seriously damage the craft. No injury or leaking took place.[9]

During this period Francis made the acquaintance of Mr. Robert Stephenson and Sir Charles Manby, the president and secretary of the English Institution of Civil Engineers that provided him many pleasant occasions to meet the best English and visiting engineers and inventors. Manby and Francis collaborated in designing a corrugated galvanized iron pontoon, jointly patented by the two. In addition to the governmental interest in metallic watercraft, Sir Charles felt that a private manufactory should develop. To that end he gathered a group of investors under the Windsor Iron Works, McClure, MacDonald & MacGregor to form a private company in Liverpool. Thus the English had two organizations using

FRANCIS AND MANBY'S CORRUGATED GALVANIZED IRON PATENT PONTOON.

6.2 Plan for Corrugated Iron Pontoon by Francis and Manby. Courtesy of Pond's *History*.

Francis's patents, the government at Woolwich and the private shipyard in Liverpool. The former could build only for its own use, while the latter carried out the full range of devices including corrugated iron steamers and floating docks. It manufactured a full set of dies to compete in the commercial world.[10]

In France the same thing happened. The experiments by the war and navy ministries alerted the private citizens of the Empire and they too established a company to buy and produce corrugated metal craft. In fact the French ordered the wooden patterns from Francis to build their own dies ahead of the English. The English, in their desire to catch up, asked Francis to go to Paris and either buy or borrow the French wooden patterns. He complied and shipped the patterns across the channel.[11]

Joseph Francis became anxious for the English War Department to formally test his metal wagon. He wrote to Lord Panmure questioning why it was taking so long. John Croomes answered, telling him that the delay was due to the absence of Colonel Tulloh, but his lordship had asked the Ordnance Committee to begin testing without waiting for the colonel.[12] Even with Lord Panmure's prodding, the committee did not meet until 2 September 1856. The examination consisted of three experiments. The first two tried to tip the wagon over while carrying various loads; however, the tests were never able to bring the water any closer to the top than ten inches. The third experiment was unique in that Francis thought that with two hammers he would be able to hammer the jagged pieces back into place after a musket ball passed through the boat's side. The wagon was placed on its running gear, and driven down to the "Proof Butt," where a marksman put two holes in the wagon with an Enfield rifle at one hundred yards. Unfortunately for Francis, each ball carried away a piece of the iron, defeating his plan.

The committee also perused the correspondence presented by Francis. Colonel Thomas's letter concerning the wagon's value on the frontier were particularly impressive. The committee "strongly recommended its adoption into the service as a substitute for wood in all descriptions of waggons and carts as far as may be considered advisable."[13]

The committee concluded by discussing how to obtain the rights to manufacture metallic wagons in light of Francis's patent. First, the government might work through the English company that was arranging with Francis to establish some form of partnership to do his work in England. Second, the government might pay a royalty for each wagon made. Third, the government might purchase the right to manufacture "by the payment of the sum demanded by Mr. Francis." The committee recommended the second method.[14] Yet later in 1857 it was determined that "a license giving Her Majesty's Government the right of manufacture of these wagons has been purchased by the payment of 3,000 l., the sum demanded by Mr. Francis."[15]

The one class of boat not discussed was the surfboat. The Royal National Institution for the Preservation of Life from Shipwreck founded in England in 1825 developed two types of lifeboats. The first was self-righting and self-bailing. The second was difficult to upset, although not self-righting. Both were unsinkable, carried a heavy keel, sat low in the water, were difficult to launch, and needed deep water immediately. Yet these features matched the English coastline. The American surfboat employed on the east coast was unsinkable, light craft ideal for shallow water, and passing through the surf. Of course, there were places in the Great Lakes that could and did use the English model.[16]

By the time Francis completed launching his three factories in England and France he had grasped the European system. He received invitations to visit Belgium, the free city of Hamburg, and the Austrian-Hungarian Empire. In 1858 he chose Hamburg where businessmen Edgar Ross, Ernst Merk, and August Jos. Ichon awaited him. They desired to establish a factory to supply all of Germany with his metal craft. They were prepared to negotiate for patent rights and to order samples from the United States. Perhaps it was the ease of doing business in a smaller political organization that gave Francis the idea to include bringing skilled workers from his factory to Hamburg immediately to jumpstart the process. He brought James Kelton over to be his overseer.

While in Hamburg, Francis completed his invention of stop corrugations. He went from concept to ordering the necessary dies from New York to produce a stop corrugation. He paid from his own account for his dies and had them shipped with the Hamburg material. This was a difficult invention. It was impossible to bend corrugated plates to form corners for his metal military pontoon wagon body. Cutting the corners for a mitered joint produced a weak connection. The solution was to apply an angle iron lap, but this greatly increased the cost. Francis's new dies produced a stop corrugation where all the corrugations would stop uniformly three inches before the end of the metal plate. His first attempt failed because as the corrugations ceased the metal beyond the corrugations "buckled, wrinkled and cracked." After more thinking he adapted a slight change to the procedure of feeding the metal to the dies and the sheet came out as desired with equal thickness throughout. The stop corrugation dies reduced the cost of metal army wagons by a third. The best engineers in Europe declared it was impossible to create a stop corrugation. Later when he showed Robert Stephenson and Sir Charles Manby a plate with stop corrugations, they said, "Yes we see it; but it can't be done."[17]

While waiting for his material to arrive from the United States, Francis accepted an invitation from Emperor Francis Joseph to visit Vienna. His demonstrations took place at Lake Klosternewburg ten miles distant from the capital. First came the boat drills that need not be repeated. Then he brought in the iron pontoon army wagon. The emperor asked many questions about the wagon and indicated that this was the device most intriguing to him. Immediately after the demonstration the emperor ordered fifty wagons.[18] Apparently the Austrians were willing to work through the factory at Hamburg. So Francis returned to complete and launch his factory on the Elbe River.

Earlier, in July and August of 1856, Francis received two letters from Robert Thal, consul for the Russian government in Brussels, Belgium, inviting him to come to St. Petersburg, Russia, to demonstrate his metal watercraft, especially his "war carriage boat." Francis did not find time to go until 1 May 1858. Yet it appeared that his arrival was a spur of the moment decision for he came unannounced, with no interpreter, no Russian official waiting for him, and armed with letters of introduction from the secretary of the U.S. Treasury James Guthrie, and his friend John A. Dix.[19]

Fortunately, Francis learned from an Englishman at his hotel that the Grand Duke Constantine, the brother of the czar, and the Grand Admiral of the Navy, was at his summer palace at Strelna only twenty miles away. Francis contacted him and received a warm welcome from the Grand Duke, who knew all about the American inventor. The Grand Duke selected the port of Cronstadt, twenty miles down the Neva River, as the place for the exhibition of the metallic boats. The route for the boat from St. Petersburg to Cronstadt entailed carrying it a number of city blocks to the dock, loading it on a steamer, and steaming down-

J. Francis.

Corrugating Metal Plates.

Nº 38,799.   *Patented Jun. 2, 1863.*

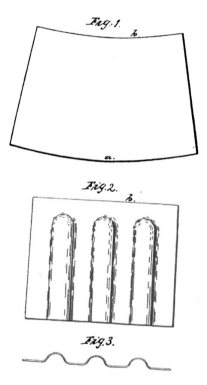

Fig. 1.

Fig. 2.

Fig. 3.

Witnesses.
A. Jones
J. J. Young.

Inventor.
Joseph Francis

6.3 Stop Corrugation Patent. Courtesy of Pond's *History.*

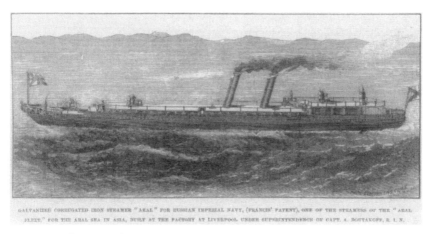

GALVANIZED CORRUGATED IRON STEAMER "ARAL" FOR RUSSIAN IMPERIAL NAVY, (FRANCIS' PATENT), ONE OF THE STEAMERS OF THE "ARAL FLEET," FOR THE ARAL SEA IN ASIA, BUILT AT THE FACTORY AT LIVERPOOL, UNDER SUPERINTENDENCE OF CAPT. A. BOUTAKOFF, R. I. N.

6.4 Corrugated Galvanized Iron Steamer *Aral*. Courtesy of Pond's *History*, p. 100.

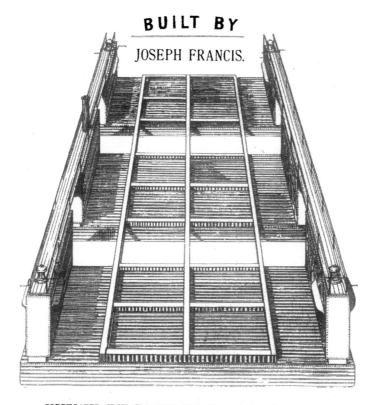

CORRUGATED IRON FLOATING DOCK FOR ARAL SEA IN ASIA.

6.5 Corrugated Iron Floating Dock. Courtesy of Pond's *History*, p. 2.

river to the port. On the morning of the journey, twenty-five sailors arrived to carry the boat through the city streets. Twelve sailors to a side on orders from their leader picked up the boat and carried it on their shoulders. The event, publicized beforehand, brought a great number of people out on the streets to watch the procession. About midway Francis saw the opportunity to entertain his audience. He asked the leader to have the sailors throw the boat over their heads on to the pavement. As it was his boat, Francis guaranteed to accept all responsibility for his actions. The sailors stopped, and on order, flung the boat over their heads to the pavement. It landed on its keel with no damage. Then Francis had the boat rolled over along the road. An inspection showed no damage, and the sailors placed the boat on their shoulders and continued marching to the dock. The onlookers were enthusiastic about the demonstration, more so because the American citizen gave his test to them before showing it to the governmental officials. A boisterous gathering escorted the metal boat to the waiting steamer.[20]

Later, when Francis gave his demonstration for the czar, he placed a sheet of galvanized iron four feet long and two feet wide on two blocks a foot high. Immediately the sheet bent under its own weight until the center touched the ground. Then Francis placed a corrugated sheet on the blocks. He jumped on the center of the sheet yet it did not bend. He followed by pounding with a sledgehammer but still the sheet remained firm and straight. This demonstration of the strength of corrugation impressed the czar.

The Russian bureaucracy was large, and its members were dispersed and poorly connected with one another. For example, the Navy Department invited the Army Department to one of Francis's exhibitions. The military received the invitation after the event, causing Francis to establish another event. All departments desired these important inventions. Russian investors wanted to build a factory in their country, but hesitated until assured that the czar supported the changes desired. Further, the delay of the patent office to grant Francis his patents kept him from building any of his inventions in Russia. So for the first two years Francis ordered his metal craft from the Hamburg and Liverpool factories. Finally, on 14 November 1859, he wrote a long letter to Czar Alexander II summarizing his frustrations and requesting assurances that he needed to begin organizing factories in Russia.[21]

When Francis received the Russian patents and an Imperial decree that allowed him to ship material, tools, and machinery to Russia duty free, he left for Hamburg and Liverpool to carry out his task. As he gathered his items, he received orders to build several steamers. The vessels were 150 and 200 feet long, built in sections for transit via St. Petersburg, Moscow, Nigni Novgorod (on the

Volga River), over the Ural Mountains to the Aral Sea. Accompanying the steamers were a metal floating dry dock and a number of metal steam tugs. Admiral Alexander Boutakoff was to supervise construction at the Liverpool factory. Ultimately Francis established a factory in Balakna where he produced corrugated iron Caspian Sea survey boats and corrugated iron mountain batteaux in sections for easy portage. These last were the Maine lumberjacks' batteaux used so successfully in the Billy Bowlegs War.

When Francis learned of the frequent serious Russian train wrecks where wooden cars splintered and train stoves overturned, setting fires that added to the disaster, leaving hundreds dead or injured, he considered these land tragedies similar to sea calamities. Thus, he invented a corrugated iron railroad car using the stop corrugation for the corners. The Russian company that made his metal wagons brought out his patented railroad cars as well. For all of his work the emperor made him "a Knight of our Imperial and Royal Order of St. Stanislaus, by a ukase of November 7. 1860."[22]

Meanwhile, Marshall Lefferts continued to run the "Francis' Metallic Life-Boat Company" in New York. After visiting Francis in London, he told General Jesup about Francis's success in England, on the continent, and with the East India Company.[23]

There were other, far more serious, changes beginning to descend upon the nation. The Civil War broke out in the spring of 1861, and Lefferts lacked the aggressiveness to sell more of his metallic army pontoon wagon bodies, especially after the stop corrugation reduced the metal army wagon to the price of a wooden wagon. Yet the United States did not take to the metal wagon as did English and Russian governments.[24]

Just before Francis left Europe to return home, he received a letter from Admiral Boutakoff written on 3 July 1862 from the Aral Sea. Boutakoff said his flotilla of steamers and the iron floating dock arrived, but until the boilers arrived he could not launch his steamers. He hoped to employ them early in 1863. He ended his letter, "With a hearty shake hands, and my sincere sympathies with your northern countrymen, of whose victories I congratulate you."[25]

7

Back Home

Joseph Francis had a successful seven-year stay in Europe promoting his metallic watercraft, but his company in New York began losing business. The Third Seminole War ended in early 1858 and in October the secretary of the treasury appointed a committee of three to evaluate surfboats. Fourteen companies participated in the trials, and Bunker's cedar clinker surfboat won approval. Henceforth, the fifty-four New Jersey and Long Island stations housed Bunker's boats. In 1861 the army quartermaster general gathered his abandoned metal surfboats from New Jersey to add to the Cape Hatteras amphibious campaign.[1] Francis's Metallic Boat Company needed its owner's guidance and salesmanship.

The outbreak of the Civil War found the Army Corps of Engineers tasked to build bridges over rivers and streams. Yet this branch of service had almost no contact with Joseph Francis or his metallic watercraft. Few engineers were aware of his devices. Engineer officers displayed an amazing lack of information concerning metal pontoons for river crossings. For example, Lieutenant Colonel Barton S. Alexander of the Corps of Engineers gave his needs and desires to Brigadier General John G. Barnard on 13 October 1861. He began by saying that they had "no bridge equipage, no engineer trains, and no instructed engineer troops." After discussing how to raise the necessary men for the corps, Alexander shifted to bridges. He began with the India-rubber pontoon bridge. He felt that it should be field tested immediately and perfected if necessary. He suggested that a proper proportion of the engineers should be sailors to handle the rubber pontoons. He wanted to make trestle bridges using the common trestle, the Birago trestle, and a combination of the Birago and pontoons to provide for various crossings. The colonel recalled that earlier he had made canvas boats for Lieutenant Joseph C. Ives's expedition on the Colorado River. He believed it would not take long to make a bridge of these boats. Then he noted that the Quartermaster Department had one hundred corrugated iron pontoon wagon bodies. Here was another type of bridge; although, he had no experience with metal wagons, but if they were as good as the testimonials implied, they would be handy. He concluded by saying that each wagon was a large boat that should convert easily to form a pontoon bridge.[2]

An even more detailed evaluation of the Corps of Engineers organization and the lack of familiarity with metal pontoons and metal wagons were contained in Brigadier General John G. Barnard's report of the Army of the Potomac and the Peninsular campaign. Barnard had been the chief engineer of operations from 23 May 1861 to 15 August 1862. He noted that the engineer forces at the opening of the campaign (17 March–2 September 1862) consisted of two regiments, the Fifteenth and Fiftieth New York Volunteers, and a three-company battalion of regular engineer troops. Their equipment consisted of 160 batteaux of wooden pontoons based upon the French model, a number of Birago trestles, and Russian canvas boats. (Barnard could not recall the exact number of trestles and canvas boats.) Originally the Engineer Brigade was organized with six regular trains, each one consisting of thirty-four French pontoons and eight Birago trestles. Thus each train could erect a bridge about 250 yards long. In addition, there was an advanced guard train of Birago trestles and Russian canvas boats. Yet, when the Army of the Potomac set out, there were only enough wagons for four trains and the advanced guard.

Barnard credited Colonel Alexander and his assistant Captain James C. Duane with assembling the army's pontoon equipment. He considered Alexander "possessed great practical ingenuity, and had had the means of knowing the best results arrived at in other services in this branch of military art. Captain Duane possessed a more extensive and thorough practical and experimental knowledge of military bridges than any other man in this country." Their best judgment was to use the French system. Barnard agreed and felt that now that the U.S. Army had grown to the magnitude of European armies, it should draw from the continental experience. Barnard felt these two officers "had before them the best modern inventions of Europe and America. The India-rubber pontoons they knew thoroughly; corrugated iron bodies and countless other inventions of American genius were before them, and the former experimented upon."

Barnard was satisfied with the results of the engineer bridges during the campaign. He thought the French pontoon was "most excellent, useful, and reliable for all military purposes"; however, he objected to the weight of the French pontoon and the size necessary to create the right floatation power. Both objections were especially critical for the American landscape, roads, and trails. He did note that "the substitution of iron for wood was one of the probable improvements well understood by the officers named, but not at that time adopted for substantial reasons." Continuing, the general said the Birago trestle proved dangerous and unreliable for a general military bridge, but useful for an advanced guard or a detachment. As for the American India-rubber and Russian canvas pontoon,

Barnard felt they had not had a fair experiment, although he had his doubts that the two devices would be suitable for a general military bridge. Returning to the iron pontoon, he suggested that "perhaps an iron sectional pontoon may be contrived which will meet these requirements, but prudence demands that the safety of an army shall not be jeopardized by giving it a bridge which experiment has not fully tested." Obviously these engineer officers had a superficial knowledge of Francis's vessels and wagons.[3]

On the other side of the continent, Colonel James H. Carleton, First California Volunteers, wrote to Major Richard C. Drum that he was preparing for his expedition from Camp Latham, California, to Fort Yuma on the Colorado River. Among the public wagons he had received were "two metallic pontoon wagon beds." If there were more available he requested four additional ones. Apparently Colonel Carleton was familiar with metal wagon bodies.[4]

Six months later in the Department of the Shenandoah General Samuel W. Crawford was mystified when a trainload of supplies "came in to-night with a lead of iron wagon-beds, which a generous Government has sent us to cross the Shenandoah. It is more than a problem to know what we shall do with them." Not knowing what to do with metal wagons, the general held on to the train dispatcher, hoping he could rectify his mistake of providing metal wagons. Obviously General Crawford was not familiar with metal wagon bodies.[5]

The epitome of command lack of knowledge about Francis's metal army wagons took place in a series of telegrams between Major General William S. Rosecrans and senior officers of the Corps of Engineers. On 22 November 1862 Rosecrans in Nashville, Tennessee, telegraphed Brigadier General Joseph G. Totten in Washington for permission to have an iron pontoon train seven hundred yards long to cross the Tennessee River. Two days later Totten replied that there were no pontoons available. He said wooden batteaux of that length would take a month to assemble, and iron boats would take much longer to create.[6]

Rosecrans replied that wooden pontoons were leaky, repairs were time-consuming and lengthy, and their care exceeded the stringent time requirements for offensive operations. Captain John D. Kurtz forwarded Rosecrans's reply to Totten, saying that he did not know the cost of a wooden pontoon train of that size. He asked the chief of engineers if the batteaux should be wood or iron? He continued saying a wooden train might be completed in six weeks; an iron train might take a month longer. To save transportation costs, Kurtz recommended building the train in Cincinnati or Louisville. He concluded with saying that the Engineer's Department did not have any models for iron batteaux nor the experience to build iron trains.[7]

On 26 November the chief of staff Brigadier General George W. Cullum

asked Rosecrans what had happened to General Don Carlos Buell's large pontoon train. Why was another one required? A new train would take six to eight
weeks to build. Rosecrans replied that same day that as far as he could learn
General Ulysses S. Grant had the India-rubber pontoons and had destroyed the
wooden batteaux to keep the enemy from getting them. Rosecrans reiterated that
the wooden batteaux were so leaky that they were of no use. When he moved
against the enemy, he did not want to "stop and tinker" with his train and allow
the enemy an advantage. Rosecrans said if he had double-canvas paulins (tarpau-
lins) and light well-made frames he could assemble them himself; but he could
not spare the time to get the material. He asked if Cullum could get them. Then
Cullum replied that General Totten authorized him to order his train from Cincinnati. Cullum continued, saying that canvas boats can't be trusted, and iron
boats take special workmen and are difficult to repair; therefore, he recommended
wooden batteaux. Cullum closed by asking once again what happened to General Buell's train.[8]

On 7 December 1862 Major General Horatio G. Wright, commanding the Engineer Department of the Ohio, wrote to Rosecrans that he could supply wooden
boats. He listed all the defects of the canvas boats and concluded that General
Buell's pontoons were made of green lumber, but he had seasoned wood, and his
end product would be better than Buell's pontoons. This episode demonstrated
the Corps of Engineers' failure to keep abreast of new developments or the actions of the army in the Third Seminole War where metal wagons and batteaux
had a successful employment.[9]

Meanwhile, Joseph Francis returned from Europe sometime in the fall of 1862
to a different world from the one he left in 1855. Those years away from the United
States played havoc with his identity at home. The military and naval officials
Francis dealt with before he left were retiring, and new leaders, less acquainted
with him, were taking their places. It was as if Francis was becoming a nonentity
at home. General Jesup, who served as quartermaster general for forty-two years,
died in 1860. Secretary of War Jefferson Davis, now president, led the Confederate States of America. Montgomery C. Meigs became quartermaster general
of the United States Army in May 1861. Edwin M. Stanton stepped up from special counsel for Secretary of War Simon Cameron to assume that cabinet post in
January 1862. Both Meigs and Stanton worked tirelessly to repair damage done to
the War Department's reputation by the initial extravagant and corrupt actions
of some contractors and supply officers who raided the public treasury as the nation geared up for hostilities.[10] Into this new era, Joseph Francis had to reintro-
duce himself and his metallic watercraft to an army locked in conflict.

Joseph Francis again turned to his friend John A. Dix, now a major general in the New York Volunteers, to furnish him with a letter of introduction to the new quartermaster general Montgomery C. Meigs. This time Francis carried a model of his corrugated iron pontoon wagon to the general, and, as in his visit years ago to Jesup, there the matter rested.

Francis also turned to Secretary of State William H. Seward, a fellow New Yorker interested in his scientific achievements, to show his stop corrugations plate. Seward was delighted with it and arranged for Francis to show it to President Abraham Lincoln. When the president looked at it and asked how he did it, Francis said that it was his secret and he wondered if the president could solve it. "Mr. Lincoln placed both elbows on his desk and rested his head on his hands in silent study for full fifteen minutes." Looking up he asked: "Is it not done so and so?" Francis replied yes and said that Lincoln was the only one to discover it.[11]

Francis told Dix of his pontoon wagon's successful test by the British and its adoption by the British and most of the German states. General Dix was interested in trying the iron pontoon wagon for his own force. The day after dispatching Francis to Washington to the quartermaster general, Dix wrote to the general-in-chief, Major General Henry W. Halleck, to tell of his plans. He had received a letter from General John G. Foster accepting Dix's offer to cooperate in a move against the enemy. Unfortunately for Dix, he would have to cross the Blackwater River in Virginia. All bridges were out from Zuni to Franklin and the fords were blocked by slashing and obstructions; however, Joseph Francis had a corrugated iron pontoon wagon that was a wagon, a pontoon, and a boat. It carried the same load as the wooden wagons, twenty-four hundred pounds, mounted on wheels of the wooden wagons, and carried its carriage as it crossed rivers. With the iron wagons he could use the same length train as with the wooden wagons. If he could have twenty of these iron wagons he could render valuable service, striking a blow at the enemy and "make a trial which will save the Government millions of dollars and thousands of lives by dispensing entirely with the heavy and expensive wooden pontoon train and giving our armies the means of crossing currents when pursued or pursuing, without delay."[12]

When Dix received his twenty iron wagons, he sent them to Major General John J. Peck to try them. He told Peck that "they are not the improved pattern. They are intended to float and hold up their running gear. When detached from the carriages they are pontoons. Try them in the Nansemond." Obviously from his explanation, Dix knew little about the iron wagons. A week later he asked Brigadier General Orris S. Ferry if he had tried the iron wagons, and Ferry replied: "Have tried the pontoons. They will not work. Will make a full report by messenger to-morrow." Unfortunately for posterity, the messenger's report was not in the *Official Records*. Thus we do not know if the unsuccessful test was the result of faulty wagons or the officer's lack of knowledge of how to use them.[13]

But Dix did not give up that easily. He wrote to Secretary of War Stanton and asked for "a sufficient number of Francis's improved iron ponton-wagons to make a bridge of nine hundred feet long." He continued citing his objections to the wooden pontoons—they were too heavy, because of their size they were difficult to handle, and, for that reason, they needed a special wagon train. If they were out of water too long, they shrank and leaked, and, if kept in the water, they were subject to worm rot.[14]

Secretary Stanton approved Dix's request and referred his letter to the quartermaster general. General Meigs immediately wrote to Francis for cost, construction, and time necessary to build his pontoon wagons. Francis replied that his patented improved corrugated iron pontoon, built in two sections, would cost $360 per section. Each half pontoon would be 13′6″ long at the top, 12′ at the bottom, 4′2″ wide, and 2′3″ deep. The two sections put together created a pontoon 27′ long. The two would include top and bottom clasps, iron rowlocks with chains and sockets, baulk hooks each side, securing rings, anchor bar with belaying cleat, and two coats of paint. Francis constructed them at his factory in New York City, and he would furnish them in one or two months after signing the contract.[15]

Meigs summarized for Stanton the description of the pontoon before adding that Francis owned the patent and would not permit others to manufacture his pontoon; therefore, there could be no competition for bids, as Congress required. Meigs calculated that a bridge 900′ long needed forty-five pontoons, whether iron or wooden, and the iron pontoon cost $720, the wooden $190 each. Thus total cost would be $32,400 for iron and $8,550 for wood, for a difference of $23,850. In the iron pontoon's favor was its lightweight compared to a wooden pontoon, but he did not think that weight compensated for price. If the army ordered this pontoon bridge it would come out of the Engineer Department's appropriation. Meigs wanted to consult with the engineers.[16]

Joseph Francis was livid when the quartermaster general turned down his proposal. He returned to the United States after seven years of European royalty's feting. He could not grasp the fact that the U.S. Army had rejected his improved iron pontoon. Being in Washington at the time, he sought out General Meigs. Yet he was not satisfied with Meigs's conversation and enlisted Senator Samuel C. Pomeroy's aid. Then Francis sent a blistering letter to Secretary Stanton. He opened his remarks by saying that Senator Pomeroy told him of his two interviews with General Meigs concerning his iron pontoons, and from Meigs the senator learned "the *cause* of his refusal to obey your order for a Pontoon Train for

Gen¹ Dix Department" was General Cullum! The engineer general was determined to use "the wooden scows in defiance of all powers above him." Further,
General Cullum said he had invented a corrugated *iron* pontoon that the engineers will use "when it suits his interest and pleasure, and has induced Gen¹Meigs
to sustain him in this course."[17]

By the second page Francis defended his patent and trusted "the Department
will not permit a subordinate to defy the power of the Secretary and violate sacred rights conferred by Government on a citizen," meaning his patent right.
Then he slipped into his sales mode and discussed the advantages of his improved
iron pontoon. He noted that the wooden pontoons General Joseph Hooker used
in crossing the Rappahannock required considerable repair after the crossing. Finally, at the end of page four, he stated that his price may seem high but he had
included in the initial cost the expense of making the dies for the pontoon. After
being in production, his price would decrease. Even before production he would
be "willing to sacrifice much of the cost of machinery for the first train, & put
the price lower, but I fear even that will not meet the view and projects of General Cullum, in his supreme power."[18]

General Meigs's endorsement of Francis's letter to Secretary Stanton stated he
did not know Cullum had invented an iron pontoon, nor did Cullum try to in-
duce him to disobey the secretary of war's order. "Other assertions in this letter
are equally groundless."[19]

When his letter to Stanton failed to produce any results, Francis wrote to President Lincoln, enclosing a copy of his letter to Secretary Stanton. He noted that
the quartermaster general refused to obey an order from the secretary. Francis
continued telling the president that Brigadier General Henry W. Benham had
tested his iron pontoon and would use it "but he cannot get them so long as sub-
ordinates overrule the power of the Secretary of War."[20]

Again General Meigs penned an endorsement to the president's letter, beginning with a quote from the *Aeneid,* "Auri sacra fames," translated as "cursed crav-
ing for gold!" Meigs then continued, "These inventors whose goods are so costly
are difficult to satisfy." Meigs reiterated that he did not know General Cullum
had a pontoon. "The Secretarys orders have not been disobeyed." He had no in-
tention of interfering with Mr. Francis's rights. Meigs thought that Francis was
"excitable & easily misunderstands what is said when his invention is not approved & his price agreed to." The general concluded: "Can not an officer of
the government exercise his judgment & advise the Secretary not to purchase
Mr. Francis expensive invention without being liable to such a tirade of abuse &
calumny as this?"[21]

In retrospect the culprit in the fiasco of the iron pontoons was Joseph Francis. A close reading of the correspondence revealed that General Dix asked for "Francis's improved iron pontoon wagons," and General Meigs asked Francis for the cost, construction, and availability of his "Improved Ponton [sic] Wagons." Had Francis provided information on his iron pontoon wagons, he would have cited a cost of $141 per wagon. That was Marshall Lefferts's last asking price. Thus the iron wagon was cheaper than the wooden pontoons and probably the quartermaster would purchase them; on the other hand, if Francis wanted to introduce a new invention, an iron pontoon, he should have laid the groundwork by talking to the ultimate users of the pontoon and demonstrating its qualities. That had been his practice in the past. It may have been his success in Europe that caused him to abandon his time-tested procedures.[22]

Two months after Francis's outburst, General Dix attempted to smooth things between Francis and Meigs. He wrote an unofficial letter to Meigs from New York, saying that he no longer had an interest in the matter of iron pontoon wagons, but as a matter of public importance "we must come to it, soon or late, wood, india rubber, canvass &c. are all liable to accidents & injury, & fail at the very moment when they are most necessary." He felt sure Francis would "do basically what you wish. If price is an objection, he will let you fix it." All he wanted was for Meigs to send for Francis and tell him what he wanted. Although Dix had been a friend of Francis for a quarter of a century, it was obvious that Dix was not aware that the object of the clash between the two men was not the iron pontoon wagon, but the newer invention of an iron pontoon.[23]

Meanwhile, Francis was perfecting his new iron pontoon and incorporating comments from Generals Thomas and Benham, and when ready he revealed his changes to General Thomas. Basically it was the same size as the one he described to Meigs except the overall length was a foot longer at 28'. He had calculated its mass displacement at 253 cubic feet, giving the pontoon a total capacity of 15,812 pounds of buoyancy. By deducting the weight of the pontoon (900 pounds) the useful capacity was 14,822 pounds, an improvement of 2,412 pounds over his earlier pontoon. This buoyancy was equal to any contingency the army might encounter because the metal pontoon did not leak or absorb water, unlike a wooden one.

Francis stated his reason for two sections for the complete pontoon was to keep the overall length within the wagon's length. Wooden pontoons far exceeded the wagon's length and made handling the bulky bodies on narrow twisting roads very difficult. If, however, the Army would like to have a one-piece unit, he could make his pontoons permanently attached, and by so doing reduce the weight and by eliminating two ends he could have the same buoyancy in a two-foot shorter pontoon. Had Francis laid his technical specifications out more completely, and apprised Meigs of the exact nature of his iron pontoon things might have been different.[24]

On 25 January 1864, General Henry W. Benham gave the chief engineer, General Totten, his views concerning modifications that could improve fitting out pontoon trains and some tactical advice. He recommended substituting canvas-covered frame boats for the French pontoon currently in use. He would eliminate the pontoon trestle, a bridge universally disliked. As for Lieutenant Colonel Ira Spaulding's suggestion that pontoon trains carry several canvas boats to transport troops to drive off the enemy from the expected landing, he disagreed emphatically. If troops were necessary to drive off the enemy, then they should be in sufficient numbers to pressure the enemy.

Benham illustrated his tactics by citing his actions at the Franklin Crossing of the Rappahannock on 29 April 1863. He initiated a surprise crossing by carrying his wooden pontoons by hand for the last mile and a half before reaching the water. He concluded that the normal pontoon trains carrying their large wooden pontoons over bad roads with difficult turns made a special noise similar to that made by artillery as it moved forward. Benham had Captain Chauncey B. Reese of the engineers test whether thirty-six men could carry a pontoon a mile and a half to the river. Reese believed it was possible with one rest stop. On the day of the crossing, two trains were to cross at different places on the river. Benham had both trains off-load their pontoons, and he doubled Reese's number of men to carry the pontoons. When Benham dismounted to direct the upper crossing, someone countermanded his orders and reloaded the pontoons on wagons for the lower crossing. Benham's upper group carried their pontoons to the river without alerting the enemy to their presence. Therefore, the crossing was a rapid, completely unexpected, engagement that overwhelmed the enemy.

The lower crossing was a different story. The pontoon train rumbled toward the Rappahannock with the loud telltale sounds of an enemy preparation for a river crossing. The result was that the Confederates were in position and waiting. The enemy fire repulsed the Union troops resulting in a several hours' delay before the bridge was ready at a cost of severe loss of life. The general concluded, "where the bridge cannot be laid by method of the simultaneous lays, and swinging the long raft with twenty men concealed in each pontoon, the whole of the boats should be first employed for the passage of the attacking forces."

Benham's modification was to reduce the size of the French pontoon by eliminating three feet from the bow and two feet from the stern. This shorter pontoon would be easier to transport. Then he posed a question: Are these wooden pontoons the best instrument for river crossings? No! Wooden pontoons might be used for permanent bridges, but "the iron pontoon of somewhat near the form proposed by Mr. Francis, when strengthened in some parts and with some slight modifications, will be altogether the best under all circumstances for field service." But of the types of pontoon bridges currently in use, he would prefer the canvas pontoon boat, at its present length of twenty-two feet. He noted that the Chancellorsville crossing in April 1863 used canvas pontoon boats, and three corps with their artillery passed over successfully. Bailing out the pontoons during the operation only required a couple of buckets.[25]

Meanwhile, Joseph Francis was not finished after his rebuke from General Meigs. In February 1864 he met engineer Colonel Edward W. Serrell in New York on a mission to recruit colored troops. Francis told him how he made pontoon trains in Europe and that a section of his train was in Washington, D.C. Serrell confided that he had two canvas pontoon trains in the Department of the South that were not satisfactory because the canvas cuts so easily. He would like "to find out all I can about any improvements in Engineer material particularly pontoons." Serrell hoped he could visit General Dix and learn more about Francis's section of his pontoon train now at the Washington Armory. Francis suggested he talk with General Dix to see if he could visit Washington.[26]

Serrell immediately contacted Dix, who wrote to Secretary Stanton, enclosing Serrell's letter. Dix told Stanton that Serrell had employed a large number of men just to keep his canvas pontoons afloat. Dix could not understand why the United States ignored the iron pontoon wagon when most European states accepted it.[27]

Stanton forwarded Dix's and Serrell's letters to the Engineer Department for comment. Major J. C. Woodruff replied on 3 March that the only thing he could find concerning "Francis' pontoon project" was General Totten's endorsement a year earlier, saying that a board of engineer and quartermaster officers had examined the metal pontoon, "but this report has not been received or seen by me." Obviously Francis had made little impression upon the engineers.[28] Then Stanton sent the two letters and the two endorsements to the Quartermaster Department. General Meigs replied that Francis's pontoon was a very expensive copper corrugated item. A board of engineer and quartermaster officers examined it. These officers with science and experience differed with Francis as to its merits. He also investigated it and found it was "not for the interest of the United States to spend more of the time of its officers, or of the money of the military appropriations upon it."[29]

Meanwhile, Francis contacted President Lincoln on behalf of Colonel Serrell's request. Lincoln wrote Stanton requesting, if expedient, to allow Serrell to visit Washington. Stanton replied that he deemed it "highly injurious to the service to grant such applications."[30]

Once again the request for iron pontoon wagons elicited a reply about Francis's iron pontoons. This time General Meigs initiated the change. The general exchanged numerous letters with Mr. Lefferts buying and assigning iron pontoon wagons from June through September 1861. A year latter, when he first met Francis, the inventor presented him with a model of his iron pontoon wagon. Surely Meigs knew the difference between a metal army pontoon wagon and the iron pontoon. Why did he discuss Francis's pontoon when the two letters he received asked about Francis's iron pontoon wagon? Why did Meigs say that "Francis's pontoon is of copper corrugated, and very expensive," when Francis described it as iron, a much cheaper metal? Why did he conclude not to spend more time or money upon the subject? Could it be that General Meigs considered this was payback for Francis's unpleasantness?

To charge Meigs with such deceit is more than plausible if one examined his feud with Thomas U. Walter, the architect who developed plans for the Capital Dome and the House and Senate wings. Meigs treated Walter as a laborer and sought credit for Walter's plans for himself. Walter wrote of Meigs: "I am under, probably, the most vain and unscrupulous man the world ever saw. . . . He seeks to rob me of every thing he can to pamper his own vanity." In the last decade of the twentieth century William D. Mohr translated Meigs's journals, written in an early form of Pitman shorthand. His journals support Walter's letter about Meigs. Similar to Francis, Meigs took his feud with Walter to the secretary of war John B. Floyd, and then to President James Buchanan. For these actions the president exiled him to Fort Jefferson on Dry Tortugas at the end of the Florida Keys in 1859. He was brought back to Washington only after the opening of the Civil War.[31] Both men were vain, confident of their talents, and inclined to go over the heads of those opposing them; except, in the iron pontoon fiasco, Meigs was in the catbird seat.

The secretary of war returned copies of letters and endorsements to General Dix. He noted that earlier he had directed the quartermaster general to investigate the invention of Francis, and Meigs had reported unfavorably upon it; therefore, the "Secry of War declines to reconsider believing that such reconsideration would but necessitate a profitless expenditure of the time & means of the Dept." Obviously, Secretary Stanton was confused by Meigs's answer and be-

lieved that General Dix's request was for the pontoon and not the wagon. Thus
the result was that the Union army lost the services of one or maybe two superior pontoons.[32]

Even the U.S. Navy, a branch of government employing Francis's metal lifeboats since the 1840s, seemed to have forgotten Joseph Francis. In the summer
of 1862, Commodore Charles Wilkes, commanding the James River Flotilla, requested the Navy Department provide him with six metal canoes for use on scout
missions up the James River. In his request he offered to provide a sketch and
working drawings to assist the naval contractor in providing him metal scout canoes. Immediately the department replied it had ordered his request to be constructed. On 1 August 1862, Wilkes received three iron-covered boats and had
them launched before he had seen them. When he came on deck and looked at
the three boats, he refused to have anything to do with them. Shortly thereafter,
one of the boats turned over in the water. Wilkes beached and ignored all three
from that time on.

By 1:55 P.M. Wilkes telegraphed Secretary of the Navy Gideon Welles of his
displeasure. "I am woefully disappointed in the reception of boats with iron clad-
ding on them, riveted as a boiler, instead of a light metallic canoe covered with
thin iron." He wanted light swift canoes propelled by paddles that could go quietly up river at night to investigate small tributaries. He got wide boats powered
by long oars incapable of traveling up small waterways that needed examination.
"There is nothing about them which corresponds to my ideas, and the person
to whom the Department intrusted their preparation can have little brains or
the knowledge of the difference between a boat and canoe." Wilkes continued,
"Francis, the galvanized iron boat builder, would have put up the six in a week at
less expense than one of these cost." Secretary Welles authorized Wilkes to pro-
cure canoes from Francis, but, as he was still in Europe, neither the navy records
nor Francis's mentioned Wilkes's scout canoes.[33]

It is strange that his metal boats and batteaux proved themselves in the Third
Seminole War and the metal army pontoon wagons succeeded on the frontier
of the trans-Mississippi West, yet the army slighted them during the Civil War.
Francis claimed that his stop corrugation invention reduced his metal army pontoon wagons to nearly the price of wooden wagons. Yet the War Department
continued using wooden wagons because of the number of competing contractors continually lowered their price. It was an example of penny-wise, pound-
foolish.[34]

On the other hand, Francis's most successful item was his last corrugated iron device prepared before leaving for Europe in 1855, his Military Portable Folding Bedstead, that during the war became an iron hospital bed.[35] The tremendous number of combat casualties and the even larger number of military patients stricken with diseases in the field made huge demands for hospital beds.[36] After the war Francis continued actively working until 1876. He retired at age seventy-five and moved from New York City to his residence at Toms River, New Jersey.

II THE IMPOSTOR

8

Retirement and Challenges

Of all his inventions Joseph Francis considered his metal life car to be the pinnacle of his achievements. He had gone where no one had gone before by devising and manufacturing watercraft able to go from shore to shoal and return under the most adverse conditions to save life. Immediately after the *Ayrshire* rescue he brought his life car back to the factory to be painted and spruced up for its journey to the U.S. Arsenal in Washington, D.C., the Capitol Rotunda, the Washington Navy Yard (where it remained during his European stay), the Brooklyn Navy Yard, and finally to his residence at Toms River, New Jersey.

As he neared retirement he looked for a place to continue exhibiting his life car for the entire world to see. In 1872 he offered his life car to the New York City Department of Public-Works. On 6 May 1872 Secretary William Irwin of the Department of Public-Works accepted the car and agreed to abide by Francis's stipulation that his car could not leave the city without his approval. Irwin placed it in the Arsenal Building.

In January 1880 Captain James H. Merryman, USRMS, asked Horatio Allan if Joseph Francis was the inventor of the metal lifeboat and car. Allan replied that there had never been any question in his mind, or his partner's, as to the role of Francis, who had stated that he had the patents for the boats, and his word was accepted. Further, there was no question raised by others as to his claim to be the inventor of the two craft. Thus the Novelty Iron Works expended large sums of money building the dies necessary to manufacture those boats. Evidently Allen told his friend about the inquiry and Francis sent the secretary of the treasury John Sherman a four-page legal-sized handwritten history of his work from 1825 through 1850. Eleven days later he followed up with a printed version that contained a list of all his inventions from 1811 to 1878.[1]

Francis wondered why the Treasury Department was so concerned about his status as the inventor of the metal life car. Almost a year later, Francis received his answer and was stunned when he read in the *Nautical Gazette* of 5 February 1881 that there was a bill before Congress to provide Captain Douglass Ottinger, USRMS, retirement with full pay. As Francis read further he learned that the basis for Ottinger's request was his extraordinary services in the Revenue Marine

Service and his inventions for the U.S. Life-Saving Service, including his metal life car. Francis recalled that Captain Ottinger had purchased eight of his life cars for the first eight-lifesaving stations on the New Jersey coast. And later, while he was in Europe, Ottinger had challenged Francis's top deck of the life car as an infringement on the captain's top deck for the life car. When he returned from Europe, Marshall Lefferts briefed him on the patent office's hearing in favor of the captain, but, believing Ottinger was dead, Francis did nothing about the challenge. Now that he knew that Ottinger was alive and stirring up the issue, not of the top deck but of the whole life car, Francis was outraged.

Three days after reading about Captain Ottinger, Joseph Francis sent off a letter to General Superintendent Sumner I. Kimball, U.S. Life-Saving Service, stating some of the many errors of fact in Ottinger's petition. First, and foremost, the captain was not the inventor of the life car. That was Francis's invention. Second, Ottinger's claim that he gave the life car to the government without compensation was false, for he had fraudulently received remuneration from an earlier Congress. Third, Captain Ottinger received compensation for his extraordinary services performed for the Revenue Marine Service through his rank and salary. Francis concluded his four-page letter by asking Kimball if there was any way "to arrest an action of Congress to make a second unjust award."

Kimball replied that he felt it would be improper for him to participate in the controversy between Francis and Ottinger. As for how to stop such actions of Congress, Kimball suggested he consult a legal adviser.[2]

Francis worried about this challenge to his invention of the life car. He was eighty years old and sickly. If he died before he gathered sufficient proof of his ownership, the world might forget or overlook his work. He was desperate to secure his place in history. On 22 April 1881 he wrote to Kimball that he had documentary evidence and many living witnesses to his rightful claim as the inventor of the life car. Yet many of his witnesses were aged and infirm, as was he; therefore, he asked to have the next annual report of the U.S. Life-Saving Service (USL-SS) mention Francis as the inventor of the life car.

Kimball replied that in view of the 1859 congressional award of $10,000, and the 1860 patent office's decision that Captain Ottinger's claim had priority, he would not be justified in recognizing Francis's claim, but if he presented his documentary evidence and his witnesses testimony to the department, they would be placed in the records of the office, and the answer as to who was the real inventor would be fairly considered.[3]

As Francis pondered Kimball's last letter, he began to think more carefully about his situation. He needed to gather his evidence more fully and plan his de-

8.1 Captain Douglass Ottinger, USRMS. Photo courtesy of the Erie County Historical Society, Erie, Pennsylvania.

fense rather than wildly assert his claim. Trying to stop congressional actions could wait. He must know more about how Captain Ottinger got Congress to approve his first bill for remuneration. He called upon friends for help gathering information (such as ex-congressman Elizur H. Prindle of Washington, D.C.) about the remuneration from Congress; Captain B. S. Osbon, editor of the *Nautical Gazette,* for information on Ottinger; and Lieutenant Charles V. Morris,

8.2 Captain Douglass Ottinger's Metal Life Car. Photo courtesy of the National Archives.

USN, for an affidavit about the early development of the life cars. He asked his agent James L. Pond to investigate the interference case in the records of the patent office.

Prindle wrote to Francis "that there was collusion and fraud practiced in getting the bill through." He believed that a friend of Ottinger waited for an opportune time to call up the bill "and had it passed without any knowledge on the part of the House as to what was being done." He continued saying that frequently during periods of confusion or stress in the House, bills will come to the floor and be passed "without having five persons know what is being done." The congressman said he had seen bills passed with only the member calling the bill voting while "the remainder of the members being interested in other matters and giving no attention to the business before the House" ignored the passage of minor requests. Prindle's information made Francis eager to know more about Captain Ottinger.[4]

Francis pursued a multifaceted approach to his problem. Besides gathering past records from the patent office and finding out more about Ottinger, he also wanted to keep his life car before the public. When he learned from Second Lieutenant and Assistant Inspector C. H. McLellan, USRMS, at Toms River, that London, England, would host the Great International Fisheries Exhibition in the summer of 1883, Francis suggested that the USL-SS might want to present an exhibit of the relics of the rescue of the British ship *Ayrshire* wrecked off New Jersey in 1850. The USL-SS already had the mortar and shot from that event, and he added that if the department made a request to the New York City Department of Public-Works for his life car, he would assist in expediting the loan.

Superintendent Kimball accepted Second Lieutenant McLellan's suggestion and assigned Captain J. H. Merryman, inspector of the U.S. Life-Saving Station, Bowling Green, New York City, to supervise the arrangements for shipping two wooden surfboats and the *Ayrshire* life car to London. Captain Merryman worried about the safety of the life car, which was highly valued by the New York Public-Works Department. According to his information the U.S. Commission of Fish and Fisheries Spencer F. Baird would ship the department's vessels by the lowest cost, which was on the deck of a steamer. Because of the loss of earlier surfboats shipped on the deck of the steamship *Glen Mowen* during a heavy sea, Merryman requested Francis's life car be crated and carried below deck. Commissioner Baird readily agreed and so the crated life car traveled below deck across the Atlantic. The United States Life-Saving Service exhibit became a popular display at the exhibition.[5]

In mid-September 1883, Superintendent Kimball received disturbing news from George Brown Goode, commissioner to the exhibition. His Excellency J. Russell Lowell, U.S. minister at the Court of St. James, sent Goode recent correspondence telling him that Francis's metal life car was not the authentic life car that saved two hundred people wrecked on the ship *Ayrshire* in 1850. Minister Lowell enclosed three items: Captain Douglass Ottinger's letter of 23 June 1883, a picture of his original, and according to him the true, metal life car photographed the day prior to his letter, and a petition of 31 July 1883 from Judge Gideon J. Ball and six other gentlemen from Erie, Pennsylvania, protesting the exhibition of a fraudulent relic. Commissioner Goode forwarded these items on to Superintendent Kimball to respond to the charges made against his exhibit.

Captain Ottinger told Minister Lowell that he had gone to the commissioner of the Department of Parks, New York City, to tell him that he observed that the covered metallic boat exhibited in Central Park was fraudulent. The commissioner showed him a letter from the superintendent of the U.S. Life-Saving Service instructing a subordinate to ship the boat to the International Fisheries Exhibition in London. In order to prove his contention, Ottinger enclosed a photograph of the original life car that saved the shipwrecked people of the *Ayrshire.* In the foreground running the length of the life car was the inscription "The Life Car at its first use saved 201 Persons wrecked on Ship Ayrshire 1850 invented by Capt Douglass Ottinger 1848." The letter continued: "The inventor of the life car gave it free of tax for patent, not to the United States alone, but to all other nations. . . . /s/ Douglass Ottinger Inventor of the life car." The captain believed it was important to expose the fraudulent impersonation.

The petition began by saying that Miss Louisa Bliss while visiting the London exhibition noticed Joseph Francis's life car displayed as the life car that saved the people of the *Ayrshire* in 1850. Being familiar with Ottinger's life car in Erie, she wrote to her parents decrying this false display. The result was the submission of a petition signed by seven distinguished gentlemen of Erie to bring this untruthful exhibit to an end. They noted that Douglass Ottinger of Erie invented the life car as proved by "The files of the Treasury Department, the Act of Congress, and the Archives of the Patent Office." They desired that the petition be publicized at the exhibition so that "it may be seen and read by the visitors."

If true, this information was a bombshell of the first magnitude. General Superintendent Kimball and his closest advisers huddled in cloistered conferences debating how to handle this news, all the while keeping outwardly calm and silent. The political damage domestically probably could be kept under control, but the international repercussions were of a much more serious matter.[6]

Meanwhile, Joseph Francis, unaware of Ottinger's latest attack, worked on a plan to place his life car in the National Museum at the Smithsonian Institution. Again using Second Lieutenant McLellan, he suggested that the secretary of the treasury Charles J. Folger initiate the process for the life car to be sent from England to Washington, D.C., while the paperwork between the secretary and the New York City Public-Works Department could be worked out with Francis's assistance to complete the change.[7]

A month later Francis told McLellan that he would like to transfer a set of cast-iron model dies and a finished model of a corrugated brass man-of-war cutter of the type furnished to the U.S. Navy to be a part of his life car exhibit. The dies would interest both the scientific and the general public, as they would demonstrate how Francis solved the difficult task of corrugating the curved lines of his life car.

In addition Francis wanted to give to the museum his gold medal and the diamond snuffbox presented to him by Emperor Napoleon III. He realized that many would question why he would donate the jeweled box, but he had no living family beyond his son Isaac, who was as broken in health as was his father. All of his other European medals had been stolen years before and he knew that the box would be secure in the museum and offer a slight indication to the public of the esteem his work had enjoyed on the continent.[8]

While Francis tried to give his life car to the national museum, Captain Ottinger seemed intent on belittling Superintendent Kimball's organization. An article in the *Erie Herald* of 21 January 1884 entitled, "Captain Ottinger's Prophesy Concerning the inefficiency of the Life Saving apparatus, Fulfilled in the wreck of the 'Fred Mercur,' and horribly realized in the loss of Fourteen lives on the New Jersey Coast," came to the attention of Secretary of the Treasury Folger. The secretary wrote a letter to Ottinger stating that it presented a serious reflection upon the Life-Saving Service that is within the Treasury Department as is the Revenue Marine Service. Secretary Folger wanted to know immediately if Captain Ottinger wrote or inspired that article. He sent his letter to Ottinger via the collector of customs in Erie with the request that the collector notify the department of the date of delivery. Collector Henry C. Stafford personally delivered the letter to Ottinger on 19 February 1884 and reported it to the secretary.[9]

It now appeared that Secretary Folger, Superintendent Kimball, and Joseph Francis, the inventor of the life car, all were wondering, "Who is Captain Douglass Ottinger?"

9

The Perfidious Captain Douglass Ottinger, USRMS

Douglass Ottinger was born in Germantown, a suburb of Philadelphia, on 11 December 1804. At a young age he shipped out in the mercantile marine and rapidly rose to command a small trading vessel. He joined the U.S. Revenue Cutter Service in 1832.[1] Of his first seventeen years of service, almost thirteen and a half were on the Great Lakes, with only three and a half years in New York City. Of this latter time he spent two years supervising boiler construction for the *Dallas* at the Novelty Iron Works.[2] At no time was Ottinger engaged in lifesaving from shore to shoal.

In 1848 he received orders to establish the first lifesaving stations on the New Jersey coast. Captain Ottinger's brief service, about seven months, establishing eight lifesaving stations, introduced him to a phase of maritime life he had not known during his career in the Revenue Marine Service. Until he received that assignment, he had not been aware of the frequency of shipwrecks, the terrible loss of life and property, or the heroic actions of the surfmen dedicated to mitigating those losses. He had a desire to participate in that exciting life not as a surfman, but as an inventor providing tools for those valiant oarsmen working the dangerous region of shore and shoals, battered by turbulent storms. Gradually it became an overwhelming obsession to be among the elite benefactors to that special niche of maritime life. As he later said, it was only after visiting the New Jersey coast that he "first heard the details of suffering and loss of life incident to the stranding of vessels in that vicinity, and of instances where wrecked vessels were so near the shore that the cries of distress of persons on board could be distinctly heard on the beach by persons who were compelled to witness hundreds of human beings washed into the sea without the means of saving a single life."[3] In retrospect, he seemed to wrap his altruistic goal in an egotistical desire for personal fame and fortune.

On 6 August 1853 Ottinger suggested to Secretary of Treasury James Guthrie to exhibit one of the department's life cars at the New York World's Fair because part of that lifesaving apparatus was his invention. He felt the public should be aware of the department's concern for public safety. Further, he said, "I did not patent the invention and am desirous that it should be used throughout the world without tax." This was said three years after the rescue of the crew and passengers from the wreck of the *Ayrshire;* however, he did not state specifically what his invention was.[4]

On 3 August 1857, two years after Joseph Francis left for Europe, Captain Ottinger submitted to the U.S. Patent Office his invention for an upper deck for Francis's metal life car. On 21 September 1857, fearing the patent office might not understand his device; he asked to personally present his invention. Three days later, worried that the patent office might analyze his application without his personal appearance, he submitted a substitute specification.[5] The next day, and before his substitute arrived, patent office clerk "E" declared that his invention was not patentable. "E" referred him to Joseph Francis's application rejected on 19 July 1851. He stated that Ottinger's request of 21 September to present his view as to why his device was new and patentable needed to await the determination of his first submission before any further consideration could take place. Thus, with the decision now made, he had the right at any convenient time to submit his views "personally, or by agent, or in writing," to show why his device should be patentable in spite of the reference supplied by the patent office.[6]

Captain Ottinger decided to use a different tact and approached Congress. He wrote a letter to the Honorable John Cochran and the members of the Committee of Commerce of the House of Representatives requesting remunerative compensation for his invention of the "life or surf car" and other apparatuses of his in use in the lifesaving stations. He appended seventeen documents to support his claim that he was "the inventor of the surf car and spiral wire, for overcoming the *vis inertia,* and fastening the line to the shot." Further, he added documentation to show the surf car had rescued passengers and crews of stranded vessels. All he asked for was just compensation from the government for past, present, and future use of his invention for the cause of humanity. To help the committee arrive at a just compensation, he noted that Congress awarded the inventor of chloroform, $100,000, Morse received $48,000 for his telegraph, and Dr. Page $24,000 for his electric motor. He then asked for, in addition to his remuneration, an extra $5,000 for him to test the practicality of the surf car at sea carrying people between ships during violent gales.

Among his documents were the following: First Lieutenant John N. Toner's report to the secretary of the treasury William M. Meredith of 4 November 1849; a letter from Thomas Bond to Walter R. Jones, president of the Life-Saving Benevolent Association, concerning the shipwreck of the ship *Georgia,* dated 7 December 1852; a letter from John Maxson to Walter Jones reporting the success of the *Ayrshire* rescue dated 13 March 1850; a letter from Governor William Newell to Ottinger dated 16 October 1857; and letters from navy commanders William Hunter and James Alden to Ottinger on 4 March 1858.[7] Amazingly few of these stated that he was the inventor of the life car.

Lieutenant Toner wrote: "The boats and life-cars were built by Mr. Francis, of New York, and are the same as those built for, and recommended by Captain Ottinger, with an important improvement of covering the whole inside bottom with galvanized iron and securing it to the wooden bottom, thereby making the boat perfectly secure and not liable to leak should the wood become rent or cracked by hard usage." Wrecking master John Maxson reported his actions during the *Ayrshire* grounding without mentioning Ottinger. Likewise, wrecking master Thomas Bond reported his actions without mentioning any inventors of his equipment. Governor Newell wrote: "I assure you I shall never cease to know or to remember you as one who has contributed very much towards lessening the dangers of the sea, and one to whom our Jersey people are almost entirely indebted for the valuable apparatus which has been the means of saving so many hundred lives and so much property. I am well satisfied that, had you not been intrusted with the erection and furnishing of the life-saving stations on our coast, my own individual effort to that end would never have amounted to much." One positive document was an extract from President Walter R. Jones, of the Life-Saving Association of the city of New York, stating that Ottinger invented the surf or life car in 1849 and that "Mr. Joseph Francis executed the mechanical part of the surf-car and life-boats under the direction and supervision of the Government officer."

Upon reading Ottinger's documents, Congressman Elihu B. Washburne sent a copy of Captain Ottinger's letter to the secretary of treasury and asked if any of his surf cars were in use? If so, how many? Was his surf car valuable? Finally, was Captain Ottinger the inventor of the surf car?

Seventeen days later Secretary Howell Cobb sent his reply. There were fifty-four lifesaving stations on the New Jersey and Long Island coasts, twenty-eight on the former and twenty-six on the latter. Captain Ottinger installed the first eight life stations in New Jersey between Sandy Hook and Egg Harbor, and from the first each station included a lifeboat and a life car. As for the life car's value, Secretary Cobb related the story of the wreck of the *Ayrshire,* and he suggested that the committee members could find a complete description of the event and of the lifeboats and life cars in Francis's book *Metallic Life-Boat Company.* As for the inventor of the life car, Cobb said that the department had no information beyond the two enclosures to his letter. The first was Captain Ottinger's letter of 21 May 1849, and the second was First Lieutenant Toner's letter of 4 November 1849. Neither of Cobb's enclosures specifically stated that Ottinger was the inventor of the life car. Cobb's answer, about the inventor, was surprising. Even a cursory reading of Francis's book would lead one to believe that Joseph Francis invented the life car.[8]

On 10 March 1858, while waiting for Congress's response, Ottinger again turned to the patent office. He requested the office to declare interference between Francis's rejected application requested in 1851 and his own rejected application requested in 1857. His demand seemed ludicrous, but the patent office was hesitant to declare itself without a thorough study of the problem proposed by the captain.[9]

Meanwhile, on 14 May 1858 Washburne reported for the Committee on Commerce that the committee members "are satisfied that Captain Ottinger is the original inventor of the life or surf car. . . . The committee then 'recommended the passage of a bill . . . as a remuneration for the use of his invention.'" Thus on 14 February 1859 an act for relief of Captain Ottinger granted him $10,000.[10]

Now that he had received remunerations from Congress under false pretenses, Captain Ottinger was more determined than ever to strengthen his claim. On 11 May 1859 he filed a new application as the inventor of an improvement for the upper deck of the life car. He claimed that the peculiar angle of his deck offered less resistance to wind and wave. The patent office rejected his application on 16 June. Patent office clerk J.F.F. stated that his arched deck was not novel, and referred him to patents issued to L. Alexander in 1850, G. F. Tewksbury in 1849, and Joseph Francis in 1839. "For the second clause of the claim you are referred to the application of Joseph Francis, rejected in August, 1858—(surf-car)."[11]

Ottinger studied his second rejection, then on 24 June he wrote to the commissioner of patents saying that he had investigated the three patents referred to in his rejection and found that "Francis alone appears to anticipate the subject-matter embraced in my first and second claims. . . . None of the references except Francis's application, rejected in 1858, possess the capabilities or resemble this car in the slightest." Four days later the patent office agreed with the captain that Francis's application rejected in 1858 seemed pertinent to Ottinger's and that both received rejections.[12]

Captain Ottinger was getting desperate. He immediately filed a third application, this time changing the curvature of his deck and claiming that the new feature would allow the life car to be used between ships at sea. On 8 November

1859, clerk "Coues" replied briefly: "Your application for improvements in surf-cars has received its third examination, and is again rejected for the reasons and the references given on its first rejection."[13]

While in Washington, D.C., on 26 November 1859, Captain Ottinger wrote again to the commissioner of patents. He acknowledged "Coues" letter of 8 November. He reiterated the facts of his earlier letter that only Francis's application of 1858 had any bearing on his application; therefore, he requested the office "declare an interference between my application and that of Joseph Francis, rejected August, 1858, for the purpose of proving priority of invention." This phrase "proving priority of invention" must have intrigued Examiner Henry Baldwin, who promptly decided to examine the case. The first step was to call the parties to a hearing. Marshall Lefferts undertook to defend Joseph Francis, who was in Russia at the time.[14]

The hearing record was voluminous as Captain Ottinger presented five witnesses who swore that Ottinger was the inventor of the life car. One witness, G. H. Penfield, whom Ottinger hired to place India-rubber floats on the sides of his life cars, testified that Ottinger claimed the invention in 1849, and that Francis denied having invented the life car. Also Captain Ottinger submitted an affidavit on 14 July 1860 stating that upon his "Second attempt he hit upon the Life or Surf Car—that himself and a committee of the board of underwriters of New York *selected* Mr. *Francis* to build a Surf Boats [*sic*] after a model furnished by a committee of Surfmen one of whom remained at the Factory and superintended the first metallic Life-Boat that was constructed for the U.S. Life-Saving stations: that the Life-Car was *built under his immediate direction.*"[15]

Henry Baldwin's investigation was interesting. He agreed that "the invention was as novel as it was bold and successful, and it consisted in the construction of a life-boat that should be strong, buoyant, and capable of containing living beings under cover, without suffocating or drowning when pulled through the surf, not be easily upset, and even safe when capsized, and at the same time the boat was protected from destruction by being violently forced either by wind or waves against the wreck, the shore, or the relieving ship" by the India-rubber floats placed on either side of the life car. He acknowledged these conditions applied to both inventions, but, from the testimony, it appeared that Joseph Francis built the boats in 1848 at the Novelty Works in New York for the U.S. government under Ottinger's direction.

Baldwin noted that the secretary of the treasury had assigned Captain Ottinger to establish lifesaving stations on the New Jersey coast. Later Ottinger asked the secretary to display one of the life cars at the New York World's Fair because part of the invention was his. He said he did not seek a patent so that the world might employ it without tax.

The examiner stated that Francis applied for a patent in April 1851, based upon his caveat of 11 February 1850, while Ottinger did not file his application until 11 May 1859. Baldwin continued, saying, "I am fully satisfied from the testimony that the invention in question was original with Ottinger, and that he was also the first inventor of the same." Baldwin believed that by giving his invention voluntarily to the public Ottinger abandoned it; therefore, he rejected both inventions. The commissioner concurred, dissolved the interference, and allowed thirty days for appeal.[16]

Years later, in either an example of a slow-moving bureaucracy or slipshod research, the commissioner of patents wrote that on 8 August 1860 the patent office dissolved Ottinger's interference request of 10 March 1858. In addition the patent office reiterated its earlier decision rejecting both applications. It based its reasoning on Francis's rejected application of 1851 and his two patents of 1839 and 1845. Yet Ottinger's second request for interference of 26 November 1859 received its rejection on the same date, 8 August 1860, reasoning that the captain freely relinquished his invention to the public. It is highly unlikely that the patent office concluded both of Ottinger's requests for interference, 10 March 1858 and 26 November 1859, on the same day.[17]

Upon reading the records of Captain Ottinger's efforts to establish a patent for a lifesaving apparatus, one can't help but notice that there was vague interchanging of words within various documents. Lifeboats, surfboats, life cars, and surf cars seem to mean the same thing: actually, as used by professionals of the time, lifeboats were boats with additional buoyancy carried by ships to save crew and passengers when some disaster necessitated leaving the ship; surfboats were specially constructed lifeboats designed to cross from shore to shipwreck through violent shoal waters; life cars were the special design of Joseph Francis for his covered lifeboats that could be used under conditions when the other open boats could not be safely used. This vagueness benefited Ottinger for it allowed him to use terms implying that his application was more than a device for a top deck to a life car and included the life car itself. The murkier the subject, the more impressive it seemed, and the more advantageous for Ottinger's design.

In the fall of 1862, when Joseph Francis returned from Europe, Marshall Lefferts told him of the interference hearing and that Ottinger's deck was the original invention. Francis said that even if he knew of the patent office's thirty-day appeal there was nothing he could do about it. At the time he learned of Ottinger's perfidy he also heard that Captain Ottinger was dead. Francis decided to remain silent rather than besmirch the grave.[18] Yet the information about his death was erroneous.

Captain Ottinger, pleased with his victory over Francis and content with his reputation within the newly created U.S. Life-Saving Service, continued his career with the Revenue Marine Service. The nascent Life-Saving Service soon noted that at several points along the Atlantic Coast shoals extended out so far that large draft ships would come to rest beyond reach of their mortar lines. Thus, when the sea state kept surfboats from launching, the station could not use its life car to provide assistance. On 23 March 1875, Acting Secretary of the Treasury Charles H. Conant detailed Captain Ottinger to make experiments to increase the range of shot-line used at the lifesaving stations. Secretary Conant recognized his previous service on the coast and "in view of your success heretofore in improving and devising apparatus for the saving of life from stranded vessels, the Department desires to avail itself of your assistance."[19]

Ottinger later wrote of his task that he worked with Robert P. Parrott, inventor of a naval gun of the Civil War. Parrott made a cannon especially for the Life-Saving Service, and designed a new way of fastening the lifesaving line to the forward end of the bolt shot. Both these devices were Parrott's. Yet, according to Ottinger, these devices came from his experiments and "belong to the apparatus I produced in executing that order." Yet again, he failed to say what his apparatus was. Before Ottinger's experiments the longest line shot was 400 yards. Using his improvements, Ottinger shot 631 yards of working strength line and 745 yards of what he called "the line of last resort."[20] It was a successful assignment for the Revenue Marine Service captain, and he basked in it.

Equally successful were Ottinger's endeavors in other areas. From May 1857 to May 1861, he commanded the cutter *Jeremiah S. Black,* one of the early cutters built specifically for the Great Lakes service. Later he served on special duty on the Examination of Officers and Applicants for the Revenue Marine Service in New York City. From October to December 1861 he was ordered to bring the five Great Lakes cutters down the Canadian canals to the St. Lawrence and around to Boston. Near the end of the war, he superintended the construction of the *Commodore Perry* in Buffalo, New York. He then commanded the *Perry* for most of her first sixteen years from 1865 to 1881. Occasionally Ottinger had auxiliary duties such as providing information to the Court of Alabama Claims in 1874, and again the next year experimenting how to increase the distance the shot-line could reach.[21]

In 1881 a new captain commanded the *Perry,* and Ottinger was placed on "waiting orders," a condition that meant a loss of one-third of his pay. Captain

Douglass Ottinger, USRMS, decided to call upon Congress once again. This time for his services to maritime commerce and to the shipping public, as noted in records of the Treasury Department and the U.S. Patent Office, "and after more than forty-five years of active service, your memorialist [*sic*] now asks, if not required for further duty by the Government, to be retired by Act of Congress with the rank and pay of a Captain in the service to which he belongs."[22] It was an impressive page and a quarter memorial delineating the most outstanding events of his career and augmented by a number of appendixes.

His "An Abridged Account of Services Rendered" was an eight-page history of his service career beginning as a second lieutenant, USRCS, aboard the cutter *Erie* in 1832, and ending with him a captain, USRMS, commanding the steamer *Perry* in 1881. It was a log of a superb seaman. One night the *Erie* was anchored in Sandusky, Ohio, under strong northeast gale winds when the captain received news that a vessel was on the rocks. At the time Second Lieutenant Ottinger served as the first lieutenant of the cutter and he told his captain that "he could beat the ship through the breakers on the bar; the Captain said: 'No vessel had done so even in day-light;' the Lieut. assured him he could take the ship out (no range lights were then on the lakes). The cutter was beat out over the bar and the vessel in distress and her cargo saved."[23]

In 1843 he served as first lieutenant aboard the iron steam propeller *Legaré*. She was at anchor in the East River when a local pilot brought orders for her to go immediately to Sandy Hook. When the pilot found that the steam machinery was not available, he refused to take the ship underway with only her sails. He said, "she could not be handled among the fleet anchored in the river; the 1st Lieut. got her under-way, wind adverse, beat her down to Sandy Hook, performed service and returned to New York." Later that year, Ottinger sailed her into Hampton Roads "with steering sails and royals set; all sails were taken in, furled and topmen piped down from aloft and ship anchored in less than nine minutes. Commander David G. Farragut remarked he had not seen more dispatch in bringing a ship to anchor."[24]

In 1848 Captain Ottinger, commanding the cutter *Dallas,* sailed from Erie, Pennsylvania, to New York Harbor via the Canadian canals. In his passage through the Gulf of St. Lawrence he had a Canadian pilot aboard. A September gale swept the gulf with violent northeast winds and misty rain. During the night the pilot lost his nerve and declared the ship must go to shore. Captain Ottinger asked the pilot for his position and he replied, "I don't know, the ship is going ashore." Ottinger called for the chief engineer and directed he produce more steam. The engineer replied, "It cannot be done; it is no use; the ship is going ashore." The first assistant engineer reported he was sick and could not take charge of the engine room. Ottinger ordered the three men to go below. Then the captain ordered the second assistant engineer "to haul fires, clean furnaces and get 50 lbs of steam as soon as practicable." He ordered the first lieutenant to take the port watch forward and set down the yards and masts. Meanwhile, he took the starboard watch to set down the yards and masts of the main and mizzen. All the yards and masts were stored on the windward side of the *Dallas* to counter the vessel's heel, for the upper part of the lee paddle box had been submerged in the water much of the time. "The Captain, with aid of log slate, made estimate of force of wind and waves so as to get place of the vessel, kept her close to the wind. Engineer Miller reported 50 pounds of steam and was ordered to go ahead and keep the pressure up; he replied: 'The leeward wheel is so submerged the shaft will probably break.' The order was not modified, the vessel moved onward so as to pass the danger. Her Captain navigated her from cape Canso [Nova Scotia] to New York without a pilot."[25]

In 1849 a group of businessmen from New York City asked the secretary of the treasury to permit Captain Ottinger to command a commercial ship to take them to California. The secretary granted Ottinger a furlough, and the revenue captain purchased and equipped a vessel for the group. Later the secretary rescinded Ottinger's furlough in order that he might continue establishing lifesaving stations. The businessmen objected, claiming that they invested their money in good faith that their captain had a furlough. The secretary granted Ottinger leave from active service without pay in June 1849.

In sailing around Cape Horn a strong gale battered Ottinger's vessel at a time when the cliffs of Staten Land became a dead lee shore. The captain reduced sails to the least amount of canvas that would give headway close by the wind. Tierra del Fuego did not provide shelter for the ship. "The leeward rail of the vessel was pressed to the water, and the billows rolled over the windward bow, sweeping aft on deck with a dash against the bulk head of the poop cabin that opened the seams and filled the leeward sleeping berths with water." Ottinger directed the steersman for over four hours. Finally, "at 1 a.m. the snow ceased to fall, the moon broke through the clouds, and the Captain got a bearing of the S. W. part of Staten land which showed that the ship had weathered it about eight miles. All sail was taken in and she was hove to under bare poles."[26]

While in California, Captain Ottinger had several commercial duties. He commanded a small steamer hauling freight on the Feather and Yuba rivers. He commanded a schooner for a group of investors interested in northern California. On that journey he discovered a bay with heavy breakers over its bar so that "no vessel had crossed its wild bar." When Ottinger crossed the bar, "the crest of a breaker drove her onward so rapidly as to *leave* the wind of a very brisk gale and her sails fell '*filled aback.*'" The investors wanted to call the bay Ottinger Bay, but he declined the honor and graciously named it Humboldt Bay, considering that it had already received that name years earlier. Later he said that he received a letter of thanks from Baron Humboldt. He opened the timber trade between Humboldt Bay and San Francisco. Next he commanded a steamer of Law's Line with a salary of $6,000 per year. His final civilian employment on the West Coast was with the Pacific Mail Steamship Company. He submitted a request to resign from the Revenue Marine Service, but the secretary of the treasury told him that his services were required. He left the Pacific Mail Steamship Company and assumed command of the revenue cutter *Lawrence* based in San Francisco, for $1,200 per year.[27]

In 1862 he brought the revenue steamer *Miami* into Washington, D.C. Shortly thereafter Secretary of the Treasury Salmon P. Chase ordered the *Miami* to transport President Abraham Lincoln, Secretary of War Stanton, General Egbert Viele, and himself to Fortress Monroe. The presidential party arrived on board on the afternoon of 5 May and spent the night anchored in the Potomac River studying maps of the Virginia coast and planning future operations.

Early on 6 May Captain Ottinger weighed anchor and headed for Fortress Monroe. When they arrived at Hampton Roads, the waters were rough from a northeast gale and Captain Ottinger did not believe these statesmen would be safe traveling in the small ship's boat. He asked the local pilot to take his vessel into the post wharf. When the local pilot declined, saying it would not be safe, Ottinger turned to the Potomac pilot to take his vessel in. The Potomac pilot replied that he was unfamiliar with the grounds. Captain Ottinger then took the helm and brought the *Miami* safely up to the wharf. After depositing his passengers, he left the wharf, steamed to an anchorage in the Roads, and anchored.[28]

As interesting as Ottinger's presidential journey was, there was another version written by Third Lieutenant A. G. Cary, USRMS, one of the watch officers of the *Miami*. His account in the ship's log was as follows:

Thursday May 6th 1862
12 Mid at Anchor off White House
3 A.M. all hands called hove up Anchor and proceeded down the Potomac
4 A.M. weather fine winds from NW
4.30 A.M. Passed Gun Boat Yankee [unintelligible] at Anchor in Mattawoman
    Creek

5.45 A.M. Passed Aquia Creek crew employed in washing down the Decks

7.45 A.M. Hove log Ship going 10 knots

8 A.M. Brailed up Mainsail passed Cedar Point

11 A.M. passed Piney Point sent top Gallant hands aloft and set sail also the squaresail

At 12 Mer the same Point look out bearing ENE dist 4 miles

12.30 P.M. abreast of Point look out

1.30 P.M. abreast Smith's Point & hauled down the Bay set Mainsail

2 P.M. set Gaff top sail

4 P.M. off Wolfstrip [Wolftrip] bearing West All hands went to quarters and expended 1 shrapnell 24 pdr. 1 shrapnell 12 pdr. 1 Hogkiss [Hotchkiss] shell from pivot guns for Practice wind and weather the same

4 to 6 Light breezes from N W

5.20 P.M. Brailed up Mainsail took in foretopsail set the awning sent down top Gallant yards

8 to 12 alongside the steamer Washington at the Wharf Fortress Monroe

Served 33 Rations

/s/ A. G. Cary
3rd Lieut.[29]

The two narratives are vastly different. Captain Ottinger's account, over twenty years later, had heroic actions in a storm-tossed bay. On the Beaufort Scale a moderate gale is a 7 indicating a wind speed of 25–35 knots and a fresh gale is 8 indicating 35–40 knots. Whereas, Third Lieutenant Cary reported the weather fine and winds from the northwest in the morning and in the evening, and, just before docking, as light breezes (number 2 on the scale or 3.5 to 6 knots) from the northwest. Thus Captain Ottinger's sailing and steaming through these gales in his narrative might contain more of a Munchausenian touch within his log rather than the traits of a superb seaman.

The next night, according to Ottinger, he anchored in Lynn Haven Bay where he then rowed two miles just off shore without receiving any fire from Confederate pickets. At midnight he gave the engineer officer at the fortress the results of his scout and the best place to land. An assault took place that night and that "same day the American flag was again flying over Norfolk."[30]

Years later General Viele wrote his version of the presidential voyage. While both Ottinger's and Viele's narrations were hazy as to dates, the *Miami*'s log provided specific hours and dates in support of the general's narrative. Thus it was Secretary Chase who proposed making a reconnaissance of General Viele's suggestion to land at the rear of Norfolk. On Friday 9 May, at 8:30 A.M., a pilot conned the *Miami* from Fortress Monroe to Lynn Haven Bay, and at 10 A.M. the first boats sent to the rebel shore. Throughout the day and night the *Miami* remained anchored off shore covering the landing party. At 11:30 A.M. Saturday, the *Miami* weighed anchor to return the expedition to Fortress Monroe. When Secretary Chase reported to Lincoln what he had done, the President insisted on going over and looking at the rebel shore for himself. At 5 P.M., as Lincoln and Chase steamed off to Lynn Haven Bay, they ordered Ottinger to bring his vessel along to cover their reconnaissance. The general wrote that under the light of the moon President Lincoln "landed on the beach and walked up and down a considerable distance to assure himself that there could be no mistake in the matter. How little the Confederacy dreamed what a visitor it had that night to the 'sacred soil.'" Early the next morning the Union transports began offloading troops on Norfolk's back door.[31] Ultimately, as the Confederates left Norfolk, they torched the navy yard and blew up the CSS *Virginia* (the former USS *Merrimac*) thereby eliminating the rebel ironclad's threat to the Union navy.

Once again Captain Ottinger's narrative contained a prevaricator's style as he modestly claimed his scout and report to the army at Fortress Monroe brought about the capture of Norfolk. In reality, his role was quite passive. He did not scout the rebel shore and when he carried Secretary Chase's party to Confederate Virginia his ship was under the control of a local pilot. One might wonder if his other occasions of relieving pilots might be in the same vein as his frequent gales.

Of course, Captain Ottinger had rendered a disclaimer at the beginning of his abridged account saying "no private journal being kept, log books not generally attainable, memory has been mainly drawn upon." Yet when President Lincoln, Secretary of War Stanton, and Secretary of the Treasury Chase boarded Captain Ottinger's small steamer, these guests should overwhelm Ottinger to the extent that his memories of even the most mundane event during the presidential voyage be in his mind a vivid mental picture. Ottinger may have, however, purposely enhanced his role to strengthen his case for full retirement.

In the opening of his memorial, he noted that in the first five years his life-saving stations, under the Life-Saving Benevolent Association of New York, saved over seven hundred people from wrecked ships. He also noted that General Superintendent of Life-Saving Service S. I. Kimball reported that between 1850 and 1870 "the life-saving stations, while mismanaged and neglected, had nevertheless reduced fatality attending shipwreck, 'in as much as 4,163 persons and $716,000 worth of property'" were saved. Near the end of his abridged account, he listed the twenty vessels he rescued while commanding the *Perry*. Then he listed three articles he had presented to the government for life-saving purposes: the use of the Life Car, the Combination Guard—(under caveat), and the Sand Wheel.[32]

Captain Ottinger prepared an impressive memorial. He stressed the number of lives saved by the lifesaving stations from 1849 through 1870. Yet again, his appendixes were vague. He used Governor William Newell, Thomas Bond, John Maxson's letters, and Samuel Metcalf's testimony from his first congressional appeal for money. To those he added Israel J. Merritt's letter of 12 November 1853 on the usefulness of the life car at the wreck of the *Western World* near Squan Beach, and, most important, the decision by the chief examiner of the U.S. Patent Office, Henry Baldwin, to provide a priority of invention to Ottinger. Then he supplied a list of his inventions and devices: the life car, the spiral wire-coil, the land or sand anchor, the gill-twine improved shot-line, the sizing first used for shot-lines, the clinometer, and the wheel adapted to sand truckage. Finally, at the very end, he appended a note saying that favorable consideration for his life car should not be included because he had been compensated for that; consideration should be based upon "the result of concerned thought that devised ways of adapting implements to a method of saving life, so plain that 'carpenters and others' have operated the apparatus with success."[33]

Ottinger was so confident that he wrote to the chairman of the Committee on Commerce suggesting he "ask the Secretary of the Treasury whether there are Departmental reasons why I should not be retired by Act of Congress as asked in accompanying memorial," and the chairman did. In turn, Secretary Folger asked General Superintendent Kimball of the Life-Saving Service for particulars on Ottinger's record within his service.[34]

Kimball began by stating that Captain Douglass Ottinger's first connection with the Life-Saving Service was in 1848. Working with a committee of the New York Board of Underwriters, he established eight stations along the New Jersey coast from Sandy Hook to Little Egg Harbor. These stations were to store and protect from the weather the articles of equipment specified on pages five through six of his memorial and were simple buildings. The structures also were temporary shelters for the rescued people from the shipwreck. There was no organization assigned to the stations. The government equipment was at the disposal of volunteers responding to the wreck.

None of the inventions and devices listed by Captain Ottinger was of a novel character, except the life car and the spiral-wire used to attach the shot-line to the shot. The life car was a most valuable invention and had rescued a large number of souls. It was an improvement upon the British hammock cot, with its canvas cover, hauled by a traveling sling and block upon a hawser. Congress recognized the value of the life car and passed a bill on 14 February 1859 paying Captain Ottinger for his invention. Kimball stated that Joseph Francis of Toms River, New Jersey, disputed Ottinger's claim. He enclosed five copies of correspondence between himself and Francis from 13 March 1880 through 26 April 1881.

Kimball could not relate the use of the spiral wire before his assignment to the service in 1871, but it had little use by the station keepers after that date. In fact, the keepers preferred to wet the shot-line three or four feet before securing the wet line to the shot; at the present time the service completely abandoned the spiral-wire because the Lyle gun and elongated shot protruding from the muzzle dispersed the hot gases from the gun barrel before it could burn the line. Nor was the elongated shot novel, for British captain Manby used it many years ago. The India-rubber attachment Ottinger mentioned on page eight failed acceptance or use in the Life-Saving Service.

Kimball offered a few remarks with respect to other inventions and devices that Ottinger claimed to have introduced. The sand anchor was not one of Ottinger's inventions, but he claimed to have discovered its usefulness for lifesaving operations. It was still in use at this time. The gill-twine-improved shot-line mentioned on page nine never saw service except for experimental purposes. Although Ottinger cast 631 yards with the normal size line and 754 yards with his "line of last resort," the material factor in reaching those distances was not his gill-twine; rather Parrott's large gun and the increased powder charge were the material factors. The gun weighed 571 pounds, an increase of 258 pounds over the standard service gun. The extra weight of the Parrott gun exceeded the normal load capacity of the USL-SS wagons. The service purchased only two guns. Later, the 182-pound Lyle gun replaced Parrott's and the standard guns. The new gun threw the "line of last resort" 695 yards and the larger line a proportionate range. Yet the service did not believe that a hawser and life car could successfully operate beyond the 400-yard range. As for the annexing of the line to the forward end of the elongated shot, that had been accomplished and described by Captain Manby in his article "Life-Preservers" years before Ottinger worked for the Life-Saving Service.

Ottinger claimed he introduced into the service the sizing for shot-lines by coating them with gum Arabic. Superintendent Kimball could find no record of its use, nor did he find that Ottinger called it to the department's attention. Waterproof lines were in use, but there appeared to be no action by Captain Ottinger to introduce it to the service.

Kimball noted that the "clinometer" mentioned by Ottinger had been a part of the gun long before Ottinger began his work for the service. All guns used it. The Life-Saving Service called it a "combination level." The unit consists of a rule, a level, and an octant.

In sum, Kimball found only two novel items, the life car and the spiral wire. Ottinger received remuneration for the life car and later Francis challenged him as the inventor of that device. The spiral wire proved unimportant and was seldom employed after Kimball became associated with the Life-Saving Service in 1871. Of the other items listed, the sand anchor and clinometer were known and used years before Ottinger became involved in the Life-Saving Service; the gill-twine-improved shot-line was never used; the India-rubber attachment was never adopted; the sizing of line with gum Arabic was never offered by Ottinger, nor used by the Life-Saving Service; and his combination guard was still under caveat with the patent office. Ottinger patented the sand-wheel and granted it to the Department; that "invention" consisted of an adaptation for the normal wagon wheel to increase the width of the wagon's tire. Kimball could not comment on it because the service had not evaluated it. Captain Ottinger reported it was "highly satisfactory" in his trial at Erie, Pennsylvania, and the superintendent of the Erie District reported it showed promise.[35] Thus Captain Ottinger's role in promoting the Life-Saving Services' efficiency was minimal.

When the Senate Committee on Commerce studied General Superintendent Kimball's letter, it cast a different light on Ottinger's memorial to Congress. The Committee hastily decided to withdraw Captain Ottinger's papers from the Senate files and terminated his request for retirement.[36]

If there was one thing Captain Ottinger learned from his dealings with the patent office it was not to give up, keep trying. Thus in the Forty-eighth Congress, 1st session, the Honorable William Mutchler of Pennsylvania introduced House Bill No. 1334 for the relief of Captain Douglass Ottinger. The bill then went to Mr. Nathan Goff of the Committee on Naval Affairs to study.[37]

While the House of Representatives plodded on with its work, the USL-SS Board for the Examination of Inventions and Services held its first examination of Ottinger's sand wheel at Buffalo, New York, on 6 September 1883. The sand wheel consisted of a wooden tire made up of four quarters of the wheel fitted over the standard surfboat wagon wheel to enlarge the tire track to ten and an eighth inches wide. With the sand wheel added to all four wagon wheels, it increased the wagon's weight 280 pounds. The test was not an overwhelming success and the board decided to continue its test at a later date.[38]

On 3 March 1884, the board tested the wheel in snow and sand and found it to be difficult to pull because the wide tires clogged up more than ordinary wheels.

John C. Patterson, who had thirteen years of service in the USL-SS, could not find any practical benefit to the sand wheel, but lots of problems with its use. Captain Ottinger immediately wrote to Secretary Folger that his sand wheel was effective for use in soft sand. The final examination took place at Shark River, New Jersey, in June 1884. This time the board unanimously voted that there was no advantages and many disadvantages over the standard wheel and recommended not to accept it for use in the service.[39]

The same month that the board rejected Ottinger's sand wheel, his second application for retirement with full pay was on the calendar of the House of Representatives for approval. This time Ottinger did not rely on patent office examiner Henry Baldwin's statement that he was the original inventor of the life car. The captain stated, "he is the original inventor of the famous life-saving device known as the surf-car, now and for many years past in use in all the life-saving stations in the United States, and which had been the means of saving the lives of thousands of human beings from wrecked ships." He said that this important invention came to him while carrying out his orders to establish the first lifesaving stations on the coast. Again, he reiterated that he did not patent the surf car because he gave it "to the public for the public use."

The Honorable N. Goff of West Virginia, presenting the Committee of Naval Affairs report, brought up Captain Ottinger's work on the Pacific coast where he explored, discovered, surveyed, and named a little known north California bay as Humboldt Bay. How the captain opened trade between the bay and San Francisco. Goff concluded: "In view of the services of Captain Ottinger, outside the line of his duty as a revenue officer, and for this reason alone, your committee are of the opinion that he should be allowed the full salary of his rank while he lives, even though, by reason of his advanced years, he may not be continued upon active duty."[40]

This time the Honorable Samuel S. Cox of New York challenged Ottinger's claims. While delving into the U.S. Patent Office records, Cox noted that that office refused Ottinger's invention for the upper deck of the life car three times because it was not a new invention. The *Statutes at Large* showed that he did not present his life car to the government for public use, but he requested and received remuneration for his life car, and the patent office said he held no invention for a surf car. The treasury records showed that Ottinger did not originate the Life-Saving Service, he merely served as superintendent of construction of early lifesaving stations. The captain did not discover Humboldt Bay in California in 1849; Captain Winship discovered the bay in 1804, as noted on a coast survey of 1848. Based upon the many exaggerations and false statements made by Ottinger, as noted by Cox, no action was forthcoming on House bill No. 1334. The *New York Sun*'s article "A Bill That Will Not Pass? Evidence, which knocks the bottom out of Capt. Ottinger's claims," expressed it all.[41]

In spite of the congressional rebuffs, Captain Ottinger persisted. When the Cleveland Administration appointed Daniel Manning to become the secretary of the treasury in April 1885, Ottinger seized the opportunity to make his presence and views known to the new secretary. He began with a list of eight wrecks from 1875 to 1885 where lives were lost because "proper implements were not used." After a disastrous shipwreck in 1875 Acting Secretary Charles H. Conant asked him "the estabisher [*sic*] of the first life saving stations and inventor of the Life Car* as I named it," to devise a method to project mortar shot farther out to sea where large draft vessels breached. (This was the time Ottinger teamed up with Parrott.) After discussing the extended ranges made by the large gun, he concluded, "It has not appeared the shipwrecked have had the benefit of all these results." He then took the subject noted by his asterisk after Life Car. "* M[r] Joseph Francis a boat builder employed in the shop of Stillman Allan & C[o] at the time they manufactured my Life Car and the surf boats (modeled by surfmen) I had made for the first life saving stations, got up a *counterfeit* of my Life Car—M[r] S. I. Kimball and Captain J. H. Merryman" sent this counterfeit to be exhibited at the International Fisheries Exhibition of 1883. He concluded his letter by asking Secretary Manning, "in the interest of the public," to allow him to compare his implements with those now being used by the USL-SS. In his endorsement the secretary wrote that "he [Ottinger] can place any inventions before the Board," but there was no need to deviate from standard procedures.[42]

It is amazing to read how Captain Ottinger parlayed a device rejected three times by the patent office as no invention and the imprecise use of several technical words such as top deck, lifeboat, surfboat, and life car into a bona fide threat to a legitimate inventor. Only a perfidious person, of whom Douglass Ottinger was among the quintessence, could accomplish this. His narration of his service career was consistent from the time he was a junior officer taking over from his captain to take the cutter out onto Lake Erie in the teeth of a gale to his exploits as the captain of his ship relieving his pilots to perform hazardous piloting during other gales. The epitome of his gale stories was when he entered Humboldt Bay upon a breaker that drove his vessel so fast that his sails, under a "very brisk gale," fell "filled aback."

Reactions to Ottinger's Charges

Of the three who were curious to know who Captain Douglass Ottinger was, the secretary of the treasury Folger was satisfied the easiest. After Ottinger told him he did not write or initiate the article "Captain Ottinger's Prophesy Concerning the Inefficiency of the Life Saving Apparatus," Folger was content until Superintendent Kimball demanded an investigation as to the allegations that he was responsible for the mismanagement at the U.S. Life-Saving Service. Folger appointed a treasury investigator to examine the charges. The agent's report found that Kimball was correct in using the Lyle gun, as it was superior to the others used. Further, the superintendent supplied every station with a life car and a breeches buoy. Thus the station keeper could call on either as the situation demanded.[1] Superintendent Kimball, who had exhibited Francis's metal life car as the *Ayrshire* car at the Fisheries Exposition in London, needed irrefutable evidence that Francis's car was the *Ayrshire* car. Joseph Francis, the inventor and owner of the *Ayrshire* car, had the most complex task of the three. He had to overcome Congress's remuneration to Ottinger for inventing the metal life car and the U.S. Patent Office's decision to proclaim that Ottinger had the priority of invention over Francis, two difficult hurdles to overcome.

General Superintendent Kimball weighed his actions concerning Captain Ottinger's bombshell that Francis's metal life car was not the one used to rescue passengers and crew of the *Ayrshire* wreck of 1850. Then, six months later on 24 March 1884, he ordered Second Lieutenant C. H. McLellan, USRMS, to investigate, compile his evidence, and forward his conclusion as to the authenticity of the life car now in Washington, D.C., awaiting acceptance to the Smithsonian Institution.[2]

Lieutenant McLellan began by finding people who were in attendance at the *Ayrshire* wreck and talking to them. Two participants had an unusual observation of the life car. Mahlon B. Chapman lived at Squan Beach at the time. He was one of the first to respond and helped carry the hawser, the life car, and other items from the boathouse to the shore. He remembered that one ring holding the life car's chain to the hawser broke and he put a rope grommet on the chain. After several trips he had to replace his rope grommet. Later he wrote on the life car asking the wrecked crew to send him a leading block to replace his jury-rigged rope grommet, but he never received the block and had to continue with his rope grommet during the two days of rescue operations. Another man, David Fleming, said that he lived at Point Pleasant, but was visiting John Maxson, who was the wreckmaster, at the time of the wreck. He also mentioned the broken ring. Lieutenant McLellan thought the information supplied by Chapman and Fleming were significant. Then, while examining the records of the Life-Saving Benevolent Association of New York, he found a letter written to the acting secretary of the treasury W. L. Hodge on 14 September 1852 mentioning an enclosed note by John Maxson "asking for repairs to the apparatus used at the Ayrshire." If the department could locate Maxson's letter it might shore up Chapman and Fleming's account. McLellan concluded his letter with saying that there were three methods to verify Joseph Francis's life car as the original one used in January 1850. First, he asked Mr. Francis to provide a detailed history of his life car from the wreck to the present. Second, he planned on developing the broken ring theory and he asked if the ring was still broken or if it could be determined if a new one had replaced the original ring. Third, he hoped to have his local witnesses examine Francis's metal life car.[3]

McLellan's initial report alerted the superintendent that he had overlooked Mr. Francis. On 17 April 1884 Kimball sent a long letter to Francis saying, "I learn it has been alleged that the Life Car which was formerly in possession of the Park Commissioners of New York, and which was exhibited at the 'International Fisheries Exhibition' in London; [sic] is not the identical Car which saved the persons from the wreck of the 'Ayrshire' in 1850." Then he asked Francis to provide him as soon as possible with an itinerary of his life car after the wreck. Kimball said that Francis "ought to be able to show it; both for your own sake, and in Justice to truth and history, and you ought to leave nothing undone to vindicate your assertions."[4]

Upon receipt of Kimball's letter Francis immediately began gathering affidavits from knowledgeable persons connected with the 1850 wreck. In all Francis gathered eight affidavits, including his own and his son's. He arranged for his friend Captain B. S Osbon to deliver them to Lieutenant McLellan. Later he directed McLellan to a number of other potential witnesses knowledgeable about the wreck. Francis suggested bringing his life car in Washington to Toms River so that those giving affidavits about the life car could examine it, and he volunteered to pay for the move.[5]

On 13 May 1884 Lieutenant McLellan telegraphed Kimball asking for the photograph Captain Ottinger had submitted of his true metal life car. Superintendent Kimball sent the photograph the same day with instructions not to injure the picture and to return it as soon as possible. Ottinger's life car was quite different. It was not corrugated on the sides and the hatch to enter was forward and along the centerline of the car. Francis's life car had corrugations along the sides and the hatch was off the centerline because Francis had an air tube running down the centerline to provide the buoyancy to keep the car upright.[6]

Two weeks later Lieutenant McLellan went to Washington, D.C., to present his evidence to Superintendent Kimball. It was a massive document with twenty-four enclosures, twenty-three affidavits and *Harper's New Monthly Magazine* of July 1851 containing Jacob Abbott's article "Some Account of Francis's Life-Boats and Life-Cars." Joseph Francis, Mahlon B. Chapman, and William Wilson each submitted two affidavits. Two of the witnesses provided an excellent history of Francis's life car. William H. Navarro said that in 1844 he was working for a manufacturer of life preservers in a house at the corner of Broadway and Anthony Street. Joseph Francis occupied the rear of the building on Anthony Street. At the time Francis was trying to construct metal boats and he often asked Navarro to help him press by hand or with a wooden press to imprint a pattern on the sheets of pasteboard and later thin sheets of iron. In 1848 Francis hired Navarro to work on his metal life car. Part of Navarro's work consisted in painting and lettering the completed metal boats and cars. Francis instructed him to always paint "Francis' Metallic Life Boat" or "Francis' Metallic Life Car" on each finished unit. Navarro remembered one time a naval officer told him not to paint a boat built for the U.S. Navy. Yet Francis gave him explicit instructions to paint the boat regardless of the officer's orders. Joseph Francis was proud of his metal boats and cars. Whenever carrying one through the city streets, big signs stating either Francis Life-boat or Francis Life-car hung on the sides of the truck.

Navarro recalled that Revenue Marine officers Ottinger and McGowan visited the shop occasionally, but at no time did he hear either of them claim that the metal boats or cars were the products of their invention.

Navarro remembered distinctly when the life car used at the *Ayrshire* wreck returned to the factory. Everyone in the factory was proud of its accomplishment and all were sure that the fame of that life car meant more work for all of them in the shop. He painted an inscription on the car immediately after the event. In 1852 Francis sent him to France to supervise the construction of lifeboats and one life car at the shipyard at Le Havre. More recently, the Department of Public Works called upon him to repaint the life car at Central Park because the original painted inscription "had become somewhat obliterated and defaced." He was sure that the original life car of *Ayrshire* fame, the Central Park exposition, and the Fisheries exhibit were one and the same car.[7]

Lieutenant Charles V. Morris, USN, of Sackets Harbor, New York, stated that in 1844 as a young officer holding the rank of master, stationed at the Brooklyn Navy Yard, he frequently visited Joseph Francis at his shop. He watched the construction of metal lifeboats and life cars. The life car particularly impressed him because it was a new concept in small boats. After the *Ayrshire* wreck, the navy's chief of the Bureau of Ordnance requested shipping the life car to the Washington Arsenal for exhibition to the president and his cabinet. By this time Master Charles Morris was in charge of the care of the life car. From the arsenal, Morris escorted the life car to the Capitol Rotunda where both Houses of Congress inspected it. Then the navy sent the life car to the Washington Navy Yard still under Morris's supervision. The metal car remained at the Washington Navy Yard until Joseph Francis returned from Europe in 1862. The secretary of the navy ordered Lieutenant Morris to take the life car to the Brooklyn Navy Yard. In 1869 Francis asked the navy to return his life car to his residence at Toms River, New Jersey. The schooner *Euphame* brought the life car to Toms River where Isaac Francis received it for his father.[8] The accounts of Navarro, Morris, C. W. Grimm (the mate of the *Euphame*), and Isaac Francis clearly document the whereabouts of the *Ayrshire* life car.

James Kelton, who did not participate in the *Ayrshire* wreck, was a longtime worker on metal boats and life cars. He started in 1852. In 1858 Francis brought him to Hamburg to supervise building metal boats and one life car, all after Francis's pattern. When Francis left the company, Kelton continued working for the company that took over. At the time of his affidavit he worked for the Continental Iron Works at Greenpoint, Brooklyn, New York, "where I make all the life cars used by the Government."

Of the seven witnesses who looked at Ottinger's photograph, none recalled seeing such a life car on the New Jersey coast. All were adamant that Francis's life car had an air tank at the top of the top deck to assist in keeping the car upright. All agreed that Francis's car had its hatch on the side below the top air tank. Eight witnesses thought the life car at Bays Head Life-Saving Station was the *Ayrshire* car. David Fleming thought that one ring of the life car was "put in at a later day than the other." Lieutenant McLellan presented an impressive study.[9]

Returning to his duty station at Toms River, Lieutenant McLellan found another witness, Alfred Hulse, who agreed with his other witnesses about Francis's life car and failed to recognize Ottinger's life car. A few days later at Long Branch,

McLellan met Edward Wardell, whose information was so important that he could not wait for the completion of Wardell's affidavit. Edward Wardell's father, Henry Wardell, was the New York underwriter agent at Long Branch from 1835 until his death in 1851. Edward Wardell remembered when Ottinger distributed Francis's life cars along the New Jersey coast in 1849. He said he was present several times when Joseph Francis, Captain Douglass Ottinger, and William Newell visited the Long Branch boathouse. At no time during these visits did he ever hear Ottinger mentioned as the inventor or co-inventor of the life cars. When the three men wanted to test a life car, they used the one at Long Branch and Edward Wardell became the first man to cross the surf in a life car. The first time that car made an actual rescue was at the wreck of the *Chauncy Jerome Jr.* on 12 January 1854. Edward Wardell told Lieutenant McLellan that he received a letter from Captain Ottinger in the summer of 1883 asking about the life car at Long Branch. Was it still in use? If not, what happened to it?

Lieutenant McLellan was curious as to why Ottinger was interested in that car. Then he remembered that Ottinger wrote his letter to the U.S. minister at the Court of St. James that summer. He began searching the records and found that the Long Branch car had been condemned and thrown into a ditch alongside the railroad arch. Later, while grading the land, the fill covered the life car. One of the locals named Valentine was sure he could locate the site. McLellan gave him directions to dig it up and send it to him. Valentine found, dug up, and brought the life car to the Long Branch Life-Saving Station. Witnesses identified the car as the one that Ottinger used on the test run when Edward Wardell made the first crossing of the surf, and that car had Francis's name on its plate! McLellan told Kimball that he would keep the car at the station and would substantiate its identity with further affidavits. He concluded, "I hope you will have Capt. Ottinger up, and settle this case soon, otherwise I shall have life car on the brain."[10]

Meanwhile, Joseph Francis continued his efforts to have the officials of the Treasury Department and the U.S. Life-Saving Service affirm that he invented the metal life car. At the same time he had his agent James L. Pond continue his research and note gathering for Francis's forthcoming book about his inventions and business ventures. At this time Francis lived in Toms River, except during periods of illness when the elderly gentleman moved to a hotel in New York City to be under his doctor's care. It must have been a frustrating phase in his life—wanting the recognition of his invention and worrying that he may not live to see that event.

It was several days after James Pond returned with his notes and copies of documents gathered from the U.S. Patent Office before Francis saw Captain Ottinger's affidavit of 14 June 1860 that he had submitted at the interference trial. Francis flew into a tirade as he wrote to Superintendent Kimball pointing out the false statements and citing his proofs against such assertions. He ended with saying, "It seems monstrous that a man whose position should be a synonom [sic] of truth, and whose office should be the badge of integrity should utter such a tissue of malicious falsehoods so readily disproved by recorded facts. They are rendered still more flagrant by his waiting until I had gone to Europe before concocting them."[11]

Less than a week later a series of letters from Francis, Captain Osbon, and James Pond, all mailed the same day and basically covering various aspects of the subject that Francis was the inventor of the life car, engulfed Secretary Folger. Francis began by saying that on 27 March he sent a letter desiring to give the government the original life car of *Ayrshire* fame for the National Museum in Washington. Then on 29 March, he presented working models of his metal dies to accompany his life car to visually complete the scope of his work. Because of his illness, he had Captain Osbon present his letter and models to Secretary Folger in his stead. Captain Osbon said that, because of claims made by an officer in the Revenue Service, the Treasury Department could not accept the life car and other articles until its officials formally established his claim as the inventor and owner. Francis said that he believed Lieutenant McLellan had overwhelmingly concluded his study in his favor. If so, he would like to have his donations officially accepted so that he could record the event in his forthcoming book. He desired to place his donations "in their final resting place, before I reach such myself."[12]

Captain Osbon's letter was brief, stating only how much Francis desired to see his life car and other objects accepted and displayed in the National Museum. The captain urged Secretary Folger to give special attention to this matter while Joseph Francis still lived; James Pond's letter was a reiteration of his findings at the patent office demonstrating that Captain Ottinger had not received a patent for his life car.[13]

Secretary Folger answered Joseph Francis to clarify his department's position. All of Francis's articles would be accepted and placed in the National Museum "on the condition that the inscription may be removed from the car ascribing its invention to you. . . . In this regard, you appear by your letter to be in some error." The recent investigation established the fact that the car was the famed car of the *Ayrshire* wreck, "and on this ground it can be accepted for a place in the Museum, . . . but I do not think the evidence of your title to the inventorship on file in the Department" justifies putting it on the car on exhibition, "in the face of the action of Congress upon the claim of Captain Douglass Ottinger, and also of a letter of the Commissioner of Patents, dated August 9, 1860, ascribing the priority of invention to him, an authenticated copy of which Captain Ottinger has filed in the Department." Further, "the General Superintendent of the Life-Saving Service informed me that the car was recently exhibited at the international Fisheries Exhibition in London with such an inscription but that if he had known it he would not have permitted it."[14]

On 10 July 1884, Francis wrote to Secretary Folger to thank him for seeing his agent. Unknown to Francis, Charles Folger had died that June. Pond told him "informally that my 'Life Car' will be accepted by the Department, and I will be allowed to inscribe on it 'This Car was manufactured by Joseph Francis of Toms River N. J.,' and recount the *Ayrshire* wreck." Francis then asked if it would be allowable for him to add "The inventor of Life Saving Appliances" after N. J. He pointed out that he had over twenty patents at home and in Europe. Then he shifted his topic back to the crux of his problem. He said the first time he saw Captain Ottinger was in 1848, and at that time the famed life car was completed and on the floor of his shop. He pointed out that Lieutenant Charles V. Morris, in his affidavit, stated he saw life cars and lifeboats in the factory four years before Ottinger arrived. He was particularly disappointed that "three score and ten years of active duty in inventing Life Boats, Cars, and other appliances, should result in my being asked technically even, to deny my own inventions which had been introduced in Europe before a public claim for a Life Car, dating 1848, was made by Captn Ottinger. Being made aware of the exact state of the case for the first time by my agent."[15]

That same day James Pond wrote to Superintendent Kimball to say that the inscription he had given him to relay to Francis had been carried out and Francis wanted to add "The inventor of Life Saving Appliances" after Toms River, N. J. Pond then enclosed a summary of his findings at the U.S. Patent Office. In 1857 Captain Ottinger claimed an interference with Francis. Twice Ottinger applied for a patent in 1859, and both times the patent office refused his applications. Then he assigned his invention that the patent office had not accepted to the world tax-free. Yet at no time had he proved the manufacture of a single car put on the U.S. coast. There were no records in the U.S. Patent Office that showed Ottinger had an invention for a life car. That same year Ottinger applied for remuneration to Congress for his life car that had saved so many lives at the *Ayrshire* wreck. Finally, in 1883 he charged that Francis's life car exhibited in London was a fraud. The next year the U.S. Life-Saving Service identified that same car displayed at the Fisheries Exhibition to be the original car at the wreck on the New

Jersey coast in 1850. The identification of the life car now in Washington proved Ottinger's "statements to Congress to have been false, and his application and receipt of $10,000—as 'the inventor of said car' to have been fraudulent." Pond requested that the commissioner of patents or other government officer should investigate the certificate of "priority of invention" to determine if it "was granted through misconception of facts, or by misstatements presented." Regardless of whether or not misconception of facts or misstatements were presented, Pond requested reopening the case or grant relief to Joseph Francis. There was no reaction to Pond's request. It appeared that even twenty-four years after the issuance of the certificate of priority, bureaucratic loyalties kept contemporary government officials from stirring up old misconceptions or misstatements.[16]

After an appropriate time subsequent to Secretary Folger's death, James Pond again wrote to Superintendent Kimball summarizing his views concerning Captain Ottinger's charges. First, the original life car had no inscriptions on it that had not been on it since 1850. That car, and the eight purchased by Ottinger for his lifesaving stations, left the manufactory with a plate stating "Francis Patent," and the captain made no objection to that statement on the life cars he purchased.

Second, three decades and three years later, Captain Ottinger mailed a letter to His Excellency J. Russell Lowell, U.S. minister at the Court of St. James that Joseph Francis's life car was not the authentic life car at the wreck of the ship *Ayrshire* in 1850. Ottinger enclosed a photograph taken 22 June 1883 of his authentic life car. Then he went to London and asked the authorities to remove Francis's name from the life car on exhibit. Instead he received the charge of *fraud* and made no further effort. Lieutenant McLellan's investigation proved that Francis's car was the original car and none of the witnesses shown Ottinger's photo recognized it.

Third, the U.S. Patent Office declared that a covered car was not a novelty nor was it patentable, and told Francis twice and Ottinger three times about its ruling. Thus the patent office award of a priority of invention to Ottinger was a contravention of law. How could there be a priority of invention if there was no invention? Pond concluded that "never until he attempted his Second fraud to use his fraudulent 'priority of invention,' and its assailment by the Hon. S. S. Cox led him to withdraw Everything, but the paper which has acted so injuriously, and unjustly against Mr. Francis." Apparently Pond was not aware of Ottinger's earlier attempt to obtain money from Forty-seventh Congress, Senate Bill S.734, in 1882 also used the priority of invention.[17]

In mid-December Joseph Francis waited for the Treasury Department to officially accept his donations of his life car, model dies, and a model man-of-war lifeboat. By now Francis was eighty-four years old and fearful that he would not live to receive the honor of having his relics placed in the Smithsonian Institution. He wrote, through Pond, to lay his case one more time before the new secretary of the treasury Hugh McCullock. He enclosed the diploma given him by the International Shipwreck Society for all Nations presented to him in 1842 for his presentation of his plans for a life car. Francis was running out of time and patience, and he had few items left to affirm his position as the inventor of the life car.[18]

In March 1885, Francis shifted his focus to his book. He was losing faith in the Treasury Department. He asked Superintendent Kimball to send copies of the affidavits gathered by Lieutenant McLellan during his investigation. Receiving no response, Francis sent James Pond to Washington to inquire. Pond discovered that Kimball would not release the affidavits gathered by McLellan because they were official government documents, but that he would send copies of the affidavits Francis had given to McLellan. Obviously once Kimball had his irrefutable evidence, he was content to stop rocking the boat. Maybe the footnote in the USL-SS Annual Report of 1876 reflected Kimball's mindset. Based upon congressional remuneration bestowed upon the captain in 1859, it acknowledged Captain Ottinger as the inventor of the life car and challenged Francis's claim. So Francis, in the final stages of his book, accepted his eight affidavits and moved on.

Yet on 10 July 1885 Francis received his first official acknowledgment while in the final page of assembly of his book. A letter from Professor Spencer F. Baird, secretary of the Smithsonian Institution and director of the U.S. National Museum, said that Francis's "Ayrshire Life Car" accompanied by his papers and models now were part of the museum. Further, "Due credit will, of course, be given you as the inventor, manufacturer and owner of the 'Life Car.'" At last vindication, and in time for his book![19]

Francis privately published his book, *History of Life-Saving Appliances and Military and Naval Construction: Invented and Manufactured by Joseph Francis, with Sketches and Incidents of His Business Life in the United States and Europe.* His book had two different title pages. Some copies had Joseph Francis as the author and others had "James L Pond, compiler," on the title page. Joseph Francis had gone public.[20]

As it turned out, his book set up a new path. On 5 November 1885 near the end of the New York Chamber of Commerce business meeting, Captain Ambrose Snow proposed: "Whereas the recent publication of the history of life-saving appliances has recalled the attention of the Chamber to the eminent services to humanity rendered by the now venerable Joseph Francis" and he listed a number of his corrugated boats, pontoons, and other devices. Snow continued: "Whereas the Chamber . . . did, on the second day of March, 1841 by resolution approve and recommend the valuable inventions of Mr. Francis to the Mercantile marine," and he stated that Francis's appliances had saved countless lives throughout the world. He recounted how great foreign nations recognized his labors with "medals, testimonials, knight-hood, and diplomas," yet there was no recognition of his works in his native land. Snow then proposed: "Therefore, resolved, that the Chamber . . . memorialize the Congress of the United States to take such action in recognition of the great services to the country and to humanity of Joseph Francis as in its wisdom it may deem most fitting and proper." Captain Snow's memorial passed unanimously, and the chamber sent it to Congress. Joseph Francis was so pleased that he ran off copies of the memorial to send to those who received his book in order to complete the book. He recommended the recipients paste the chamber's action on the flyleaf opposite the presentation card.[21]

The rapid outpouring of approval for the memorial from diverse sources seem more than coincidental. The responses belie a true spontaneous upwelling for the memorial. It resembled a guided movement directed by Joseph Francis or a group of his friends or both. Yet this is only speculation for none of the files examined carried such hypothesis. By 3 December 1885, William J. McAlpine of the Harlem River Bridge Commission sent to the secretary of the treasury Daniel Manning a copy of a letter that Reverend Morgan Dix sent to Francis with the earnest hope he would read it. Dix noted the long friendship enjoyed between his parents and Francis and said, "you may understand with what pleasure I received, and with what attention I am reading the book you recently presented to me." Morgan Dix noted that "it is a strange thing, that, to this day, that work remains unrecognized by any official act of the American Government; Your own Country is behind the rest of the civilized world." Horatio Allen's letter of 7 December 1885 dealing with the honors due to Joseph Francis went to the superintendent of the USL-SS. Then Allen's affidavit of 30 December 1885 attesting to Francis's invention of the life car followed in February 1886. Also on 4 February at the annual meeting of the American Institute of the City of New York Mr. R. H. Shannon submitted a resolution reminiscent of the chamber of commerce memorial, except it went to the U.S. Senate. That same day the House of Representatives Committee on Commerce began work on recognition of the services of Joseph Francis. The chair of the Sub-Committee in Life-Saving Services, Alfred B. Irion, requested Secretary Manning to forward all documents related to the identification of Francis's life car at the London exposition to his committee. Manning asked if copies would suffice instead of original documents, and Irion was agreeable to that suggestion. The rapidity of the House of Representatives to begin action indicated that it received a deluge of support for Joseph Francis. Now it was Francis's turn to appeal to Congress for recognition.[22]

II

The Forty-ninth Congress
and Beyond

The House of Representatives lost little time moving forward toward recognizing Joseph Francis. By 20 February 1886 the Honorable Abram S. Hewitt, of New York, asked for joint resolution (H. Res. 125) that the Committee of Commerce reported on favorably may be read subject to objections. The Speaker replied that first the resolution would be read and then he would ask for objections.

The Clerk read:

> Joint resolution (H. Res. 125) in recognition of the services of Joseph Francis.
> *Resolved by the Senate and House of Representatives of the United States of America in Congress assembled,* That in view of the life-long services to humanity and to his country of the now venerable Joseph Francis, in the construction and perfection of life-saving appliances by which many thousands of lives have been saved, the thanks of Congress be, and are hereby, tendered to Joseph Francis; and that the President of the United States is hereby authorized to cause to be prepared a gold medal, with a suitable inscription, to be presented to Mr. Francis, in recognition of his eminent services.[1]

The Speaker asked if there was an objection to discharging the Committee of the Whole House and proceeding to the consideration of the resolution. The Honorable William R. Cox, of North Carolina, wanted to know the effect of this resolution. Would it confer privileges or emoluments? The Honorable Hewitt replied that no privileges follow Congress's vote of thanks except to officers of the army or the navy. Thus Mr. Francis received nothing beyond recognition of his services. That, according to the Committee of Commerce, is the recognized procedure.

Congressman William L. Scott, of Pennsylvania, asked if the resolution gave Francis credit for inventing the surfboat? Hewitt replied that it did not address that question. Scott reiterated his concern. He said there had been a serious dispute between a gentleman in his district and Mr. Francis over that question.

Hewitt answered that the question of invention of a surfboat did not arise in the resolution. With no objection, the discharging of the Committee of the Whole House took place, and the House turned its attention to the resolution. It ordered a third reading for the resolution.

Following the reading, the Speaker stated that the question before the House was for the passage of the resolution. Adoniram J. Warner, of Ohio, asked to have the whole report read to the members. The Speaker ordered the clerk to read the report. It was a seven-paragraph report initially describing Francis's early life. It told of the young man striving to develop a lifeboat to rescue people from stranded vessels during severe storms. The focus of the report was that Francis "persevered in making improvement after improvement until his inventive genius culminated in the construction of the first perfect life-car in the year 1848. It was not, however, until January, 1850, that he had the opportunity to test the efficiency of his invention. . . . Through the instrumentality of the mortar and line a hawser was stretched from the shore to the ship, and along this passway the life-car made frequent trips, until two hundred out of the two hundred and one persons on board were carried over the boiling surf in safety to the land." Then followed the recognition by other nations for his services. Yet no recognition came from his own country, "and now in the eighty-fifth year of his age, as the last honor which is to crown his well-spent life, he asks his own Government to award him a suitable testimonial" for his lifelong devotion to the welfare of his fellow man.[2]

Upon completion of the reading Mr. Scott addressed the Speaker, stating that he would have to object. "The question as to who originated or conceived the idea of the life-saving boat was between Mr. Joseph Francis and Captain Douglass Ottinger, of the United States revenue marine. Some fifteen years ago the Congress of the United States voted to Captain Ottinger, as a reward for the invention and origination of the life-boat, the sum of $10,000, which was a voluntary contribution on the part of the Government of the United States to Captain Ottinger, made entirely without his solicitation.

"Now sir, this resolution is introduced here in behalf of Mr. Francis, and as a reward for the same invention. Captain Ottinger is a man of over ninety years of age." (Actually, he was three years younger than Joseph Francis.) Scott said that if the Committee on Commerce talked to Captain Ottinger it would know his history: "Thus, I must submit my objection and, if necessary, move to return this resolution back to the Committee of Commerce for further consideration."

Mr. Hewitt arose and said that the gentleman from Pennsylvania misunderstood the resolution, as it did not concern itself with passing judgment upon the success of any other man. If Captain Ottinger received recognition and $10,000 from Congress then there should be no reason to object to congressional recognition of another man for his work for humanity.

Mr. Scott rose to reply that it boiled down to who invented the surfboat. When Congress reached that decision Mr. Francis had the opportunity to appear before that body and state his claim, but he did not do so. Yet the $10,000 Captain Ottinger received meant nothing compared to his reputation. The captain wanted his children to know "that he had invented the surf-boat by which all those lives had been saved and by which all the lives in the future will be saved."[3] This appeal to let his children know that he had invented the surfboat was a ploy used by Captain Ottinger to elicit sympathy from the congressmen. In truth, the Ottingers were childless.[4]

Congressman Scott declared that the passage of this joint resolution "robs that old man of the credit to which he is entitled and puts it into the hands of one who was not the inventor" and one whom the Congress of the United States did not consider as the inventor.

A lively exchange followed. Hewitt asked Scott whose lifeboat saved all the people from the *Ayrshire*. Scott replied that that was the question needing an answer. Hewitt responded, "Who built the car at the wreck?" Scott said, "Wait a minute," but Hewitt plunged on, asking who furnished the life car. Scott said, "I would answer if you give me time. The question should not be made by the Chamber in New York, it should be answered by this body." Hewitt said that the gentleman from Pennsylvania had not answered any of his questions. At this point Nelson Dingley, of Maine, interrupted the conversation between the two to interject that, as he read the resolution, it did refer to the inventor of the surfboat. Hewitt said that he had already told the gentleman from Pennsylvania that the resolution solely recognized the services of Mr. Francis to humanity with lifesaving apparatuses. Mr. Dingley responded, "It refers to the life-car." Hewitt replied that it referred to the life car, not the surfboat. Mr. Scott replied that he would not object if the life car were not in the report, but otherwise he would make a motion to recommit.

Shortly thereafter, the Speaker stated that the question before the House was on the motion to recommit. In the following vote there were 56 yeas and 76 nays. The motion to recommit failed. The House then shifted to another topic.[5]

The men who arranged the report and the resolution were astute. They were aware that to challenge Captain Ottinger's claim to the inventorship of the life car would lead to questioning the actions of the Thirty-fifth Congress over a twenty-seven-year-old insignificant matter. This would antagonize members who were not closely concerned with the question of who invented the life car. To a lesser degree impugning the actions of the patent office would be, as stated earlier, against bureaucratic loyalties that would dampen any enthusiasm to probe another branch of government over such a small issue. Thus by playing up the lifetime effort to aid humanity and sliding over the inventorship issue more members would be willing to aid a venerable man's desire for recognition. Yet the framers of the resolution may not have recognized the tenacity of Captain Ottinger.

It was not until 2 July 1886 that the Senate brought up the joint resolution 125. Senator William M. Evarts of New York moved to have the Senate consider recognizing the services of Joseph Francis. Senator William B. Allison, of Iowa, hoped it would not take much time, but if it did, he would object to hearing the resolution at the present time. Evarts said he did not expect to occupy much time. The president *pro tempore* called up the resolution and had the clerk read it. Senator Allison again cautioned that he would object if it were time consuming. Senator William P. Frye, of Maine, predicted there would be a regular fight over it. Senator Orville H. Platt, of Connecticut, said he had no objection if the purpose was to allow the senator from New York to say a few words. Platt said that he knew nothing about the matter, except that a Captain Ottinger had called upon him to claim he was the inventor of the device "for which it is now proposed to thank Mr. Francis." Senator George G. Vest, of Missouri, then said he had kind feelings for Mr. Francis and for the integrity of the Committee on Commerce, but after the committee reported favorably on Mr. Francis, he was visited by a gentleman asserting "that Mr. Francis was not entitled to any recognition on the part of Congress, and that, to use plain language, he had robbed this Captain Ottinger of his patent, and now was asking credit for services in the interest of humanity which he had never rendered." Senator Vest said that he had received papers to prove this accusation and he felt there must be considerable debate before the Senate proceeded with this resolution.[6] Senator John R. McPherson, of New Jersey, presented his views. Mr. Douglas Ottinger sent a communication to every senator, saying that Mr. Francis was depriving him of his rights and invention. Contrary to Captain Ottinger's view, McPherson had evidence to convince every senator that the opposite was true, and it would not take longer than a half hour to prove it. Ottinger "has undertaken to deprive, and has by a vote of Congress deprived, Joseph Francis of the rights that belong to him. He received $10,000 from the Government on a fraudulent representation, as can be made to appear by the papers here in my possession to the satisfaction of every Senator."[7]

Senator James A. Beck, of Kentucky, noted that on 1 July the law closes all branches of government until passage of the appropriation bills. Senator Evarts withdrew the question to consider his resolution, and the Senate turned to the appropriation bills.

It was 12 February 1887 before Senator Evarts again brought up Joint Resolution 125 and expressed his hope that the procedure would be brief. The president *pro tempore* said that the question was whether or not to proceed in recognition of Joseph Francis's services. Immediately Senator Francis M. Cockrell, of Missouri, said it would take all day, and he asked for the ayes and nays on the motion. The clerk read the joint resolution. Then the secretary called the roll and announced that there were 30 yeas, 17 nays, and 29 absent. The motion to proceed passed and the Senate began considering Joint Resolution 125.

Senator Evarts again told the story of the obstacles faced by Joseph Francis and how "as early as the year 1845 in progressive steps he had brought the invention to the complete perfection and practical application that have made the saving of live [life] at shipwrecks now the common rule where before the almost universal rule was the loss of life." The senator concluded by saying that this recognition given by the U.S. government should add to the honors bestowed upon him by the principal states of Europe.[8]

Senator Cockrell asked if Mr. Francis had secured a patent from the government as the original inventor of the lifesaving boats. Evarts replied that he had obtained numerous patents as he progressively worked toward his goal of saving life and property from shipwrecked vessels along the coast. Senator John T. Morgan, of Alabama, then submitted a letter from the commissioner of patents summarizing the patents issued and the refusals for both Francis and Ottinger. Mr. Francis had patents for a portable screw boat in 1833, a life and anchor boat in 1839, life and other boats in 1841, boats and other vessels of sheet-iron in 1845, and an application for patent for a life car that was rejected in 1851 because Mr. Greene already had a patent for a covered boat. Mr. Ottinger filed an application in 1857 for a life car and received a rejection in the same year. In 1858 he filed for interference from Mr. Francis based on Francis's rejected application of 1851. In 1859 Ottinger filed another application for a surf car and was again rejected. The commissioner concluded that "long prior to the proceedings in interference referred to, and long prior to the filing of either of the applications involved therein, patents had been granted to Mr. Francis for life-boats of the same general character" in 1839 and 1845. "Neither of these patents was involved in the interference, and that adjudication did not therefore affect any way the validity of these patents."[9]

Senator James D. Cameron, of Pennsylvania, addressed the presiding officer saying that this claim is old and musty. From his examination of the subject he did not believe Mr. Francis to be the inventor, "and that the life-boat was first made by Joseph [*sic*] Ottinger."[10] Cameron then told the history of it as he gathered it. Ottinger was the inventor and Congress recognized him, but he did not patent his invention. Ottinger had his boat made in a factory in New York where Francis was working. Francis later applied for a patent but the patent office refused it.

Senator Morgan rose to challenge his colleague, stating that it might not be necessary for Congress to grant this recognition to Francis except that his fame had been blemished "by a man who had no right to do anything, a man who had pirated or attempted to pirate his patent." The letter just read from the patent office clearly noted that Mr. Francis obtained patents years before Ottinger applied for his first patent, which was refused. At this time the presiding officer closed the hearings because it was time to address another topic.[11]

Finally, on 2 March 1887, Senator Evarts moved that the Senate receive the joint resolution (H. Res. 125) in recognition of Joseph Francis's services. The Senate accepted the motion and, acting as in Committee of the Whole, began consideration of the resolution. The president *pro tempore* said that if no amendment presented, it would proceed to the Senate. Senator Cockrell of Missouri said that before sending it to the Senate he wished to state that "this is a very remarkable measure, and it had been pressed with a great deal of pertinacity. It is an individual measure for the relief of this gentleman. It seems that he is exceedingly anxious to get a gold medal, and that he has—the effrontery, one of my friends suggests—to come here and beg the Senate to confer upon him a gold medal. I appeal for another gentleman, who contests the right with this claimant. May the clerk read and spread his views upon the *Record.*"

The president ordered the paper read. The clerk read for some time before Senator Sherman asked to print the document in the *Record* and dispensed with the reading, as he supposed the senator from Missouri only wanted to put it in the record. Senator Cockrell had no objection to that suggestion. The paper began as follows:

> Appeal of Capt. Douglass Ottinger against the passage in the Senate of House Resolution 125, First Session Forty-ninth Congress.
>
> This resolution proposes the thanks of Congress and a gold medal to Joseph Francis for the "construction and perfection of life-saving appliances." The House Report No. 529, first session Forty-ninth Congress goes further and gives him the credit of the "invention" of the life car. For this reason Capt. Douglass Ottinger (the actual inventor) objects to the pas-

sage of the resolution in the Senate, and respectfully asks the Senate to consider the following facts in the case, taken from Official or other reliable sources.

There followed ten sections of Ottinger's argument. Within the section there were numerous letters and extracts of letters from the 1848 appropriation for life-saving stations on the coast and testimony submitted to the patent office during the interference case.

At the completion of Ottinger's case against Francis, Senator Cockrell asked to have printed the report of the House of Representatives in 1858 submitted by the Honorable Elihu B. Washburne, Report No. 403 of the Thirty-fifth Congress, first session, that gave the history of Congress's decision to award Ottinger $10,000. This included eleven sections of letters supporting Ottinger's first appeal to Congress. After accepting all of the documentation, the presiding officer asked Senator Cockrell if he wanted any thing else from the floor. Senator Cockrell suggested to the senator from New York in his desire to do justice to all parties that he ought to accept an amendment to this resolution to read this way: "That in view of the life-long services to humanity and to his country of the now venerable Joseph Francis and Captain Douglass Ottinger in the construction and perfection of life-saving appliances by which many thousands of lives have been saved, the thanks of Congress be, and are hereby, tendered to Joseph Francis and Captain Douglass Ottinger; and that the President of the United States is hereby authorized to cause to be prepared gold medals with a suitable inscription, to be presented to Mr. Francis and Captain Ottinger in recognition of their eminent services."

Senator Evarts said he would accept it as a suggestion, but not as an amendment. The presiding officer turned to the senator from Missouri to ask if he would press his amendment. Senator Cockrell said he thought Senator Evarts would accept it. Senator Evarts replied that he had answered Senator Cockrell in his hearing that he would accept it as a suggestion, but not as an amendment.[12]

Senator Evarts said that memoranda presented to the committees detailing the complete matter of the competing claims were on his desk. He asked to insert them into the *Record.* The presiding officer accepted that information for the *Record,* unless opposition arose from the floor. Evarts's information filled seven pages of the *Record.* Thereafter, "the joint resolution was reported to the Senate without amendment, ordered to a third reading, read a third time, and passed."[13]

Thus the *Congressional Record* contains copious documents and statements from both sides of the debate. Members of Congress closely associated with either side had documentation to satisfy their cause, but for the majority of members the initial approach of emphasizing the lifetime efforts of the venerable Joseph Francis to aid humanity while glossing over the minutia of inventorship seemed to be the just course to follow. Congress tendered its thanks to Joseph Francis.

The joint resolution then went to the White House for the president's signature, but President Grover Cleveland failed to sign it. Without his signature, the process of striking a gold medal could not begin. There was no reason given for not signing the congressional resolution, but Cleveland served as a lawyer in Buffalo, New York, a sheriff, and later mayor of Buffalo before becoming governor of New York. It may be that he had close ties to Erie politicians or even knew Ottinger personally. Three days after the resolution passed, Senator John T. Morgan wrote to Francis to tell him how pleased he was to have voted for the resolution. Morgan went on to say that the thanks of Congress was an expression of the people, and the only effect of the lack of the presidential signature was the loss of a gold medal. Yet it could not diminish the respect of the people or tarnish the gratitude of the country.[14]

Although disappointed by the loss of the gold medal, Joseph Francis purchased a large number of copies of the daily *Congressional Record* before the revised *Record* in its permanent form appeared. He appended a rough index to the front, added a page after page 2674 that showed the reader the pages where Ottinger had obtained his $10,000 by fraud, listed the places where bogus letters were submitted by Ottinger, noted where to find the conclusive and incontrovertible facts that Ottinger was not the inventor of the life car, and included diagrams and illustrations. Francis had this material bound into a book and privately printed under the title of *The Life Saving Appliances of Joseph Francis: Action of Congress of the United States in Recognition of His Services, March, 1887*. This was his way of clearing his name and ending the long-standing dispute over who invented the life car.

Yet Francis's friends in Congress were not ready to give up. On 13 April 1890 the *New York Times* wrote that the day before a small group had gathered in the Blue Parlor of the White House at noon to observe President Benjamin Harrison bestow a gold medal upon Mr. Joseph Francis for "his services in the construction and perfection of life-saving appliances." It was a brief and simple ceremony. Senator Evarts spoke for Congress; the president gave a short address; and there was "a brief response of thanks by Mr. Francis, who was so overcome that he could not complete his remarks."[15]

A recent publication, *Legacies: Collecting America's History in the Smithsonian*, noted that for the first three decades after Francis's donation, when shipwrecks were still common, the exhibit was quite popular and Joseph Francis was regarded

The likeness of Joseph Francis on a medal commemorating the inventor.

11.1 Joseph Francis's Commemorative Medal, from Robert F. Bennett's *Surfboats, Rockets, and Carronades* Washington, D.C.: U.S. Government Printing Office, U.S. Coast Guard, 1978.

as an eminent figure in American history. Later, as this form of maritime disaster diminished, the display moved from the main exhibit to a smaller room.[16]

Joseph Francis died on 10 May 1893 at Otsego Lake, New York, where he had gone to spend the summer. He was ninety-two. His obituary told of his inventive genius. It recounted that the U.S. Congress was slow to recognize his ability, but it did, eventually, pass a resolution tendering him a gold medal, that "he never obtained, as the resolution was not approved by the President." Evidently the *New York Times* had the same American affliction of forgetting about Francis when he was not in the limelight. It was the same affliction that the U.S. Army and Navy had after he returned from Europe during the Civil War.[17]

But what had happened to his nemesis, Captain Douglass Ottinger? After his letter of June 1883 to the U.S. minister at the Court of St. James, Ottinger visited

Europe and later reported receiving many testimonials of respect while in England. About 1887 he left Erie and returned to his birthplace, Germantown. As the years passed, Ottinger left the minutest details on how to carry out his wishes after death with an intimate friend in Erie. He wanted to return to Erie for burial next to his wife. He prepared his obituary under three topics: "Sketch of a Long Life," "In the Exciting War Times," and "Invented the Life Car." This last section stated "Captain Ottinger was made historical on account of his invention of the life car an appliance to rescue persons from stranded vessels in storms where life boats would be swamped. The Congress of 1858 recognized the value of his invention by voting to Capt. Ottinger the sum of $10,000." He died at Mount Holly, New Jersey, on 13 January 1899. Captain Ottinger set his last comments in stone on his tombstone so that later generations could read: "Established the first life-saving stations in the United States and invented the Life Car in 1848–49 as per patent office record."[18]

Thus the two venerable gentlemen, the inventor and the impostor, fought their battle to the bitter end. They both desired to be the inventor of the metal life car that was the new and strange metallic boat that could go from shore to shoal and back carrying shipwrecked victims to land. The life car became a true historical turning point. Before the life car, shipwrecked passengers and crew had little hope for survival if the weather kept surfboats from venturing out. After the life car, passenger and crew survival rates improved considerably.

A little over a century and a half later, neither Francis nor Ottinger were household names. The Forty-ninth Congress still provided documentation for both men's claims. If one wanted to see the object of this struggle, one had to visit the Smithsonian Institution to view Francis's metal life car, the patent model of his metallic life boat, the commemorative gold medal with die cast by Louis St. Gaudens presented by President Benjamin Harrison, and the jeweled snuffbox presented by Emperor Napoleon III.[19]

12

Epilogue

In the second half of the twentieth century, like the Flying Dutchman, Captain Douglass Ottinger, USRMS, sailed back on the scene through a series of events. In February 1969, the U.S. Department of the Interior Museum Laboratory, Springfield, Virginia, received a metal life car to treat. When it completed its task, the life car went to the Museum Warehouse in Springfield for storage. In July 1974, the warehouse sent its accumulation of historical artifacts to various destinations. The life car went to the National Parks Service, Outer Banks Group, Manteo, North Carolina. Two years later, Commander Robert F. Bennett, USCG, published *Surfboats, Rockets, and Carronades* for the Department of Transportation, U.S. Coast Guard. Finally, in 1989, the National Parks Service loaned the life car to the North Carolina Maritime Museum in Beaufort. The only background information accompanying the life car was the Museum Catalog Record revealing that the life car was galvanized sheet iron hull, canvas fenders hanging by rope around its edge, two iron bails with an iron ring at the center of each bail, and each bail set one-third inboard from the bow and stern. The life car was eleven feet long and was estimated to have been built in 1890. It carried two manufacturer's plaques, one at each end, on the top deck: "T. F. ROWLAND/BUILDER/ CONTINENTAL WORKS/Greenpoint/BROOKLYN, N.Y."[1]

With such a paucity of information the North Carolina Maritime Museum staff began a search for metal life cars and found Bennett's *Surfboats, Rockets, and Carronades*. His sketch of a life car looked as if he used the Maritime Museum's life car for a model. His theory of who invented the life car follows:

> If what transpired during the first few months of 1849 had been recorded at the time, a great deal of later confusion and controversy might have been avoided. In essence, it appears that Captain Ottinger, having conferred with such practical surfmen as Major Henry Wardell and other underwriters' agents, brought to Mr. Joseph Francis, the surfboat maker at the Novelty Iron Works, a concept for a small converted lifeboat. This craft was to be capable of floating; but principally it was to be made to ride suspended beneath a hawser from the beach to the stranded ship and back again. . . .

12.1a North Carolina Maritime Museum Life Car (Broadside view). Courtesy of the National Park Service Outer Banks Group

12.1b North Carolina Maritime Museum Life Car (Bow view). Courtesy of the National Park Service Outer Banks Group.

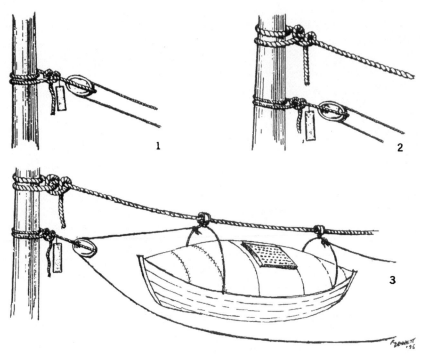

Three steps in connecting the rescue apparatus to a ship. 1. Whip and tally board made fast to a ship's spar. 2. Hawser made fast to a spar above the whip. 3. Surfcar riding the hawser.

12.2 Bennett's Life Car Rigging for Rescue Operations, from Bennett's *Surfboats*.

Mr. Francis, who was already embarked in the construction of surfboats for the new government boathouses, and who was well-versed in the design and construction of iron craft, implemented Captain Ottinger's ideas. Francis was not a practical seaman, let along a surfman, nor was he particularly well-versed in the subject of rescue operations; he was a very competent, experienced, innovative constructor of metal lifeboats and had been so for 12 years, and he apparently had a considerable amount of business sense. . . .

Together, Captain Ottinger and Joseph Francis produced what was first called a "surfcar" and later a "lifecar.". . . Captain Ottinger declined any patent rights on the surfcar which he, in essence, designed on the decent, but perhaps naïve, basis that the credit for such a noble instrument belonged to all mankind.

Joseph Francis, shortly to found the Francis Life-Boat Company, was not quite so magnanimous; after all, he was "in business" and therein came the "rub." In later years Francis, over Ottinger's protestations, claimed credit for the invention of the "lifecar"; Ottinger in turn claimed the "surfcar."

. . . The differences between the Francis lifecar and the Ottinger surfcar were so insignificant that it would require a patent attorney to tell them apart properly.[2]

Presently the museum displays its life car with the legend that "Captain Douglas [sic] Ottinger of the United States Revenue Cutter Service designed the first life-car in the early 1840s."[3] Actually that life car, and all life cars made in the United States, was fashioned on Francis's original and only set of life car dies for the hull portion of the vessel. The top deck underwent several changes in shape. When Francis stopped making life cars, Mr. T. A. Rowland acquired his life car dies. James Kelton worked for Francis "from 1852 until he [Francis] left the business and until 1868 for the company which carried on the manufacture" of making metal cars and boats. In 1884 Kelton worked for the Continental Iron Works of Greenpoint, Brooklyn, making "all the life cars used by the Government." He stated that he never "heard any other name [than Joseph Francis] mentioned as the inventor of the car while employed in their manufacture."[4]

It was almost as if these two deceased gentlemen, Ottinger and Francis, still were controlling earthly events. In the spring of 1982 the Florida Maritime Heritage Program learned that Park DeVane, a regional historian of south Florida, claimed he knew the burial place of some copper canoes from the Third Seminole War. The Florida Maritime Heritage Program contacted DeVane and offered to assist him in finding grant money to unearth the copper boats. DeVane replied that he had been studying the copper canoes for twenty-five years and had many personal diaries and official documents relating to the subject. Yet it had taken him many years to gain the confidence of the owners of the property. At the time of his writing he had full access to the area and he hoped he could "work very quietly and without any fanfare." He was vague about his copper canoes and was reluctant to divulge any information. Two years later the Florida Maritime Heritage Program heard from a friend of Park DeVane that DeVane had died without revealing where his copper canoes were located.[5]

It can only be assumed that maybe somewhere beneath the muck and mud of south Florida several metallic canoes or batteaux from the Billy Bowlegs War, Joseph Francis's products, await discovery. Only after finding Park DeVane's source of information could one uncover these interesting relics of the Third Seminole War.

Similarly, Joseph Francis's reputation as the inventor of the life car lies buried in the muck and mud of congressional debate. Yet in spite of arguments pro and con, the basic facts remain unchanged. In 1844 William H. Navarro assisted Francis as the inventor developed his concept of using dies to build metal lifeboats. In 1846 Thomas McLeary went to work for Francis building metal life cars. In early 1848 Navarro joined Francis's work force building metal life cars. Between 1845 and 1849 Francis built nine prototype metal life cars and sold them to the U.S. Navy and to the Collins Line of steamers. Note that all of these events happened before the secretary of the treasury issued orders on 18 October 1848 to Captain Ottinger to establish eight lifesaving stations along the New Jersey shore. As for Ottinger's attempt in 1883 to establish his claim of inventing the true *Ayrshire* life car, supported by his photograph of the car, that claim disintegrated under Second Lieutenant C. H. McLellan's massive document of 23 May 1884 sent to General Superintendent Kimball of the U.S. Life-Saving Service. Thus, historical evidence overwhelmingly delineates that Joseph Francis was the inventor and Douglass Ottinger was the impostor of the famed metal life car that brought countless numbers of shipwrecked survivors safely from shoal to shore.

Notes

Chapter 1

1. *Cong., Record,* 49th Cong., 2d sess., 2676, in Joseph Francis, *The Life-Saving Appliances of Joseph Francis: Action of Congress of the United States in Recognition of His Services, March, 1887* (privately printed 1887), this book is composed of copies of the daily *Congressional Record* before it was revised and issued in permanent form, thus the pagination differs from the permanent *Congressional Record,* all citations refer to the daily issue, hereafter cited as Francis, *Life-Saving,* no. sess., page; John L. Everhart, "Life Saver: Inventor Joseph Francis Spent a Lifetime Looking for Ways to Save Victims of Shipwrecks," *The SandPaper* [Cape May, N.J.?] (12 September 1986), 9; *Dictionary of American Biography,* s.v. "Francis, Joseph," hereafter cited as "Francis," DAB.

2. Francis, deposition of 23 April 1884 enclosure in 2d Lt. C. H. McLellan to General Superintendent, U.S. Life-Saving Service, S. I. Kimball, 26 May 1884, Records of the U.S. Life-Saving Service, Joseph Francis Lifeboat, RG 26, hereafter cited as RG 26; George Henry Preble, *History of the Flag of the United States of America: Symbols, Standards, Banners, and Flags of Ancient and Modern Nations* (Boston: H. Williams and Co., 1880), 704.

3. Francis, deposition of 23 April 1884, RG 26; Everhart, "Life Saver," 9; *The National Cyclopaedia of American Biography,* s.v. "Francis, Joseph."

4. Francis, *Life-Saving,* 2d sess., 2676; "Francis," DAB; Everhart, "Life Saver"; *A Naval Encyclopaedia: Comprising a Dictionary of Nautical Words and Phrases* (Philadelphia: L. R. Hamersly, 1881), 435–36.

5. Francis, *Life-Saving,* 2d sess., 2676.

6. Edward Wardell, deposition of 4 June 1884, in McLellan to Kimball, 26 May 1884, RG 26.

7. Francis to Secretary of Treasury John Sherman, 13 March 1880, filed 15 March 1880, ibid.

8. Francis, *Life-Saving,* 2d sess., 2676.

9. Francis to Secretary of War Joel R. Poinsett, New York, 30 October 1840, Consolidated Correspondence File: Francis Iron Wagons and Metallic Life Boats, Record Group 92, National Archives, hereafter cited as RG 92.

10. Francis, *Life-Saving,* 1st and 2d sess., 1740, 2676, 2677.

11. Francis, deposition of 23 April 1884, RG 26.

12. Ibid.

13. Francis to Secretary of War John C. Spencer, 4 February 1843, RG 92; Everhart, "Life Saver," 9.

14. Horatio Allen to Francis, 7 December 1885, filed 19 December 1885; Allen, deposition of 30 December 1885, filed 20 February 1886, RG 26.

15. For a more complete explanation of the hydraulic press, see Jacob Abbott, "Some Account of Francis's Life-Boats and Life-Cars," *Harper's New Monthly Magazine* 3 (July 1851): 164–66; for a more complete description of the assembly of Francis's boat, see the U.S. Army Board on Francis' Metallic Life Boats, 10 January 1852, 1–2, RG 92; Francis to Secretary of the Treasury John Sherman, 2 March 1880, RG 26.

16. In Francis's publications he italicized phrases complimentary of his metallic boats; although an examination of some of the originals did not contain the italics. M. Berry to Senator John Davis, 6 August 1850, New York, Joseph Francis, *Francis' Metallic Life-Boat Company* (New York: William C. Bryant & Co., 1852), 48.

17. Awful Collision at Sea, ibid., 47–48.

18. Extract of a letter from Capt. Samuel L. Breese, 16 August 1847, ibid., 64.

19. Robert Grant to Francis, 30 September 1850, ibid., 63–64.

20. Lt. William F. Lynch to Secretary of the Navy John Mason, U.S. Store-ship *Supply*, November 1848 in the "Report of the Secretary of the Navy with a Report made by Lieutenant W. F. Lynch of an Examination of the Dead Sea, 26 February 1849," Thomas C. Cochran, gen. ed. *The New American State Papers*, vol. 9 (Wilmington, DE: Scholarly Resources, Inc., 1972), 1–4, and Appendix B, 30; Francis, *Metallic Life-Boat Company*, 81.

21. Francis, *Metallic Life-Boat Company*, 81.

22. Ibid., 83; Cochran, "Report of Secretary of the Navy," vol. 9, Appendix B, 43.

23. CDR. Charles W. Skinner to Alex. Vattemare, 1 July 1848, Francis, *Metallic Life-Boat Company*, 60–61.

24. Skinner to Senator Daniel S. Dickinson, 19 July 1850, ibid., 61.

25. James L. Pond, comp., *History of Life-Saving Appliances and Military and Naval Construction: Invented and Manufactured by Joseph Francis, with Sketches and Incidents of His Business Life in the United States and Europe* (New York: E. D. Slater 1885), 121.

26. William G. Temple to Francis, 30 August 1851, enclosure in Francis to General Jesup, 14 November 1851, RG 92.

27. Extracts from Crabtree letters of 19 June 1848, 13 August 1850, and 1 February 1851 in Francis, *Metallic Life-Boat Company*, 60–61.

28. Ibid., 10.

29. Treasury Department orders, 28 May, 1851, 7 November 1851, 21 October 1852, 27 April 1853, and 5 August 1853, enclosures in Francis to Kimball, 4 April 1884, RG 26.

30. U.S. Navy Yard, Boston, to Francis, 5 November 1851; Navy Department, Bureau of Const. &c to Francis, 22 December 1851, ibid.

31. Captain Napoleon N. Coste to Francis 8 August 1850, Francis, *Metallic Life-Boat Company*, 48–49.

32. Everet & Brown to Francis, 30 August 1852, ibid., 49.

33. Maillefert to E. Meriam, 10 February 1852, ibid., 70–71.

34. Ibid.

35. Brown to Francis, 21 February 1852, ibid., 69.

36. John Dix, ibid., 72.

Chapter 2

1. J. H. Merryman, "The United States Life-Saving Service," *Scribner's Monthly* 19 (January 1880): 321, 329–30.

2. *A Naval Encyclopaedia,* 524–27.

3. Dennis R. Means, "A Heavy Sea Running: The Formation of the U.S. Life-Saving Service, 1846–1878," *Prologue: Journal of the National Archives* 19 (Winter 1987): 4.

4. *A Naval Encyclopaedia,* 91, 795–96; Thomas W. McMahon, "Beach Erosion and Conservation Problem in Northeast Florida," unpublished manuscript in Jacksonville University Library, 2–5.

5. George J. Hagar, "The United States Life-Saving Service, Its Origin, Progress, and Present Condition," *Frank Leslie's Popular Monthly* 5 (February 1878): 166.

6. Means, "A Heavy Sea Running," footnote 2, p. 13.

7. Rebecca Harding Davis, "Life-Saving Stations," *Lippincott's Magazine* 17 (March 1876): 302–3.

8. Some accounts list the brig as the *Count Terasto.*

9. Fitch, "The Inventor," 98; Abbott, "Some Account," 162.

10. Edward Warren to Francis, 4 July 1843, in Fitch, "The Inventor," 98.

11. Means, "A Heavy Sea Running," 2; Hagar, "U.S. Life-Saving Service," 166.

12. Hagar, "U.S. Life-Saving Service," 166.

13. Ibid., 166–67.

14. Francis to Kimball, 20 April 1884, filed 22 April 1884, RG 26.

15. Joseph Casey, deposition of 17 April 1884, enclosure in Lt. McLellan to Kimball, 23 May 1884; Francis to Secretary of Treasury John Sherman, 13 March 1880, RG 26; Francis, *Life-Saving,* 2d sess., 2677.

16. Extract from Ottinger's affidavit made at Erie, Pennsylvania, 14 July 1860, filed in the Patent Office and no longer extant, ibid., 2677.

17. Robert F. Bennett, *Surfboats, Rockets, and Carronades* (Washington, D.C.: U.S. Government Printing Office, Department of Transportation, United States Coast Guard, 1976), 19–27, 38–39.

18. Ibid., 40.

19. Ottinger to Newell, 16 January 1849, 30th Cong., 2d sess., Appendix 133–34, *Congressional Globe.*

20. Hagar, "U.S. Life-Saving Service," 167.

21. Ottinger to Meredith, 21 May 1849, Francis, *Life-Saving,* 2d sess., 2670–71.

22. Deposition of Edward Wardell, 4 June 1884, filed 7 June 1884, RG 26; Extract from testimony of McGowan, Francis, *Life-Saving,* 2d sess., 2672; Abbott, "Some Account," 163–64; Service Record of Ottinger compiled for author, 31 January 2005, RG 26.

23. Extract of Captain John McGowan to the Commissioner of Patents, Francis, *Life-Saving,* 2d sess., 2672.

24. Bennett, *Surfboats,* 28.

25. Toner to Secretary of the Treasury, 4 November 1849, Francis, *Life-Saving,* 2d sess., 2673.

26. Holmes to Walter R. Jones, 3 December 1849, Francis, *Metallic Life-Boat Company,* 40.

27. Maxson to Jones, 13 March 1850, ibid., 43; Mahlon B. Chapman, deposition, 26 April 1884, enclosure in McLellan to Kimball, 23 May 1884, RG 26.

28. Abbott, "Some Account," 162–63.

29. Davis, "Life-Saving Stations," 310.

30. Fitch, "The Inventor," 97.

31. Maxson to Jones, 13 March 1850, Francis, *Metallic Life-Boat Company,* 43.

32. Abbott, "Some Account," 168–71.

33. Strong to Francis, 14 April 1852, Francis, *Metallic Life-Boat Company,* 42.

34. Extract from "A description of the wreck of the 'Georgia'" made by Capt. Thomas Bonde, RG 26.

35. Service Records for Douglass Ottinger, transcribed from the bound volumes, 31 January 2005.

36. Davis, "Life-Saving Stations," 305.

37. Robert G. Albion, *The Rise of New York Port*, renewal copyright, 1967, by author, 347.

38. Hagar, "U.S. Life-Saving Service," 167–68; Means, "A Heavy Sea Running," 2–3.

39. *New York Times*, 20 January 1857.

40. S. S. Cox, "The Life-Saving Service," *North American Review* 132 (May 1881): 489; Merryman compares surfmen and sailors in Merryman, "Life-Saving Service," 322–23.

41. M. V. Montgomery, commissioner, U.S. Patent Office to Hon. John T. Morgan, 20 December 1886, Francis, *Life-Saving*, 1st sess., 1740, 2d sess., 2672, 2678.

Chapter 3

1. General Orders 55 of 10 November 1851, RG 92.

2. Francis to Jesup, 14 November 1851, ibid.; Maillefert to Meriam, 10 February 1852, Francis, *Metallic Life-Boat Company*, 70–71; Dix to Jesup, 14 January 1852, RG 92.

3. Report of the Army Board on Francis' Metallic Life Boats, 23 January 1852, RG 92.

4. Francis to Davis, 15 June 1853, ibid.; Davis to Francis, 20 June 1853, Records of the Office of the Secretary of War, file F-50 (June) 1853, RG 107.

5. Francis to Jesup, 27 June 1853, RG 92.

6. George E. Buker, *Swamp Sailors in the Second Seminole War* (Gainesville: University Presses of Florida, 1997), 115–35.

7. Letters from Commissioner General Land Office, 1853–56, 7:233; U.S. Field Notes, 3:489, Florida, Department of Natural Resources, Division of State Lands, Bureau of State Land Management; Francis N. Page, *Memoir of Reconnaissances With Maps During the Florida Campaign, April 1854–February 1858*, microfilm M-1090, 1980, National Archives, 1:28, frames 29–30, hereafter cited as Page, *Memoir*, number, M-1090.

8. "Governor's Office, Letterbooks, 1836–1909," Record Group 101, Series 777, Box 2, Folder 3, Florida, Division of Archives, History & Records Management; Munroe to commanding officers at Forts Myers and Thompson, 13 December 1854, microfilm, M-1084, 10 rolls, RG 393, National Archives, Roll 1, Target 5, no. 181, hereafter cited as R-, T-, number, M-1084.

9. Agar to his parents, 9 February 1856, in "Editor's Corner," *Florida Historical Quarterly* 42 (July 1963): 95.

10. Page, *Memoir*, 1:passim, M-1090.

11. Francis to Jesup, 4 November 1853, RG 92.

12. Munroe to Cooper, 10 October 1854, R-1, T-5, 141, M-1084.

13. Jesup to Munroe, 7 December 1854, R- 3, T-3, J-1, ibid.; "Barge . . . a spacious light-draft river boat for the transportation of heavy merchandise. . . . Whale-boat. A long narrow boat, from 20 to 50 feet in length, and from 4 to 10 feet beam, sharp at both ends, and admirably fitted for all uses at sea, . . . These boats are best in a surf, and they should then be steered with a long oar instead of a rudder," *Naval Encyclopaedia*, 64, 843; Durham boat, designed by Robert Durham ca. 1750, was a long, narrow, flat-bottomed craft to carry pig iron from the Durham furnace down the Delaware River over a series of rapids. "These boats were like large canoes, some thirty or forty feet long . . . pointed at each end . . . a steering oar adjustable at

either end." William S. Stryker, *The Battles of Trenton and Princeton* (Boston, 1898; facsimile ed., Spartanburg, 1967), 129.

14. John Gardner, *The Dory Book* (Camden, ME International Marine Publishing, 1978), 21; Paul K. Walker, *Engineers of Independence: A Documentary History of the Army Engineers in the American Revolution, 1775–1783* (Washington, D.C.: U.S. Government Printing Office, 1981), 144; M. V. Brewington, "Washington's Boat at the Delaware Crossing," *American Neptune* 2 (April 1942): 168, 170.

15. Alexander S. Webb, "Campaigning in Florida in 1855," *Journal of the Military Service Institution* 45 (November/December 1909): 424; "Barge," *Naval Encyclopaedia*, 64.

16. "*Bateau* (plural, *Bateaux*) is French for any small boat, *Batteau* (plural, *Batteaux*) seems generally to have been adopted in English as the name of one particular boat, or rather class of boats, the double-ended river boats . . . *Batoe* (plural, *Batoes*) is the spelling generally employed in the British colonies during the French and Indian Wars." Gardner, *The Dory Book,* 10; Thomas to Francis, 2 November 1854, Records of the Office of the Quartermaster General, letters sent, vol. 43:336, RG 92.

17. Mason to Thomas, 9 November 1854, RG 92.

18. Francis to Thomas, 9 and 24 November 1854, ibid.

19. The Mackinaw boat was a small craft, 35′ long, 8′ beam, 3′ depth, developed on the Canadian side of Lake Huron on Georgian Bay about 1850. "The traditional Mackinaw was double ended, cat rigged, with no bowsprit or jib, and a full-frame, clinker built hull with a centerboard. The foresail was larger than the aftersail and both were gaff rigged." John F. Polacsek, curator, Dossin Great Lakes Museum Belle Isle, Detroit Historical Department, to Martin D. Sugden, Jacksonville University, Jacksonville, Fla., 26 April 1982, in possession of the author; Hill to Maj. J. A. Haskin, 12 December 1854, R-3, T-3, H-24, and 14 January 1855, R-4, T-2, H-8; Haskin to Munroe, 22 December 1855, 3d enclosure, R-4, T-1, H-42; Haskin to headquarters, 22 January 1855, R-4, T-1, H-9, M-1084.

20. Montgomery to Munroe, 14 January 1855, R-4, T-1, M-1, M-1084.

21. Allen to Brown, 3 March 1855, R-4, T-1, B-9, ibid.

22. Brown to Hays, 23 February 1855, R-4, T-1, B-7, ibid.

23. Allen to Brown, 3 March 1855, R-4, T-1, B-9, ibid.; His map "Lake Okeechobee showing locations of Fort McRae & Cypress Point," Page, *Memoir,* I, 35, frame 40, M-1090.

24. Allen to Brown, 3 March 1855, R-4, T-1, B-9, M-1084; Records of U.S. Army Continental Commands, 1821–1920, Letters Received 1854–1857, entry 1641, RG 393 (hereafter cited as entry-number, RG 393).

25. Dawson to Hill, 9 March 1855, R-4, T-1, H-14, M-1084; Patricia R. Wickman, "'A Trifling Affair': Loomis Lyman Langdon and the Third Seminole War," *Florida Historical Quarterly* 63 (January 1985): 308.

26. Pratt to Brown, 5 May 1855, R-4, T-2, unregistered letters, M-1084.

27. Brown to Harris, 11 June 1855, R-4, T-1, B-26, ibid.

28. Ray B. Seley Jr., "Lieutenant Hartsuff and the Banana Plant," *Tequesta* 23 (1963): 6–8.

29. Munroe to Pratt and Arnold, 13 December 1854, R-1, T-5, 181; Haines to Hays, 24 December 1854, R-1, T-5, 186; Weed to Munroe, 9 January 1855, R-4, T-1, W-1, M-1084.

Chapter 4

1. Harney to Thomas, 23 November 1856, R-1, T-7, 256; Loomis to Thomas, 1 May 1857, R-1, T-7, 238, M-1084.

2. Buker, *Swamp Sailors,* 134.

3. James W. Covington, *The Billy Bowlegs War, 1855–1858: The Final Stand of the Seminoles against the Whites* (Chuluota, FL: Mickler House Publishers, 1982), 42–44.

4. John and Mary Lou Missall, *The Seminole Wars: America's Longest Indian Conflict* (Gainesville: University Presses of Florida, 2004), 216–17.

5. Casey memo, [?] December 1855, T-1, last item, M-1090.

6. Covington, *The Billy Bowlegs War,* 37.

7. Munroe to Broome, 20 January 1856, R-1, T-6, 13, M-1084.

8. Covington, *The Billy Bowlegs War,* 37.

9. Munroe to Broome, 20 January 1856, R-1, T-6, 13, M-1084.

10. Munroe to Tompkins, 28 January 1856, R-1, T-6, 26, ibid.

11. Tompkins to Munroe, 11 and 12 February 1856, R-4, T-3, T-2, and T-4, ibid.

12. Thomas to Munroe, 18 February 1856, R-4, T-3, T-5; Vincent to Brown, 4 March 1856, R-1, T-6, 86, ibid.

13. Vogdes to Vincent, 9 February 1856, R-4, T-3, V-3, ibid.

14. Brown to Munroe, 3 February 1856, R-4, T-3, B-17, ibid.

15. Stemson to Brown, [?] February 1856, entry 1645, RG 393.

16. Molinard's Journal, 6 January 1856, entry 1641, ibid.; Molinard's Journal, R-4, T-3, B-18, no. 2, and R-4, T-3, M-1, M-1084.

17. Munroe to Broome, 11 February 1856, R-1, T-6, 44, M-1084.

18. Munroe to Cooper, 13 February 1856, R-1, T-6, 45, ibid.

19. Broome to Munroe, 19 February 1856, R-4, T-3, E-2, ibid.

20. Munroe to Brown, 2 February 1856, R-1, T-6, 30, ibid.

21. Fort Dallas, Orders No. 3, 13 February 1856, R-4, T-3, H-10, ibid.; Wickman, "A Trifling Affair," 310.

22. Munroe to Broome, 4 March 1856, R-1, T-6, 85, M-1084.

23. Munroe to Cooper, 6 April 1856, R-1, T-6, 128, and 20 March 1856, R-1. T-6, 113; Pratt to Brown, 12 April 1856, R-4, T-3, B-51, ibid.

24. Casey, 28 March 1856, T-2, C-3, first item, Page, *Memoir,* M-1090.

25. Munroe to Cooper, 20 March 1856, R-1, T-6, 113; Pratt to Brown, 12 April 1856, R-4, T-3, B-51, M-1084.

26. Pratt to Brown, 31 March 1856, R-4, T-3, B-44, no. 3, ibid.

27. Pratt to Brown, 12 April 1856, R-4, T-3, B-51, ibid.

28. Pratt to Brown, R-5, T-1, B-7, ibid.

29. Pratt to Brown, 17 April 1856, R-5, T-1, B-7, no. 2; 5 May 1856, R-5, T-1, B-7, no. 1, ibid.

30. Duryea to H. B. Hill, 5 April 1856, R-5, H-10, ibid.

31. Munroe to Gen. Carter, 16 April 1856, R-1, T-7, 14, ibid.

32. Munroe to Brown, 16 April 1856, R-1, T-7, 16, ibid.

33. Munroe to Cooper, 7 June 1856, R-1, T-7, 89; Munroe to Broome, 20 June 1856, R-1, T-7, 96, ibid.

34. Munroe to Cooper, 18 May 1856, R-1, T-7, 64, ibid.

35. Munroe to Cooper, 18 May 1856, R-1, T-7, 66, ibid.

36. Munroe to Broome, 19 May 1856, R-1, T-7, 71, ibid.

37. Adjutant General to Munroe, 14 June 1856, R-5, A-15, ibid.

38. Munroe to Broome, 6 July 1856, R-1, T-7, 129; Munroe to Cooper, 6 July 1856, R-1, T-7, 131, ibid.

39. Munroe to Broome, 1 August 1856, R-1, T-7, 151, ibid.

40. Maj. McKinsty to Quartermaster for stores and property, 15 September 1856, R-6, M-17, ibid.

41. Quartermaster inventory, Fort Myers, 15 September 1856, R-6, M-17; 30 September 1856, R-5, H-65, and Fort Dallas, R-5, H-82; Fort Dallas, 10 November 1856, R-6, T-21, ibid.

42. Colonel J. J. Abert, Topographical Engineers, to Captain J. W. Abert, Topographical Engineers, Fort Brooke, 20 September 1856, R-5, A-31, ibid.

43. Frank N. Schubert, *Vanguard of Expansion: Army Engineers in the Trans-Mississippi West, 1819–1879* (Fort Belvoir, VA: History Division, Office of the Chief of Engineers, 1980), 118–22; Logan V. Reavis, *The Life and Military Service of General William Selby Harney* (St. Louis, MO: Bryan, Brant & Co., 1875), 246–67; Buker, *Swamp Sailors*, 106–13.

44. Harney to Davis, 31 August 1856, filed under date of 21 November 1856, R-5, A-40, M-1084.

45. Cooper to Harney, 25 September 1856, R-5, A-40; Davis to Harney, 4 November 1856, R-5, A-39, ibid.; Casey, 9 October 1856, T-1, last item, Page, *Memoir*, M-1090.

46. Harney to Thomas, 23 November 1856, R-1, T-7, 256, M-1084.

47. Memorandum was an enclosure in Cooper to Loomis, 6 May 1857, R-7, A-38, ibid.

48. Ibid.

49. Harney to McKinstry, 28 December 1856, R-5, A-52, ibid.

50. Roberts to Harney, 4 January 1857, R-9, R-5; 12 January 1857, R-9, R-6, ibid.

51. Harney to commander at Cape Sable, 30 January 1857, R-1, T-7, 71, ibid.

52. Whitehalls were copied from the fast gigs of the late eighteenth century built at the Brooklyn Navy Yard. The classic Whitehall had "slack bilges, tucked up run, small heart-shaped transom, and straight keel" usually about 17′ long. Robert W. Stephens, "Survival of the Fastest," *Wooden Boat* (September/October 1995): 48; David Ramsey, ed., "Abner Doubleday and the Third Seminole War," *Florida Historical Quarterly* 59 (January 1981): 322, 325; John Brannan to Dimick, 6 February 1857, R-7, D-11; Dimick to Harney, 6 February 1857, R-7, D-10, M-1084.

53. Harney to Howard, 10 March 1857, R-1, T-7, 157; Harney to Cooper, 22 April 1857, R-1, T-7, 226, M-1084.

54. Cooper to Loomis, 6 May 1857, R-7, A-38; Secretary of War to Harney, 14 May 1857, R-7, A-41, ibid.

55. David J. Coles and Zack C. Waters, "Indian Fighter, Confederate Soldier, Blockade Runner, and Scout: The Life and Letters of Jacob E. Mickler, " *El Escribano: The St. Augustine Journal of History* 34 (1997): 36; Williams to Harney, 26 April 1857, R-9, W-21, M-1084.

56. Munroe to commanding officer at Fort Kissimmee, 10 April 1857, R-8, M-48; Lynde to Maj. J. C. Pemberton, 5 June 1857, R-8, P-37; Col. F. S. Belton to Loomis, 4 September 1857, R-7, B-54; and Lt. C. L Best to Capt. G. A. De Russy, 3 September 1857, R-7, B-54, M-1084.

57. Loomis to Cooper, 23 June 1857, R-1, T-7, 311, ibid.

58. Ibid.; Loomis to McKinstry, 25 June 1857, R-1, T-7, 312; Loomis to Mickler, 1 July 1857, R-1, T-7, 319; Loomis to McKinstry, 6 July 1857, R-1, T-7, 323; Munroe to Geo. H. Bunker, 8 June 1856, R-1, T-7, 92, ibid.

59. In the voluminous records of the Billy Bowlegs War only two references were made to the Durham boats, yet from the skimpy description I believe Mickler used Durham boats on his first scout with his boat company. Mickler to Loomis, 28 August 1857, R-8, M-143, ibid.

60. Interesting Letter Relative to the Seminole Indian War, *St. Augustine Evening Record,*

Tuesday, 4 May 1914; Loomis to Pacetty, 7 August 1857, R-1, T-7, 348; Pacetty to Loomis, 23 September 1857, R-8, P-44 and 31 October 1857, R-8, P-45, M-1084.

61. Loomis to Adj. Gen., 30 September 1857, R-1, T-7, 408, ibid.

62. Rogers to Loomis, 1 November 1857, R-9, T-1, 55, 17 November 1857, R-9, T-1, R-62, and 16 October 1857, R-9, T-1, R-53, ibid.

63. Loomis to Irvin McDowell, 6 December 1857, R-1, T-7, 450, ibid.

64. Rogers to Loomis, 2 December 1857, R-9, T-1, R-63, ibid.

65. Rogers to Loomis, 31 December 1857, R-9, T-1, R-66, ibid.

66. Ibid.

67. Interesting Letter, *St. Augustine Evening Record.*

Chapter 5

1. Francis to Jesup, 27 June 1853, RG 92.

2. Ibid.

3. Francis to Jesup, 4 March 1854, ibid.

4. Francis to Gordon, 5 May 1854, ibid.

5. Francis to Jesup, 19 July 1854, ibid.

6. Br. Genl Harry Stanton to Jesup, 27 September 1854; Francis to Jesup, 17 October 1854, ibid.

7. Francis to Jesup, 8 and 24 November 1854; War Department to Francis, 16 February 1855; Lefferts to Thomas, 23 February 1855, ibid.

8. Thomas to Francis, 30 April 1855, ibid.

9. Van Vliet to Thomas, 19 December 1855, ibid.

10. Van Vliet to Jesup, 3 October 1856, ibid.

11. Brown to Arnold, 5 December 1855, R-4, T-1, B-49, M-1084.

12. Arnold to Brown, 11 December 1855, R-4, T-1, B-50, ibid; Arnold to Brown, 15 December 1855, Entry 1639, RG 393.

13. Dimick to Page, 6 February 1856? [1867], R-7, D-9, M-1084.

14. Ramsey, ed., "Abner Doubleday," 318–34.

15. Smith to Jesup, 30 December 1856; Forney to Jesup, 12 January 1857, RG 92.

16. Harney to commander at Fort Kissimmee and McKinstry, 22 January 1857, R-1, T-7, 56, 57, M-1084.

Chapter 6

1. Thomas to Francis, 30 April 1855, Major Henry C. Wayne, USA, Hotel Du Rhin, Paris, 12 July 1855, and T. Y. Mason, U.S. Minister in France, U.S. Legation, Paris, 12 July 1855, Pond, *History of Life-Saving,* 65–66.

2. Vincent Eyre, "On the Application of Corrugated Metal to Ships, Boats and Other Floating Bodies," *Journal of the Society of Arts* (London), 4, no. 196 (22 August 1856): 665.

3. Tulloh's letter of 12 December 1855, RG 92.

4. Wood to Francis, 1 January 1856, with Tulloh's letter of 12 December 1855, as an enclosure, ibid.

5. Brooke's letter of 22 July 1856; Pollock excerpts, Eyre, "On the Application," 667.

6. Ibid., 666,

7. Ibid., 666–67.

8. Wood to Eyre, 9 August 1856, reprinted in Eyre, "On the Application," 667.

9. Pond, *History of Life-Saving,* 68–69.

10. Ibid., 73, 77.

11. Ibid., 69, 73.

12. Croomes to Francis, 29 July 1856, RG-92.

13. The Ordnance Select Committee, 4 September 1856, No. 911, ibid.

14. Ibid.

15. Michael McGrady, Research and Editorial Services Department, Public Record Office, to George Buker, 17 June 2002, citing SUPP 6/1 Ordnance Select Committee Proceedings.

16. *A Naval Encyclopaedia,* 435–36.

17. Pond, *History of Life-Saving,* 78–79.

18. Ibid., 82–83.

19. Ibid., 74–75, 83–84.

20. Ibid., 86.

21. Ibid., 87–92.

22. Ibid., 99, 102.

23. Lefferts to Jesup, London, 16 December 1856, RG 92.

24. Pond, *History of Life-Saving,* 102.

25. Ibid., 99–101.

Chapter 7

1. Bennett, *Surfboats,* 53–56.

2. Alexander to Barnard, 13 October 1861, U.S. War Department, *The War of the Rebellion: A Compilation of the Official Records of the Union and Confederate Armies,* 130 vols. (Washington, D.C.: U.S. Government Printing Office, 1880–1901), ser. I, vol. 5:617–19, hereafter cited series, vol., page, OR.

3. Barnard to Gen. R. B. Marcy, 26 January 1863, I:11, part 1: 127–28, OR.

4. Carleton to Drum, 21 December 1861, I:50, part 1:773–78, ibid.

5. Crawford to Williams, 21 June 1862, I:12, part 3:419, ibid.

6. Rosecrans to Totten, 22 November 1862; Totten to Rosecrans, 24 November 1862, I:20, part 2: 82, 94, ibid.

7. Rosecrans to Totten, 24 November 1862; Kurtz endorsement, 25 November 1862, 96, ibid.

8. Cullum to Rosecrans, 26 November 1862; Rosecrans to Cullum, 26 November 1862; Cullum to Rosecrans, 98, 102, ibid.

9. Wright to Rosecrans, 7 December 1862, 133, ibid.

10. Russell F. Weigley, *History of the United States Army,* enlarged ed. (Bloomington: Indiana University Press, 1984), 216–19.

11. Pond, *History of Life-Saving,* 60.

12. Dix to Halleck, 29 November 1862, I: 18: 467, OR.

13. Dix to Peck, 10 December 1862, I: 18: 476; Dix to Ferry, 17 December 1862; and Ferry to Dix, 17 December 1862, I:18: 483, ibid.

14. Dix to Stanton, 13 May 1863, RG 92.

15. Francis to Meigs, 22 May 1863, ibid.

16. Meigs to Stanton, 26 May 1863, ibid.

17. Francis to Stanton, 10 June 1863, ibid.

18. Ibid.

19. Ibid.

20. Francis to Lincoln, 15 June 1863, ibid.

21. Ibid.; *The Oxford Dictionary of Quotations,* 3d ed. (New York: Oxford University Press, 1979), 558:10.

22. Lefferts to Meigs, 27 August 1861, RG 92.

23. Dix to Meigs, 20 August 1863, ibid.

24. Francis to Thomas, 13 November 1863, ibid.

25. Benham to Totten, 25 January 1864, I: 33:411–15, OR.

26. Serrell to Dix, 11 February 1864, RG 92.

27. Dix to Stanton, 11 February 1864, ibid.

28. Woodruff's 1st endorsement and Totten's 2d endorsement, 3 March 1864, of Dix to Stanton, ibid.

29. Meigs to Stanton, 25 March 1864, 3d endorsement of Dix to Stanton, 11 February 1864, ibid.

30. Roy P. Basler, editor, *The Collected Works of Abraham Lincoln,* vol. 7 (New Brunswick, NJ: Rutgers University Press, 1953), 221, fn.

31. Lawrence L. Knutson, "Capital Feud Is Revisited," *Bangor* (Maine) *Daily News,* 26 June 2001, A-9; Wendy Wolff, ed., *Capital Builder: The Shorthand Journals of Montgomery C. Meigs, 1853–1859, 1861,* Senate Document 106–20 (Washington, D.C.: U.S. Government Printing Office, 2001), xxxiv–xxxv, 181, 183, 199, 593, 643–44, 752–53.

32. Stanton to Dix, 31 March 1864, RG 92.

33. Comdr. B. J. Totten to Flag Officer L. M. Goldsborough, 1 August 1862, I, 7:609; Wilkes to Welles, 1 August 1862, I, 7:610. U.S. Navy Department. *Official Records of the Union and Confederate Navies in the War of the Rebellion,* 30 vols. (Washington, D.C.: U.S. Government Printing Office, 1894–1927), Series I, vol. 7.

34. Pond, *History of Life-Saving,* 122.

35. Ibid., 45.

36. Francis to Jesup, 2 April 1855, RG 92; Deposition of Horatio Allen, 30 December 1883, filed 20 February 1886, RG 26.

Chapter 8

1. Merryman to Allan, 5 February 1880, filed 15 March 1880; Francis to Sherman, 2 March 1880, filed the same day, and 13 March 1880, filed 15 March 1880, RG 26.

2. Francis to Kimball, 8 February 1881, Kimball to Francis, 10 February 1881, enclosures 2 and 3 of Kimball to Secretary of the Treasury Charles J. Folger, 10 February 1882, History of Senate Bill No. 734 for the relief of Captain Douglass Ottinger, USRMS, introduced by Senator McDill on 9 January 1882, RG 46, hereafter cited as S. 734, RG 46.

3. Francis to Kimball, 22 April 1881, enclosure 4, ibid.

4. Prindle to Francis, 23 February 1881, enclosure in James L. Pond, agent for Francis, to Kimball, 28 July 1884, RG 26.

5. Merryman to Kimball, 20 April 1883, filed 21 April 1883, 26 April 1883, filed 27 April 1883; Baird to Kimball, 23 April 1883, ibid.

6. Goode to Kimball, 8 September 1883, filed 18 September 1883 with three enclosures:

Ottinger to Russell, 23 June 1883, photograph of Ottinger's life car, and Ball to Russell, 31 July 1883, ibid.

7. McLellan to Kimball, 16 December 1883, with enclosure Francis to McLellan, 15 December 1883, filed 18 December 1883, ibid.

8. Francis to McLellan, 17 January 1884, ibid.

9. Folger to Collector of Customs, Erie, Pa., 16 February 1884; Stafford to Folger, 19 February 1884, filed 29 February 1884, ibid.

Chapter 9

1. The service was known as the Revenue Cutter Service, 1790-1843, the Revenue Marine Service, 1843–1915, and the Coast Guard thereafter. John A. Tilley, "Coast Guard, U.S.," in *The Oxford Companion to American Military History* (New York: Oxford University Press, 1999), 145.

2. Service Records for Douglass Ottinger—Attachment B in T. Juliette Arai, National Archives to George E. Buker, 31 January 2005; An Abridged Account of Services Rendered by Capt. Douglass Ottinger, U.S. Revenue Marine, S. 734, 1–2, RG 46.

3. Ottinger's affidavit made at Erie, Pa., 14 July 1860, on file in the Patent Office, but no longer extant, Francis, *Life-Saving,* 2d sess., 2677; Ottinger Obituary, *Erie Dispatch,* 16 January 1899.

4. Francis, *Life-Saving,* 2d sess., 2678.

5. Ibid., 1st and 2d sess., 1740, 2678.

6. "E" to Ottinger, 25 September 1857, enclosure in Pond to Kimball, 28 July 1884, filed 29 July 1884, RG 26.

7. Francis, *Life-Saving,* 2d sess., 2673–75.

8. Ibid.

9. Ibid., 1st sess., 1740.

10. Ibid., 2d sess., 2672, 2675.

11. J. F. F. to Ottinger, 16 June 1859, ibid., 2d and 1st sess., 2678 and 1740.

12. Ibid., 2d sess., 2678.

13. "Coues" to Ottinger and F. S. Smith, his attorney, 8 November 1859, ibid.

14. Ibid.; Ottinger to Commissioner of Patents, 26 November 1859, enclosure in Pond to Kimball, 28 July 1884, filed 29 July 1884, RG 26.

15. Extract from testimony of Penfield, Francis, *Life-Saving,* 2d sess., 2672; Francis to Kimball, 17 June 1884, containing this excerpt from Ottinger's affidavit made at Erie, Pa., 14 July 1860, for the interference case, Patent Office, RG 26.

16. Baldwin to Philip F. Thomas, Commissioner of Patents, 8 August 1860, and Thomas's concurrence, 8 August 1860, Francis, *Life-Saving,* 2d sess., 2672, 2678.

17. Commissioner M. V. Montgomery to Senator John T. Morgan, 20 December 1886, ibid., 2d sess., 1739–1740; Ottinger to Commissioner of Patents, 26 November 1859, enclosure in Pond to Kimball, 28 July 1884, filed 29 July 1884, RG 26; Baldwin to Thomas, 8 August 1860, Francis, *Life-Saving,* 2d sess., 2672.

18. Francis, *Life-Saving,* 2d sess., 2680.

19. Conant to Ottinger, 23 March 1875, enclosure in Ottinger to Secretary Daniel Manning, no date, filed 21 April 1885, RG 26.

20. Ibid.

21. Local History Scrapbook, roll C, p. 56, Erie County Historical Society; An Abridged Account of Services Rendered by Capt. Douglass Ottinger, U.S. Revenue Marine, S. 734, 4–5, RG 46.

22. Memorial of Captain Douglass Ottinger, 1–2, S. 734, RG 46.

23. The Revenue Marine Service had a commissioned officer's rank of first lieutenant, and, similar to the U.S. Navy, a commissioned officer's duty station of first lieutenant. The latter was the officer in charge of seamanship and the safety of the vessel. Ottinger, An Abridged Account, 1, ibid.

24. Ibid., 1.

25. Ibid., 2.

26. Ibid., 2–3.

27. Ibid., 3.

28. Ibid., 6.

29. Log of the U.S. revenue steamer *Miami,* RG 26; the journey from Washington to Fortress Monroe may be seen in *The Official Military Atlas of the Civil War* (reprint, New York: Arno Press, 1983), Plate CXXXVII.

30. Ottinger, An Abridged Account, 1–2, S. 734, RG 46.

31. [Viele], "A Trip With Lincoln, Chase and Stanton," *Scribner's* 16 (October 1878): 819; *Miami's* log, 9–11 May 1862, S. 734, RG 46.

32. Memorial of Captain Douglass Ottinger, 1; An Abridged Account, 8, S. 734, RG 46.

33. Memorial, ibid.

34. Ottinger to Chairman of Committee on Commerce, 19 January 1882, ibid.

35. Kimball to Folger, 10 February 1882, ibid.

36. Undated and unsigned memo from the Office of Secretary, United States Senate, 47th Cong. Accompanying Papers Ottinger, Douglass, RG 233; Francis, *Life-Saving,* 2d sess., 2680.

37. Francis, *Life-Saving,* 2d sess., 2680.

38. *Annual Report of the Operations of the United States Life-Saving Service for the Fiscal Year Ending June 30, 1883* (Washington, D.C.: U.S. Government Printing Office, 1884), 420–21.

39. *Annual Report of the Operations of the United States Life-Saving Service for the Fiscal Year Ending June 30, 1884* (Washington, D.C.: U.S. Government Printing Office, 1885), 442, 455, 457–58.

40. Francis, *Life-Saving,* 2d sess., 2680.

41. 35th Cong., 1st sess., 2488, *Cong. Globe;* Francis, *Life-Saving,* 2d sess., 2680–81; "A Bill That Will Not Pass?" *New York Sun,* 22 June 1884, 7.

42. Ottinger to Manning, n.d., filed 21 April 1885, RG 26.

Chapter 10

1. Pond, *History of Live-Saving,* 107.

2. Kimball to McLellan, 24 March 1884, RG 26.

3. McLellan to Kimball, 11 April 1884, ibid.

4. Excerpts from Kimball to Francis, 17 April 1884, are found in Francis to Kimball, 7 April 1885, ibid.

5. Francis to Kimball, 20 April 1884, filed 22 April 1884, ibid.

6. Kimball to McLellan, 13 May 1884, ibid.

7. William H. Navarro affidavit of 3 April 1884, enclosure in McLellan to Kimball, 23 May 1884, ibid.

8. Morris affidavit of 9 April 1884; C. W. Grimm, mate of the *Euphame,* affidavit of 10 May 1884; Isaac Francis affidavit of 14 April 1884, ibid.

9. McLellan to Kimball, 26 May 1884, ibid.

10. McLellan to Kimball, 2 June 1884; Edward Wardell affidavit of 4 June 1884, ibid.

11. Francis to Kimball, 17 June 1884, ibid.

12. Francis to Folger, 23 June 1884, filed 24 June 1884, ibid.

13. Osbon to Folger, 23 June 1884; Pond to Folger, 23 June 1884, ibid.

14. Folger to Francis, 28 June 1884, ibid.

15. Francis to Folger, 10 July 1884, ibid.

16. Pond to Kimball, 10 July 1884, ibid.

17. Pond to Kimball, 30 August 1884; McLellan to Kimball, 26 May 1884, ibid.

18. Pond to McCullock, 11 December 1884, ibid.

19. Pond, *History of Life-Saving,* 62.

20. Francis to Kimball, 24 March, 7 April, and 23 April 1885, RG 26; USL-SS *Annual Report of 1876* (Washington, D.C.: U.S. Government Printing Office, 1876), 42–43.

21. Chamber of Commerce memorial of 5 November 1885, with three enclosures, filed 21 November 1885, RG 26.

22. McAlpine to Manning, 3 December 1885, with enclosure Dix to Francis, 19 November 1885; Allen to Francis, 7 December 1885, and affidavit, 30 December 1885; Irion to Manning, 4 and 10 February 1886, ibid.

Chapter 11

1. Francis, *Life-Saving,* 1st sess., 1599.

2. Ibid., 1600.

3. Ibid.

4. Obituary, Mrs. Capt. Douglas Ottinger, *Erie Morning Dispatch,* 26 January 1883; Obituary, Capt. Douglass Ottinger, *Erie Dispatch,* 16 January 1899; Tom Sterrett, "What D'ye Know?" *Erie Dispatch-Herald,* 26 May 1940.

5. Francis, *Life-Saving,* 1st sess., 1600.

6. Ibid., 6737.

7. Ibid.

8. Ibid., 2d sess., 1739.

9. Ibid., 1740.

10. Ibid.

11. Ibid.

12. Ibid., 2670–75.

13. Ibid., 2682.

14. Morgan to Francis, 5 March 1887, RG 92.

15. *New York Times,* 13 April 1890, 5.

16. Steven Lubar and Kathleen M. Kendrick, *Legacies: Collecting America's History in the Smithsonian* (Washington, D.C.: Smithsonian Institution Press, 2001); Smithsonian Legacies, http://www.smithsonianlegacies.si.edu/objectdescription.cfm?ID=21.

17. *New York Times,* 11 May 1893, 4–7.

18. *Erie Dispatch,* 16 January 1899; Sterrett, "What D'ye Know?"

19. Robert Post, curator of the Division of Transportation, Smithsonian Institution to author, 23 July 1982.

Chapter 12

1. Cynthia Ploucher, Archive Technician, Outer Banks Group, to author, 30 November 2005, with enclosures: the catalog record, three photographs from the 1970s, a shipping inventory from July 1974, and a letter from 1976 discussing the July 1974 shipping of artifacts.

2. Bennett, *Surfboats,* 46, 47, 48, 52.

3. One of the Plexiglas legends around the life car.

4. James Kelton affidavit of 3 April 1884, enclosure in McLellan to Kimball, 26 May 1884, RG 26; Pond, *History of Life-Saving,* 112.

5. Buker to DeVane, 17 November 1982; DeVane to Buker, 26 November 1982; Allen C. Altvater to Buker, 27 February 1985, in author's possession.

Bibliography

Archival Sources

Unpublished

Florida, Department of Natural Resources, Division of State Lands, Bureau of State Land Management. U.S. Field Notes, 3:489. Letters from Commissioner General Land Office, 1853–1856.

Florida, Division of Archives, History & Records Management. Florida Governor's Office, Letterbooks, 1836–1909. Record Group 101, Series 777, Box 2, Folder 3.

National Archives and Records Administration.

Microfilm

Microfilm M-1084, Letters Sent, Registers of Letters Received, and Letters Received by Headquarters, Troops in Florida, and Headquarters, Department of Florida, 1850–1858, 10 rolls, RG 393.

Microfilm M-1090, Page, Francis N. *Memoir of Reconnaissances With Maps During the Florida Campaign,* April 1854–February 1858.

Record Groups

RG 26 Records of the U.S. Life-Saving Service: 2 Files, (1) Joseph Francis Lifeboat, (2) Log of the U.S. Revenue Steamer *Miami;* Service Records for Douglass Ottinger (transcribed from the bound volumes, 31 January 2005).

RG 46 Records of the U.S. Senate, Senate Bill for the Relief of Captain Douglass Ottinger.

RG 92 Entry 255 Consolidated Correspondence File: 3 Files, (1) Francis Joseph 1855, (2) Francis Joseph Metallic Lifeboat, (3) Francis' Iron Wagon Bodies. Records of the Quartermaster General, Letters Sent, vol. 43:336.

RG 107 Records of the Office of the Secretary of War.

RG 233 47th Congress Accompanying Papers Ottinger, Douglass.

RG 393 Records of the U.S. Army Continental Commands, 1821–1920, Letters Received 1854–1857, entries 1639, 1641, and 1645.

Published

Annual Report of the Operations of the United States Life-Saving Service for the Fiscal Year Ending June 30, 1876, 1883, 1884. Washington, D.C.: U.S. Government Printing Office, 1876, 1884, 1885.

Congressional Globe. 30th Cong., 2d sess.

Congressional Globe. 35th Cong., 1st sess.

Congressional Record. 49th Congress (daily issue and different pagination from edited edition), found in Francis, *The Life-Saving Appliances.*

Cochran, Thomas C., gen. ed. *The New American State Papers.* Wilmington, DE: Scholarly Resources, Inc., 1972. vol. 9.

The Official Military Atlas of the Civil War. Revised ed. New York: Arno Press, 1983.

U.S. Navy Department. *Official Records of the Union and Confederate Navies in the War of the Rebellion.* 30 vols. Washington, D.C.: U.S. Government Printing Office, 1894–1927. Series I, vol. 7.

U.S. War Department. *The War of the Rebellion: A Compilation of the Official Records of the Union and Confederate Armies.* 130 vols. Washington, D.C.: U.S. Government Printing Office, 1880–1901. Series I.

Wolff, Wendy, ed. *Capital Builder: The Shorthand Journals of Montgomery C. Meigs, 1853–1859, 1861.* Senate Document, 106–20. Washington, D.C.: U.S. Government Printing Office, 2001.

Newspapers

Bangor (Maine) *Daily News*
Erie (Pennsylvania) *Dispatch*
Erie (Pennsylvania) *Dispatch-Herald*
Erie (Pennsylvania) *Morning Dispatch*
New York Sun
New York Times
St. Augustine (Florida) *Evening Record*
The SandPaper (Cape May, NJ)

Secondary Sources

Abbott, Jacob. "Some Account of Francis's Life-Boats and Life-Cars." *Harper's New Monthly Magazine* 3 (July 1851): 161–71.

———. "The Novelty Works, With Some Description of the Machinery and the Processes Employed in the Construction of Marine Steam-engines of the largest Class." *Harper's New Monthly Magazine* 2 (May 1851): 721–34.

Agar to his parents, 9 February 1856, in "Editor's Corner." *Florida Historical Quarterly* 42 (July 1963): 91–100.

Albion, Robert G. *The Rise of New York Port.* Renewal copyright, 1967, by author.

Altvater, Allen C., to author, 27 February 1985.

Arai, T. Juliette, to author, 31 January 2005.

Basler, Roy P., editor. *The Collected Works of Abraham Lincoln,* vol. 7. New Brunswick, NJ: Rutgers University Press, 1953.

Bennett, Robert F. *Surfboats, Rockets, and Carronades.* Washington, D.C.: U.S. Government Printing Office, Department of Transportation, United States Coast Guard, 1976.

"A Bill That Will Not Pass? Evidence, which knocks the bottom out of Capt. Ottinger's claims, Washington, June 21." *New York Sun,* 22 June 1884.

Brewington, M. V. "Washington's Boat at the Delaware Crossing." *American Neptune* 2 (April 1942): 168–70.

Buker, George E. *Swamp Sailors in the Second Seminole War.* Gainesville: University Presses of Florida, 1997.

———. "Francis's Metallic Lifeboats and the Third Seminole War." *Florida Historical Quarterly* 63 (October 1984): 139–51.

———. *Environment—The Third E.* Jacksonville, FL: Jacksonville District, U.S. Army Corps of Engineers, 2000.

"Coast Guard Pioneer." *Coast Guard Magazine* (November 1931): 12.

Coles, David J., and Zack C. Waters. "Indian Fighter, Confederate Soldier, Blockade Runner, and Scout: The Life and Letters of Jacob E. Mickler." *El Escribano: The St. Augustine Journal of History* 34 (1997): 35–69.

Covington, James W. *The Billy Bowlegs War, 1855–1858: The Final Stand of the Seminoles against the Whites.* Chuluota, FL: Mickler House Publishers, 1982.

Cox, S. S. "The Life-Saving Service." *North American Review* 132 (May 1881): 482–90.

Davis, Rebecca Harding. "Life-Saving Stations." *Lippincott's Magazine* 17 (March 1876): 301–10.

DeVane, Park T., to author, 26 November 1982.

Dictionary of American Biography. Edited by Allen Johnson and Dumas Malone. New York: Charles Scribner's Sons, 1931.

Ehrhardt, John Bohne. *Joseph Francis (1801–1893): Shipbuilder Father of the U.S. Life-Saving Service.* Princeton, NJ: Princeton University Press for the Newcomen Society, 1950.

Everhart, John L. "Life Saver: Inventor Joseph Francis Spent a Lifetime Looking for Ways to Save Victims of Shipwrecks." *The SandPaper* (Cape May, NJ) (12 September 1986): 9.

Eyre, Vincent, Maj. "On the Application of Corrugated Metal to Ships, Boats and Other Floating Bodies." *Journal of the Society of Arts* (London), no. 196 4 (22 August 1856): 664–68.

Fitch, C. W. "The Inventor of the 'Ayrshire Life-Car.'" *Lippincott's Magazine* 35 (January 1885): 96–100.

Francis, Joseph. *Francis' Metallic Life-Boat Company.* New York: William C. Bryant & Co., 1852.

———. *History of Life-Saving Appliances and Military and Naval Construction: Invented and Manufactured by Joseph Francis, with Sketches and Incidents of His Business Life in the United States and Europe.* New York: E. D. Slater, 1885.

———. *The Life-Saving Appliances of Joseph Francis: Action of Congress of the United States in Recognition of his Services, March, 1887.* (n.p., 1887).

"Francis, Joseph, Obituary." *New York Times,* 11 May 1893.

Gardner, John. *The Dory Book.* Camden, ME: International Marine Publishing, 1978.

Hagar, George J. "The U.S. Life-Saving Service, Its Origin, Progress, and Present Condition." *Frank Leslie's Popular Monthly* 5 (February 1878): 165–78.

"Interesting Letter Relating to the Seminole Indian War," *St. Augustine Evening Record,* 5 May 1914.

Knutson, Lawrence L. "Capital Feud Is Revisited." *Bangor* (Maine) *Daily News,* 26 June 2001.

Local History Scrapbook, roll C, Erie County Historical Society. Erie, Pennsylvania.

Lubar, Steven, and Kathleen M. Kendrick. *Legacies: Collecting America's History in the Smithsonian.* Washington, D.C.: Smithsonian Institution Press, 2001.

McGrady, Michael. Public Record Office, 27 May 2002, to author.

McMahon, Thomas W. "Beach Erosion and Conservation Problem in Northeast Florida." Manuscript in Jacksonville University Library.

Means, Dennis R. "A Heavy Sea Running Formation of the U.S. Life-Saving Service, 1846–1878." *Prologue: Journal of the National Archives* 19 (Winter 1987).

Merryman, J. H. "The United States Life-Saving Service." *Scribner's Monthly* 19 (January 1880): 321–38.

Missall, John, and Mary Lou Missall. *The Seminole Wars: America's Longest Indian Conflict.* Gainesville: University Presses of Florida, 2004.

National Cyclopaedia of American Biography. 47 vols. New York: J. T. White & Co. 1892–1966.

A Naval Encyclopaedia: Comprising a Dictionary of Nautical Words and Phrases. Philadelphia: L. R. Hamersly, 1881.

The Official Military Atlas of the Civil War. Reprint. New York: Arno Press, 1983, Plate, cxxx-vii.

"Ottinger, Douglass, Obituary." *Erie Dispatch,* 16 January 1899.

———. Service Records for Douglass Ottinger transcribed from the bound volumes, 31 January 2005, in author's files.

"Ottinger, Emily, Obituary." *Erie Morning Dispatch,* 26 January 1883.

The Oxford Dictionary of Quotations. 3d ed. New York: Oxford University Press, 1979.

Polacsek, John F., Curator, Dossin Great Lakes Museum Belle Isle, Detroit Historical Department, to Martin D. Sugden, 26 April 1982, in author's files.

Pond, James L., comp. *History of Life-Saving Appliances and Military and Naval Construction: Invented and Manufactured by Joseph Francis, with Sketches and Incidents of His Business Life in the United States and Europe.* New York: E. D. Slater, 1885.

Post, Robert C., Curator, Division of Transportation, The National Museum of American History, Smithsonian Institution, to author, 23 July 1982.

Preble, George Henry. *History of the Flag of the United States of America: Symbols, Standards, Banners, and Flags of Ancient and Modern Nations.* Boston: H. Williams and Co., 1880.

Ramsey, David, ed. "Abner Doubleday and the Third Seminole War." *Florida Historical Quarterly* 59 (January 1981): 318–34.

Reavis, Logan V. *The Life and Military Service of General William Selby Harney.* St. Louis, MO.: Bryan, Brant & Co., 1875.

Schubert, Frank N. *Vanguard of Expansion: Army Engineers in the Trans-Mississippi West, 1819– 1879.* Fort Belvoir, VA: History Division, Office of the Chief of Engineers, 1980.

Seley, Ray B., Jr. "Lieutenant Hartsuff and the Banana Plant." *Tequesta* 23 (1963): 6–8.

Smithsonian Legacies: http://www.smithsonianlegacies.si.edu/objectdescription.cfm?ID=21.

Stephens, Robert W. "Survival of the Fastest." *Wooden Boat* (September/October 1995).

Sterrett, Tom. "What D'ye Know?" *Erie Dispatch-Herald,* 26 May 1940.

Stryker, William S. *The Battles of Trenton and Princeton.* 1898. Facsimile ed. New Jersey: Spartanburg, 1967.

Tilley, John A. "Coast Guard, U.S." In *The Oxford Companion to American Military History.* New York: Oxford University Press, 1999.

[Viele, Egbert L.] "A Trip With Lincoln, Chase and Stanton." *Scribner's* 16 (October 1878): 813–22.

Walker, Paul. *Engineers of Independence: A Documentary History of the Army Engineers in the American Revolution, 1775–1783* (Washington, D.C.: U.S. Government Printing Office, 1981), 144.

Webb, Alexander S. "Campaigning in Florida in 1855." *Journal of the Military Service Institution* 45 (November/December 1909): 398–429.

Weigley, Russell F. *History of the United States Army.* Enlarged ed. Bloomington: Indiana University Press, 1984.

Wickman, Patricia R. "'A Trifling Affair': Loomis Lyman Langdon and the Third Seminole War." *Florida Historical Quarterly* 63 (January 1985): 303–17.

"The Wreck of the *Metropolis.*" *Prologue: Journal of the National Archives* 19 (Winter 1987).

Index